Diary of a Wartime Traveler, 1941-1945

Best Wish

Margaret B. Mc Cullogh

3-23-02

Diary of a Wartime Traveler, 1941-1945

Margaret B. McCullough

To order additional copies of this book, contact:
Xlibris Corporation
1-888-7-XLIBRIS
www.Xlibris.com
Orders@Xlibris.com

To my mother,
who gave me wings and let me fly

CONTENTS

Acknowledgements

Blest with a loving family and a host of helpful friends, I hardly know where to begin. I'll start with my pastor Father Bill Spencer, O.F.M. because he was the first one to read my diary and to find it interesting. Thanks also to Millie Prasifka and Anne Jones, who laboriously made Xerox copies, page by page, from the fragile original. Thanks to Jackie Butler, who took me to my first writer's conference in Albuquerque and introduced me to her writers' club in Santa Fe. Jackie also designed the book jacket. Thanks also to Dr. Wildred Guerin, emeritus professor of the English department at LSU in Shreveport; he offered valuable advice. Paul Nice, a square dance friend, put all my pages on computer disk.

Peter Wooten, a British naval researcher, provided a passenger list from the *S.S.Malda*, and Barbara Galvin, my cousin, helped me make contact again with Tony and his family after 58 years.

Finally, my thanks go to a very special lady without whose generous and expert help this "baby" would never have come to term. Mimi Winterton worked with me from beginning and later, when macular degeneration took most of my sight, she read the pages to me as we edited them together.

To all who have helped me, I can only say a humble and grateful, "Thank you!"

M.B.M.

Author's Note

Perhaps the title to my journal needs some explanation. After all, traveling in wartime is unusual, exciting, purposeful, possibly dangerous, but seldom for pleasure.

In the spring of 1941 after I had graduated from the Froebel Training College in London, I was teaching at a convent boarding school in Harrogate, Yorkshire when I received a letter from a college friend inviting me to take her place in a school in Sumatra.

Normally overseas assignments are sealed with a three-year contract since the employer usually pays the travel expenses of the future employee. My friend Rosalind had signed such a contract, but her marriage intervened. She asked me to take her place and fill out the contract.

Excitement was my first reaction; then the reality of crossing the high seas caused me to hesitate. I think my Aunt Dolly clinched the decision when she said to me, "You know, Margaret, we only hear about the ships that *don't* get through."

So I accepted, and my uncle, who lived in Singapore, made all the arrangements.

My mother traveled with me by train to Greenock, Scotland, my port of embarkation, and the next day saw me board an unknown ship for an unknown destination. In wartime all orders were sealed and only opened by the Captain once the ship was under way. So, although our final destination was surmised, the route was not known.

Only now, all these years later, have I begun to appreciate the courage it took for my mother to let her only child leave under such circumstances.

Sadly, my mother returned to her job as housekeeper in a large house in Sussex. Incidentally, it was her kind employer who later had his secretary re-type and assemble all my entries.

My mother and I were very close, as illustrated by an incident related to me many months later. She told me that one night after she returned from Scotland, she awakened suddenly, turned over in bed, and for a split second vividly saw me standing in the doorway of her bedroom. I was wearing my new green tweed coat, and my hair was flying in the wind. Instantly she sensed that I was in some kind of danger.

We figured later that just at that moment I must have been standing at boat stations, wondering if I really had to get into that lifeboat on that green and windy sea!

So that explains how I came to be traveling in wartime, and it turned out to be most pleasurable.

The Diary

Part I

The Long Voyage

15 June 1941

[I had an opportunity to mail a letter to my mother
before we sailed. While it is not part of the journal,
it serves as an introduction.]
Aboard ship anchored in the Clyde

My own darling Mummy,

You will surely think that I have missed the boat, hearing from me so soon, but rest assured this is not the case. We are not off just yet, so there is a chance of posting at least once. This is grand as it will give me a chance to tell you something of my new surroundings before we sail. Otherwise, goodness knows when you would have heard! There are many speculations as to the route we shall take, but, of course, no one knows, although there are many who think they do and hold forth with much authority. I do hope that you had a not too uncomfortable journey home; I thought of you all the time and wondered how you managed to pass the time in Glasgow all by your ownsome. We had a good deal of waiting about, but not as much as I had anticipated. It was getting on to 4 o'clock before we were aboard. After I left you, I ambled down to the end of that shed and found a place on the bench, where I settled myself quite comfortably, ate many sandwiches—or rather some of them—for there was such a lot! Eventually when the queue became less, I joined on the back and got through very quickly. They seemed to have some particulars of me, for my passport was the only thing they asked to see at that point. Once through the barrier, we had to wait again on a hard bench before going into the baggage room. We were allowed through only four or five at a time, so that everyone was assured of a seat. Passports were inspected; ration books, gas masks and identity cards were handed over. I was asked how much money I had, the purpose of my journey, and that was all: my carefully tidied handbag was not even looked at! From this table we passed into the baggage room itself where I found all my belongings neatly together on the table. I was asked what was in each bag, but nothing was opened. My camera was handed over, and I was given a chit for it so that I could claim it as soon as we sailed. So far, I have not bothered to ask for it because the poor officials seem to have more than enough to cope with in the way of baggage. I shall lie low for a couple of days.

All my baggage I left in the hands of a porter, who assured me that I should find it on board. The typewriter, however, I took with me and very glad I was, as it turned out, that I had done so. By this time it was pouring with rain, but luckily for me I was one of the last and had only an hour to wait on the tender. The first ones through the baggage room were standing on deck for literally hours. All the baggage was brought on board by hand and dumped together on the deck. Finally when all was aboard and well soaked, it was covered up with tarpaulin! I found that nice woman we saw on the station at Glasgow with her little girl wearing a perky blue tamashanta. She, too, is going to Singapore to join her husband, Mr. Doig—naval folk, I think, though Auntie may know the name. We stood together under what shelter the bridge provided, and about half-past three we moved slowly off.

We were one of the first to embark and were shown straight up to the cabins. Here I found Mrs. Alstone already

seated rather despondently on the bunk. We were both relieved to discover that each of us is young! She, indeed, is
only just twenty and a widow. Poor soul, what a time she
must have had! Her husband, a lad of twenty-three, was
killed recently in a submarine, and a baby born a few
months later died of a weak heart. Only a few months ago
she lost her mother, who was on her way out to Colombo
when the ship was sunk. It does seem terrible that one person should lose so much. I think we shall get on very well
together. She is in a very nervy state, as you can imagine.
But she has a friend Mrs. Griffiths, a very nice middle-aged
woman, who is in the next cabin. I'm sure she will look
after Bunty; I think we shall see quite a lot of her in here.
Mrs. Alstone and her friend Mrs. Griffiths did not know
that they were going to be on the same boat and only discovered it yesterday. Otherwise, no doubt, they would have
had a cabin together. Still, then, I might have been landed
with the apparition in slacks and pink mackintosh! You
remember the one! She and this Mrs. Griffiths are both survivors from a previous attempt to get out to India, and Miss
Wilson can talk of nothing else. I think the whole ship knows
about her adventure. How trying people can be!

The cabin is very nice indeed. We each have a bed and
not the two bunks, one above the other as I had imagined.
This is, of course, much nicer. On the left as you enter, there
is a washbasin with a tap for cold fresh water, a sponge
rack each, hooks behind the door for dressing gowns, and
more hooks at the side for towels. Facing the door is a large
wardrobe with masses of room for hanging all our dresses
and coats. This is truly marvelous. On top are the life belts,
which have to be carried as soon as we sail, and below is
plenty of space for shoes. Along the same side is Mrs. A's
bunk under the two portholes, and between the bunks is a
dressing table containing four drawers, two each, and two
little trinket drawers. Over each bunk is a reading light and

by the side a pull-down shelf. I have found my hanging pockets that I made for camping trips most useful. There is masses of room underneath the beds for trunks and suitcases. My big trunk has not come up so far, but when it does, I shall repack my cotton dresses in one of the suitcases and have them put down in the baggage room. But for the present I have all I need.

A sad misfortune occurred yesterday when the baggage was being hauled in nets over to the ship from the tender. The net swung over, hitting the railing and sending a hat box, together with a couple of suitcases overboard. Of all the unfortunate things, it *would* be Mrs. A's hat box. Oh dear, there was a terrible scene! She burst into tears, rushed off to find the Captain, the purser, the stewardess, etc. However, Mrs. Griffiths and I managed to calm her. I proceeded to wash out the stockings and handkerchiefs that had got soaked. The stewardess came along and brought hot fresh water and took all the things away to be dried below. This morning most of them have come back dry, and the hats can be steamed later on. The company's insurance representative was on board. He told her to put a claim through Cook's, who will deal with the whole thing. All the same, it was most unfortunate and very disappointing as all the hats were new and had never been worn. Although it had not actually been in the sea, my own hat box was very wet. The hats were crinkling at the brims. However, they have been hanging up all night and have dried off this morning. They will be quite all right. We got up too early this morning by mistake! Most unusual for me! We were called with tea, biscuits and an apple at 7:30. Thinking it was 8:30, I rushed over my bath and hurried down to 9:00 breakfast to find nobody there. However, there were plenty of people up, and we walked round the decks until breakfast was ready. Tomorrow I shall be wiser.

While we were waiting to find table places this morning and before going into the dining room, the purser came up to talk to us and inquire about yesterday's mishap. He fully understood the circumstances and made allowance for the fuss that had been caused. I mentioned that my trunk had not yet come up but that I was in no hurry for it for a few days. He insisted at once on my coming into his office while he made a note of the trunk. There I discovered the ship's cat, and we at once made friends! I have just heard that the trunk is on the way up, so I shall be able to unpack after lunch.

Lunch is over. My goodness! What an amount of good food one is supposed to consume. I shall certainly grow very fat on this trip.

Whilst I was typing this morning, Mrs. A. came in with that girl we thought was a school teacher or a governess. It turns out that she knows Mrs. Paton. She went to say goodbye to her the other day and was told to look out for me. She is on her way out to China as secretary to the students' branch of the YWCA. A very nice girl, I should think, in spite of her capacity for talking!

She was green with envy on seeing our cabin and exclaimed at its size. Hers is also a two-berth cabin, but of the double bunk type and with half the baggage accommodation and wardrobe space. So I think we are very lucky indeed. The other passengers are just about as we thought! That group of naval men consists mainly of R.N.V.R.s [Royal Naval Volunteer Reserves], most of them about twenty or twenty-three, on their first trip. Do you remember that man and woman who were standing at the barrier on the station at Greenock? The man is on board. His wife was not able to get a passage on the same boat.

My trunk has just come up with a great dent on top, alas! Bashed right through the lid. I hope and pray that the fiddle inside is all right. I hardly dare to look.

To continue with the passengers: most of the women seem to be either wives going out to their husbands or women going out to be married. People are beginning to sort themselves out. Unfortunately, I have not seen much of my little friend of the blue felt hat! There are very few children, two little boys of about four or five, two girls of about seven and a couple of older children. On the whole we are an odd lot, I fear; one or two of the women seem very nice indeed, but the others—well! Some, I notice have got to work already on the Naval Babies! This is going to be a very amusing trip, I can foresee.

I will now see if this can be posted, and if so, will write again tomorrow, but whether *that* can be posted or not remains to be seen. No one, of course, knows how long we shall be here.

Darling, all my love. I'm thinking of you all the time. And of Auntie and Uncle, too. How I wish you were all here, too.

Lots and lots of love to you all,
Margaret

Monday, 15 June 1941

Well, this really begins my journal, although we have not yet sailed. She has been working up steam for the last two or three days, so we may be off soon. On Saturday we moved down the river a little and are anchored in a perfectly heavenly spot, within sight of Ben Lomond. On either side of the ship are long ridges of hills, which seem to go back and back into the distance, each line appearing more rugged and beautiful than the last. In the evening it is quite perfect to watch the mists slowly coming down to cover the highest peaks. The light is continually changing over them as each different cloud formation gives place to another. During the night I thought we had moved again, but it appears that we are still here! The engine worked all night, so I suppose that is a sign that we shall be under way before long.

I shall not say anything about the speculations as to the route we shall take, in case there is a chance of posting at some port, but most people think we shall be three months over it. So one can imagine the roundabout way we may go. I already have a bet on with one of the naval V.R.s who is bound for India as to who will leave the boat first. I'm afraid I shall lose the bet! Still I shall see the world!

This morning we had lifeboat drill again and were allotted boats. Yesterday we just mustered on the promenade deck in two lines while life jackets were inspected. But today we have been given boats, twenty-three passengers to each boat, plus crew, about forty in all. The Naval Reserves are in charge; they feel very important indeed and are busy at the moment checking over stuff in the boats, washing out the drinking tubes, etc. Somehow I got separated from my cabin mate, who is in boat 3, and she doesn't want to be dislodged. I wandered on deck with a very nice girl this morning, one Sylvia Collins, who is going out to India to get married. We found ourselves together in boat 6, both separated from our cabin mates, and have decided to stick together. As a matter of fact, the whole thing was rather a mix-up. One boat was left without anyone in it at all. There will probably be a reshuffle tomorrow when someone with authority takes over. Our group was dismissed without names being taken as the others' were. Sylvia Collins and I wandered round the deck, picked on two nice looking V.R.s, went up to them and asked if their boat were full! It was. They had twenty-six but hit on the plan of putting our names down in the middle of the list, so that when the number of passengers is questioned, they will strike off three names at the end! We are having a lot of fun over this, I can say!

Our table places are not quite so successful. Mrs. Alstone, Mrs. Griffiths and I sit next to each other, two places down from the end of the middle table, which I gather is the commander's table when he appears. There is a very mixed crowd aboard, and our female companions are not the ones we should have chosen had we got to know them sooner. However, that cannot be helped, and one need not see much of them apart from meals. I gather there are about a hundred and seventy passengers, all told; we just fit into the saloon, so there is no need for two sittings. There are some very nice girls about my age, and I expect we shall get together in time.

Very few people wore anything different for dinner last

night than they had been wearing all day. A few changed into silk blouses or put on a different jumper. Nearly all the women were in slacks. My cabin mate felt she must change and so decked herself out in a black crepe frock and made up her face heavily, but I fear she was the only one who had bothered to change. I shall not do so. I may go to the length of washing my face but no more.

Until the ship sails, there is no hot salt water for baths; one is only supplied with a tub of hot, fresh water and a mat in the bath. This is really quite adequate and, provided you remember to swill the mat with hot water first, it is not so bad: otherwise, you step onto a cold, clammy, sodden mass. I have arranged with the stewardess to have my bath in the morning. As we are called at 7:30 and breakfast is not until 9:00, there is plenty of time.

There was great excitement last night, or rather this morning at 3 A.M., when a man tried to visit the cabins on our deck. There are a lot of workmen aboard at the moment doing repairs or something, and I suppose they sleep here. Anyway, we woke up to find a man trying to get in. We both shouted to him to get out, which he did—trying the next cabin, but with the same result! The trouble is we may not lock the door of the cabin as it has to be kept ajar. However, I reported the matter to the stewardess in the morning, as did the others, and she, in turn, is going to inform the chief steward.

Tuesday, 17 June 1941

Yesterday afternoon the air was full of rumors of our imminent departure, and when two tugs and an oil tanker came alongside, it seemed pretty obvious that we should be off before the night was out. It was very cold, but most of the passengers gathered along the sides to watch preparations. An enormous pipe from the tanker was fitted over the pipe hole on the lower deck. It was hauled up in the most perilous manner, one man hanging onto the side of the ship by the railing and pushing the pipe into position with both feet, whilst his colleague connected it with nuts and bolts, which were flung up to him from the tanker below. The tea bell rang before we could see what happened after that, and by the time we came up again, we were pushing off, nosing our way out of the lock through a narrow strip between moored boats and flying boats. It was grand to be really moving at last, though I must admit that I felt a little lump in my throat as we moved on past the land, out to the sea, or rather lower down the Clyde to the rendezvous of the convoy.

I spent a most amusing evening, if a somewhat noisy one, with four of the naval lads. One, I discovered,—Tony Prichard-Davies—comes from just outside Covington. They are a jolly crowd and will liven up the party, I should think. They are taking it in turns to man one of the guns, and as there are sixteen of them (men, I mean), they get a watch about once in three days.

No alarms or excursions last night, I am glad to say. We had a very peaceful night. In fact, I don't think I woke until the stewardess came in at 7:15 with the tea. Oh, it's grand to see apples again. I do enjoy mine in the morning. Once out of bed there was no mistaking the Atlantic swell!! It got steadily worse all morning. I just managed to stagger round the deck before breakfast to get a last look of the Scottish coast. We were steaming north along the coast, with the coast of Ireland just visible off the starboard side. I believe we are making for the rest of the convoy.

After breakfast I again walked round the deck but decided that it was wiser to sit! The swell was pretty bad by this time, and I was feeling not exactly sick, but very drunk! Oh no, I didn't sit until later because of boat stations. It was announced at breakfast that there would be boat stations every morning at 10:00 until further notice. We were also issued with strict instructions to carry our life belts everywhere with us and were warned that unless this was done, no food or drink would be served to those without them.

Accordingly, at 10 o'clock, complete with life jackets, we all assembled on the promenade deck and lined up in two rows, men at the back and women and children in front. We had previously been told to assemble on our own sides of the ship, those in port cabins on the port side and those in starboard cabins on starboard side. (At last, I know which is which!) This is, of course, a much better arrangement; also, I am with my cabin mate, which is really better than being separated. The V.R.s are still boat wardens as before, but the arrangements are somewhat better. In our boat we have the ship's doctor, the cook and the wireless operator, and amongst the passengers are two, myself one,

who are supposed to know something about First Aid, so
we should be all right. There are several survivors on this
boat from the *Stafford*, and all are very cheerful at making
a second attempt. They had only been four days out when
she was hit, and they scrambled to the lifeboats. They had
no drill at all, which seems odd; however, they all got away,
were picked up twenty-two hours later by a destroyer and
landed back in England. Their chief concern is that they
have lost everything in the way of equipment.

After dismissal, I found a quiet spot and settled down
to read. My Crawley's friend came along, however, and
settled himself next to me, so we spent the rest of the morning chattering. Eleven o'clock brought the deck steward
along with cups of hot boiling beef tea and biscuits. I can
see that I shall do little else but sleep and eat on this trip. By
lunchtime I was feeling rather green, at least as soon as I
stood up. Determined not to be beaten, I descended with
the rest to the saloon, but I'm afraid that most of the lunch
was beyond me. It's all very well to say one should eat; the
food just will not go down! I struggled through soup; fish I
had to leave—it was horrible, rather dry, coddling, hidden
under white sauce. Next, I tried salad and finally had a go
at a sultana roll, delicious in the ordinary way, but I could
not finish it. Coffee—and then I was rather glad to get away.
I thought I should have to give in when I got up to the
cabin, but I laid down for half a minute and immediately
felt better. I decided to find a suitable spot on deck in the
open air and go to sleep. So, taking my knitting, a book and
a rug [a throw, similar to an afghan], I put on my old coat
and proceeded down to the deck. I had just settled to read
when two of my naval friends came along. They rolled themselves up in coats, and the three of us slept soundly all afternoon!

Much revived from my afternoon sleep, I ate an enormous tea and have retired to my cabin to write this. The

swell is much less this afternoon, and I think everyone is feeling the better for it! The stewardess has just come in for a chat. She is a kindly soul—has been with the B.I. [British India Co.] for twenty-five years and comes from Box Hill, near Dorking. I was glad of the opportunity of having a talk with her for I was rather ashamed of the scene caused on our arrival over the hats. My cabinmate is in the habit of ringing the bell for everything she wants and does not seem to think that these people might want a little rest, nor that certain hours are busy times for them and that it is kinder not to call them then. However, in spite of this, I think she (Mrs. A.) will be quite easy to manage. After all, she has been through a great deal, so one must make every allowance.

Well, I think that brings my journal up to date, so I will go on deck and rescue my knitting. One or two of the V.R.s rather fancy themselves on the plain rows!!

Wednesday, 18 June 1941

By evening yesterday we were somewhere in the region of Skye and were making leeward. The steep mountainous outline of the coast was clearly visible through the mist, which seemed to have suddenly enveloped us. We were practically stationary and seemed to remain so all night. Most people appeared relieved at the stillness of the boat and took the opportunity of coming out in full force on the decks. These are small and apt to get rather crowded. I believe nine and a half times round is the mile, but no one seems to know if this refers to the nautical mile or not! However, I just walk and sit when I have had enough, not bothering to count the number of times round. I spent most of the evening, in fact, walking the promenade deck.

Once more we had a calm and peaceful night and both would have slept soundly throughout had it not been for the cold. Tonight, however, we have extra blankets and so should be warm enough.

I've just finished bathing. It is amazing how warm one can get by this method of pouring hot water over oneself. The process of soaping is a very cold one, but with a beaker of hot water, one soon gets warm. Apparently, it does not matter how much splashing is made. After the bath, I had just time to dress and take one or two turns round the deck before the breakfast gong rang. It is a pity I cannot cope with cooked things in the morning as there is no end to the menu offered. And do you know! I had All Bran yesterday, which gave rise to many derisive comments from my table companions! Nevertheless, I enjoyed it very much.

After breakfast, boat stations as usual, and this time everyone assembled in the right places. We were given instructions as to what to do in the event of the boat's being made useless by shelling or the like. It appears that we have to proceed aft to the port raft, which will be slipped into the sea from its position where it is at present, secured to a kind of shoot from the mast to the side of the boat. Passengers will then descend by means of a rope ladder! For those who cannot get into this, there are two others each side. But these will be just thrown overboard, and we shall have to jump for it, holding the life belt well down. I do not suppose for a moment this will happen, at least I hope not, but it is just as well that the passengers should know what to do in an emergency.

After boat stations I spent the whole morning doing nothing but wandering round the deck with my Birmingham friend Mr. Pike. We inspected the convoy, trying to identify the different types of ships, all of which were by this time steaming ahead at a considerably greater speed than the night before. The sun came out, although the wind was still high. It is marvelous to be able to stand and do nothing but gaze out to sea and feel that you need not be doing anything else if you do not want to! No doubt this will lose its novelty after a few weeks at sea, but for now it is very pleasant.

The afternoon was spent in reading and sleeping. It was very windy indeed, but the sun was still out, so Bunty and I found a sunny spot on the well deck where, we were soon joined by the others. Thus we slept until tea. I am finding my rug a useful investment. After tea we again walked the deck—I think this time we did do the nine times—and then both retired to our cabin to write.

Thursday, 19 June 1941

There is a howling gale, so I have been obliged to close the porthole and type by artificial light. As this is rather meager, there will be many mistakes. Being compelled to keep the door ajar on the hook, one cannot have the porthole open at the same time, or the result is disastrous. Yesterday I spent some time trying to put the sheets and carbons back together in the right order, but in the end had to give it up as a bad job.

Yesterday I sat in the smoking room all evening after dinner and did quite a bit of my cardigan, but I have grave doubts as to whether I have enough wool. I shall be very annoyed if I have not as there will be no chance of getting any more. However, I may be wrong in my calculations. I have started the back first and that will take the most wool, so when that is finished, I shall be better able to tell.

Boat stations as usual this morning, followed by a demonstration of equipment on the after deck by our Naval friends, one or two of whom proved to be budding lecturers. On each raft is a red box containing matches, rather like Mr. Horne's [my mother's employer] special ones, but they will light in a wind and burn for several seconds. There are also flares, both ends of which are sealed and have to be broken before the thing "ackles" [family term meaning "works"]; this appears quite simple—all that is required is a sharp strike on the ignition end with the top of the matchbox. This starts a pinkish flame, lighted from the bottom, which is used for signaling by covering and uncovering it with a bucket, for a flashing light is more visible than a stationary one. Next, we were shown the sea-anchor—a kind of canvas bag, or rather cylinder, attached to a large round frame on one end and tapering to a tiny hole on the other. Thick and thin ropes are fastened to each end respectively, and this is lowered into the sea and allowed to fill with water. It is then dragged by the force of the current, so as to steady the raft somewhat. At the same time another bag that contains thick oil is lowered, and this has three valves at the end which enable the oil to seep through and cover the sea round the raft with oil. That concluded the demonstrations, and we were dismissed.

It was very blowy, but we struggled round the deck several times before the Chief Steward came up to say that those with cameras [being held for security reasons] could now claim them in the dining saloon, so I went below and got mine back. As soon as the weather gets a little brighter, I shall endeavor to take some snaps to send home with this, or maybe I shall have to wait until I get to Singapore.

I have acquired the terrible habit of spending the afternoon in a deck chair, doing nothing in particular but reading and sleeping. It was very cold indeed, but we wrapped ourselves up well and snuggled down into deck chairs on the after deck until the gong announced tea. How terribly bad it is—but on the other hand how very nice—always to have new bread. We get lovely little rolls for breakfast and for tea, small loaves, always new and fresh. It is really delicious. I shall get so fat with all the good food, and there is always such a quantity of everything, and—what do you think?—curry every day for lunch. I fall for it nearly every day!

There was some excitement caused this morning by gun practice from the ships of the convoy. Each ship seemed to fire several bursts in succession, trying to keep them as close to each other as possible—it was quite exciting. I feel very safe as I look out and see all the ships steaming round us. My goodness, some of them pitch and toss in the choppy sea, and it is choppy today.

This evening there is to be a cinema show of Jessie Mathews in *Sailing Along*; in order to avoid overcrowding, we have to get tickets from the purser's office in the morning. But as there are to be several showings of the same film, I have decided to go tomorrow. There will probably be more room. I see that a deck tennis court has been put down on the forward deck with netting all round, but I doubt if it will be patronized until the wind drops. Also, the court markings on the promenade deck have been re-painted. I am afraid that when these begin to be used, they will be rather in the way of the promenaders. I can see that we shall have to be up before breakfast if any serious walk-ing is to be done. Yesterday I suggested to the Navy that we should organize a P.T. [physical training] class at seven o'clock every morning. I am rather afraid now that I may be taken at my word! *When* the warmer weather comes, however, I may be persuaded to get up a little earlier. But not at the moment. It is still too cold in the mornings.

Our table companions are improving on acquaintance, and I think we shall resolve into quite a jolly party after all.

Friday, 20 June 1941

Yesterday evening was spent very pleasantly in the smoking room with a jolly party, which included Bunty and that girl of whom I spoke earlier who knows Mrs. Paton. She is on her way out to China for four years on kind of missionary work for the Students' Christian Movement in connection with the YMCA. A very nice person indeed. Just before 11:00 we went for a breather round the deck. By this time it was very cold and a mist was coming down, so that the other ships of the convoy were scarcely visible. Needless to say, we did not stay long.

Hot seawater is now available in the morning, in addition to the tub of hot fresh water. This is since yesterday, but this morning the water was cold; nevertheless, the bath was filled just the same! Apparently, there is likely to be severe rationing of fresh water as the ship is carrying so many passengers. They seem to be using more than the supply will guarantee, so I should think that it would be turned off during the day. The question of washing is very acute. The laundry is not yet functioning, so we have nowhere to dry our things. Washing, of course, can be done in the hand basin in the cabin, but one will not be allowed to hang things up there as soon as the captain begins his tours of inspection. The stewardess told me the other day that, in the usual way, they have a Mongolian crew, who are excellent *doebes* (Malay phonetics!). The present crew are all Singhalese (Roman Catholics, too, by the way), and it appears that they are not as good. The stewardess said that she would be doing her own aprons herself, but that later on we should be able to have the use of the laundry for our own washing and drying. On the lower deck there are two ironing boards and electric irons. I expect it will be impossible to get a look in as soon as the hot weather comes, and everyone will be wanting to iron their cotton dresses. Bunty is down there at this moment, and I am going to join her shortly as soon as a board is free. I have a shirt to iron! One of the naval lads came up to me and asked if I could possibly do it for him. I think his cabin mate has washed it by mistake, and he, Donald, whose father owns a laundry, is terrified he will ruin it altogether! They have to do all their own washing and ironing. There is no means of getting it done for them, and I don't think one of them knows how to use an iron!

The sea is still rather choppy, and several people have not appeared today. I spent most of the morning out on the deck. This afternoon, wrapped up in raincoat, woolly coat, tweed coat, cardigan and rug, I went to sleep in a deck chair on the after well deck. It is lovely, believe it or not, to sit with the wind blowing over one's face and to be gently rocked by the motion of the ship! Yes, I like it!

This morning after boat stations I went to the Chief Steward and asked him if I could type in the dining saloon after tea, or at any other time that was convenient, and it has been arranged that I can use the saloon after 2:30 until tea time. This is a great improvement on the cabin as I have now a steady table and room in which to think. I am so sorry that yesterday's entry was so scrappy, but I was writing under difficulties.

Tonight we are going to the cinema show, the same film that was shown the other day. They clear out the music room or lounge and erect the projector at one end. This means an overcrowding in the smoking room as it is still too cold to sit out on deck after dinner. In fact, it is too cold at all today for most people. If only this wretched weather would change—but I suppose we will have it all across the Atlantic. It is voiced abroad that we shall be in Halifax by today week, but I should think it will be longer. At any rate, I shall try to send a cable from there and will post this—a copy to Mummy and one to Singapore. My journal is the cause of much interest and not a little teasing!

I have been persuaded to play deck tennis after tea, but I think that it will be far too cold. I can see through the window of the saloon onto the court, and the players appear to be well wrapped up!

At 12 o'clock this morning, I went down to the nursery

where a dancing class was in progress. Miss Collins is a dancing teacher, and she has been asked by two of the men on board to teach them a few steps. She asked me to go down as partner, thus making four of us, but I do not think the class will last very long. One of the men is a naval officer, but the other is a terrible old bore—calls everybody by their Christian names!

We had a grand curry today for lunch! A vegetable one and really hot. I think so far I have had curry most days. I expect later on I shall get tired of it, but at present I am enjoying it very much. The food is really very good indeed, lashings of butter and sugar, and marmalade and oranges. It seems a shame that I should be enjoying so much here while those at home cannot get these things. I was speaking to the cook this morning whilst waiting to see the Chief Steward. He says that they have had to cut down a lot as the ship does not normally go for voyages of longer than seven days before being able to pick up fresh supplies. But now we are likely to be fourteen days or more crossing the Atlantic, and it is a problem keeping enough supplies for the number of passengers on board.

Today I have really started to learn Malay—there are several people on board who speak it fluently—and I have had many offers of help. There are also two Dutch girls, one going to Singapore and one to the Dutch East Indies, but I have not met them yet. That little book that I got from the Dutch Shipping Office is most useful, and once I get the hang of the pronunciation, I shall be able to get along very fast.

I visited the barber's shop yesterday and was able to get a huge slab of chocolate and a Kodak film for my camera. I do not want to use those I got in London just yet; in any case, they are not the right ones for this dull weather. The barber's shop is a perfectly marvelous place; he seems to have everything that one can want in the way of soaps,

toothpaste, sweets, etc., a second Mr. Adams [country gro-
cer back home], in fact. At the bar the other night I got fifty
Players cigarettes for two shillings. They were not allowed
to sell them until we were out of the three-mile limit, but so
far there seems to be no shortage whatsoever. At the moment I have gone off smoking, which is a pity when there
is the opportunity of getting them so cheaply.

In the lounge is a piano, which is unfortunate, as it is
played almost continually all evening and a good part of
the day, and when that is not happening, there is usually a
gramophone. I do think it rude of people to bring a
gramophone into a public room like that and play it continually—Radio Three sort of music [dance music]! Even in
the afternoon on deck they have it, and in the evenings the
ship's gramophone is usually functioning through a loud
speaker for dancers on deck. The other night it was going
until after 12 o'clock. The dancing on deck is not so bad,
but there is a receiver in the lounge, which broadcasts it, so
that all the ship must suffer for a few dancers. However,
there may be some rules about this later on, for I doubt if
the captain will allow music until after midnight every night!

After tea Tony and I had a very good game of deck tennis. I had never played it before, but we managed to have an amusing afternoon. The game is very popular with all the passengers, so I expect it will be a question of queuing up for the court. Even in the early morning it is quite popular, and last night at 11 o'clock people were still playing.

We got into the cinema show last evening. I enjoyed seeing the film again. Jessie Matthews is always very good, and her dancing is beautiful. It seemed hard to realize that we were in the middle of the Atlantic Ocean as we sat there watching the film. It was quite a typical Saturday night at the pictures! First we had a nature film about seagulls, followed by a very old Mickey Mouse, one of the early black and white ones. Then came *Sailing Along*. We were out by eleven, but just at the end the purser made the announcement that clocks and watches should be put back two hours, thus making it 9 o'clock, with an additional two hours' sleep in the morning. However, as it turned out, this was not the case, for we walked round the deck until eleven o'clock new time, or nearly that. We were not much better off in the way of sleep after all.

Remarkable unconcern over the war news this morning that Russia is at war with Germany. There was a little stir at breakfast, but by the middle of the morning everyone seemed to have forgotten about it! With no news or papers, one seems too aloof at sea and out of touch with things to do with land. There is a wireless in the Chief Steward's cabin, and generally at lunch time there is a little knot of people round his door, listening to the news—he does not seem to mind. Thus, news is usually second hand and not always very reliable. However, there seems to be no doubt this time.

Poor Bunty got the wind up thoroughly this morning and was terribly worried as to the possibility of getting to Colombo: she was afraid that we might all be stranded in Canada or some such place without funds, etc. But there is absolutely no chance of that, for probably we should not be allowed to leave the ship. In any case, they would not leave us stranded. Nevertheless, we may be considerably delayed. How nice it is to feel that I am earning money all this time! How frightful it would have been if I had my salary only on landing—we shall be weeks and weeks.

After boat stations, those who wanted went down to the dining saloon where a woman doctor, one of the passengers, was giving a lecture on First Aid. She has very kindly offered to give a series every day at 10:30 for any who are interested. I think I shall attend them, for it is something to do, besides being very helpful.

Thank goodness, the sun has come out at last, and there is a warm spot in which to sit on deck. The well deck is crowded this afternoon. I was out there until 2:30 when I came in to the saloon to do my typing, and I shall go out there again before tea. It really is marvelous being able to type here in the dining saloon. The Chief Steward just put his head round the corner to see if I was all right. The table is just next to his cabin. I was afraid I should disturb him, but he assures me that typing will not keep him awake. Depth charges do not waken him, so I think I shall be fairly safe! A few were dropped yesterday at dinnertime; at least, that is what I think they were. Some say yes, and some say no, but I have it on naval authority that they were!! However, our escort has left us this morning, so that seems to indicate that we are more or less out of danger. At least I hope so, anyway until we get into the Pacific!

I had curry again for lunch today, Kashmere curry this time. I don't think one is really any different from the other, but the name sounds important. Anyway, it was nice and hot, and also I had Bombay duck. The first lot they brought round was crawling with red ants, but the next lot seemed all right.

I shall try to get some more photographs this afternoon as the sun seems quite strong. They can be developed at the barber's shop, only not until after today, as the barber has been on watch and has no time. His watch comes just at the time he usually does his developing and printing. Anyway, this is not a vital matter, and one will possibly be able to get them done in Halifax. Really, there is not much one wants to take; the only subjects seem people in deck chairs!

Monday, 23 June 1941

What a perfectly horrible day! The sea is rough, and the decks are wet with spray: it's cold and dreadful. A few brave people are walking round the decks, but the majority are comfortably settled in the lounge or smoking room and, no doubt, in the bar. But it is really too cold for even me to be sitting outside. We are tossing about a bit, more than just swell, but it is not too bad.

Yesterday after tea I had a good game of deck tennis. We had two very close sets, my Birmingham friend Reggie Pike and myself winning one and losing the second. The ring is rope, and this is very hard on the hands. In fact, I bruised my hand so much that, had the game not been canceled, I should not have been able to play at all today. It is hard on the tips of the fingers and the thumb. All the same, it is a very good game, and we get lots of fun out of it. One or two brave souls were playing this morning before breakfast. I got up early and had a few turns round the deck, but it was raining already and looked very nasty on the court.

A party of us played one of the deck games [shuffleboard] after dinner. There are two circles marked out in squares on the deck. In the squares are numbers, some plus and others minus. Four can play at a time, and they stand in twos behind a line, the partners at opposite ends. Each player has a billiard cue with a wooden disc on the end and six round flat wooden discs. Then, in turn, each player sends the discs to the opposite end, trying to get the highest score in numbers by either getting into a square himself or knocking his opponent's disc out. It is quite amusing but rather noisy, and of course, the rolling of the ship makes it more difficult. Still that adds to the fun! About 10:30 we had had enough and repaired to the bar, but there was such a din in there that we retired in disgust to the smoking room. My goodness, there are a horrible lot of people on this boat—a really unpleasant type. This does not, of course, apply to all of them! It is a very good thing that all deck games have been stopped between two and four in the afternoon, for the noise was really too bad, especially for people trying to rest in their cabins on the lower deck.

Today we danced at 12 o'clock, and tonight I think we are really getting the gramophone. We can use the nursery after the children are in bed, and it will be quiet down there. I think one or two more are anxious to join the class, but there is not much room and I don't think that Sylvia is too keen to have many there.

Yesterday as I went upstairs, I saw the assistant purser struggling away with one finger on the typewriter, doing menus or something of the like. So I said, half in fun, "Oh, I'll do those for you," and today he has asked me if I would mind doing out some forms for a crossword puzzle. He has come in just this moment, but unfortunately, the paper won't fit into my machine. I must say I am rather glad, as it was one of those wax stencils and I have never done any of them. I should be sure to make many mistakes, which, of course, is fatal. I have, however, offered to do any other typing they may have, within reason! I should be quite glad of the occupation.

Before dinner yesterday we all crowded round the Chief Steward's door to listen to Churchill's speech, and later a summary was typed out and put up on the notice board. I think they will do that with at least one news bulletin every day.

Alas, no entry yesterday, and what a horrible day it was. But thank God, we are all safe. I am taking the precaution to write early on in the day in case there is not another opportunity. Yesterday I had just gone down to the dining saloon when the alarm sounded to take to boat stations. It is seven short blasts on the Klaxon, followed by a long one. Everyone heard the first blast. There was a moment's dead silence and then one rush from the saloon. It is very difficult getting out of the chairs, which are heavy and close together. We all got out without much panic, although one or two did get a little flustered. But the boat wardens were very good and kept calling out to everyone to take it easy. Once on deck, I piloted Bunty to the cabin, where we picked up our belongings and hurried to our boat. There were a good many "bonkings" by this time, and I am afraid the boat astern of us was lost. We heard later on in the day that all survivors had been picked up. She was hit by a torpedo and sank in a quarter of an hour. ["The ship *SS Malda* (official no. 146286) was a British registered vessel owned by the British India Steam Navigation Company. The name of the Master was H N Edmondson. The vessel sailed from Greenock in June 1941 as part of convoy OB336 (UK—North America). On the 24th June the convoy was attacked by U203 (K/Lt Mutzburg) at approx 0913hrs in position 52 deg 23' N 38deg 49' W. Two ships were sunk as a result of this attack, the *SS Kinross* and the Dutch registered *Schie*," British naval researcher Peter Wooten, email to M. McCullough, 29 July 1999]. I think some people saw her, but I did not. The sub, I understand, surfaced but had to crash dive as soon as our guns opened fire. Oh, it was horrible, standing there on deck, wondering if we were going to be next. Somehow I had a feeling that we should pull through, although I wished it could be soon.

Then all the ships in the convoy dropped smoke flares and set off full speed, each boat pursuing its own way and changing course every few minutes. Anyway, we made a wonderful get-away, and one cannot be grateful enough to all those concerned. After a little while, we were allowed to disperse, boat by boat, to collect belongings and get what food we could from the saloon. One or two sat down to cold fried eggs, but the majority of us grabbed toast and marmalade. The Chief Steward came on deck at one point with a huge dish of cold sausages, and they were most appreciated!

People began to appear, carrying bundles of food or plates of bread and butter. One man caused much amusement by carrying up a dish of prunes. A bucket of coffee was also produced, and everyone began to feel much better. I think we must have been well away by this time, for the "bonkings" had ceased and the smoke screen was most effective. Gradually, one by one, as the tension eased, people brought out their cameras. I managed to get one or two snaps. I hope they come out, but the light was not good; also, it was difficult to keep absolutely still, as the wind was so strong and it was bitterly cold. Very soon after this, we were told that we could wander about. The immediate danger seemed over. It was a wonderful feeling of relief.

I got up to the cabin and made the bunks, as the boys had all the mess in the saloon to clear up, as well as the cabins. Having got the bunks straight, I put our bundles in order on the end of the beds, ready for another emergency, so that one could just rush up and snatch hold of them. Then I went on deck, determined to enjoy the rest of the day. The sea was beautiful, as blue as could be, the strong wind tossing it up into little white breakers and tearing the white clouds that filled the sky. Four of us started a game of deck tennis, but we could hardly stand up against the wind, and every now and then one or other of us would be drenched with spray. We played until the tips of our fingers became so sore from the quoit that we were forced to call it off. Still, we had two hectic sets.

How they managed to feed us at all I don't know, but sure enough there was a sumptuous meal at 1:30, as always. But, alas! we had just reached the cheese stage when the Klaxon sounded again, and once more we rushed to boat stations. I must admit that again I had the feeling, *Shall we get away with it this time?* And the sea looked awfully rough for an open boat. However, we were much comforted by one of our boat wardens' telling us that a ship had been sighted on the horizon and it had not yet been identified, so that this was merely a precaution. The wind was bitter, and after a time we were told to go into the smoking room or lounge until further orders were issued. It was warm in there, and we settled down in a little group on the floor by the door. Conversation started by being lively, but before long most of us were attempting to sleep. After about another hour, the alarm sounded once more, and we "upped and outed" to the boats. Once again we were not kept long and soon went in again. This time we were asked to keep to either one or other of these two rooms, and about four o'clock, tea was announced for the smoking room, the others going down later.

We came up from tea and hung about until dinner when again we went in relays so as to avoid overcrowding in the saloon and also probably to facilitate the catering. By this time we had been told that we could once more wander, but we kept to the promenade deck and the smoking room. In fact, none of us had any energy at all and spent the evening just sitting and talking. After tea, volunteers were called upon from among the male passengers to take a submarine lookout watch from the boat deck. Also, the Sub-Lieutenants took watches with the gun crews. It must have been absolutely bitter, for the wind never dropped all day. This morning it is still very strong.

Many people sat up all night in the bar or lounge, but our cabins being on the boat deck, that was not necessary. We turned in about eleven—did not undress but just took off coats and shoes and lay down under masses of blankets. I slept very well indeed, rather too heavily, in fact, but a hurried bath this morning helped to freshen me. One man was caught in his bath yesterday, but, all the same, I felt I would risk it. And I am very glad I did, for there is nothing worse than waking up in your clothes and then having to go about all day without a wash!

There was a marked improvement in the absence of latecomers to breakfast! I think everyone was determined to get a bite in before it was too late. I, for one, had a huge meal, which included beans on toast, preceded by All Bran and followed by large quantities of bread, toast and marmalade. And yesterday I managed to get a Madras curry before we had to go!

On Monday evening we had the gramophone in the nursery for the purpose of continuing our dancing lesson, but others also got wind of it and we were crowded out to start with. However, we were most polite and took up as much room as we could, practicing steps down the center of the room and bumping heavily whenever the ship lurched!

Wednesday, 26 June 1941

There is a terrific gale blowing, and it is practically impossible to stand on the deck. One just sways from one side to the other. Just before lunch it was trying to snow or sleet: it was bitter. Oh, for some hot weather! Thank goodness, though, we had an otherwise quiet day with no alarms. All the same, we did not dress last night, just in case of emergencies. But I think it will be all right to do so tonight, for the submarine and gun watches have been suspended for the time being, though we have been asked to keep as alert as before. I think the general suggestion is that we shall have sight of land the day after tomorrow, but how true that is no one can tell. All I hope is that we run into some warmer weather soon!

I discovered an amazing thing today: Donald Westcotte, one of the Sub. Lts., is the son of the proprietor of Westcotte Laundries Ltd. at Chingford, and he knows Uncle [Charley Wilkes], or rather his father does, and until the war he was acting as manager at his father's laundry in London. At least, he knows a Mr. Wilkes from St. Albans, so I should think there can be no doubt but that it is Uncle. Isn't it amazing?

I had a date to play deck tennis this morning before breakfast, but neither of us kept it. I did attempt to struggle round the deck once, but it was far too cold to do more than that. One could hardly stand up round the corners, the wind was so strong. We had to put our watches back half an hour last night, and I forgot to do so; as a result, I came down half an hour too soon for breakfast. We have put them back yet another half hour this morning, so by now I think we are about three hours back from time at home.

A party of us is going to the flicks tonight; they are showing *Dr. Syn*, and I think there should be a good audience. We have tickets, but nevertheless, we shall take the precaution of getting there early. Otherwise, the most comfortable seats will be taken.

There is a movement on foot to discover the hidden talent on board, with a view to getting up some sort of an entertainment, but I do not think it will meet with much success. Everyone is far too cold to bother about that sort of thing, besides being rather keyed up. That very nice woman with the little girl, Sally, is going to Singapore, and I have offered to help her with the child in any way I can. She said she would be very grateful for Sally to have a few lessons as soon as the weather gets a little better, for after Halifax most of the other children will have left the ship. I said that I would be only too pleased to help her.

I spent this morning in the music room, as it was far too cold to sit out on deck. I managed to get quite a bit done to my cardigan, but I am afraid that the wool was not a very good investment. I am sorry now that I did not get plain wool; I think it would have been much more successful. I shall probably leave it and begin on the bathing costume before long.

Bunty is lying down in the cabin. She rather wanted me to stay up there and type, but it is so much more comfortable down here in the dining saloon. Besides, she will probably go to sleep. I think she is rather nervous being up there alone, so I make a point of going up to bed when she does. But, I expect, once we are across the Atlantic, she will get over that. However, I should not like her to be up there alone if the alarm went. She was the other day and fell down the stairs in a panic. It was amazing she did not hurt herself badly, for they are very steep. However, we now have ourselves beautifully organized and can sprint with all our belongings at the shortest notice.

The purser has been in here talking to me. He comes from Sussex, near East Grinstead, and knows the part round Turner's Hill quite well.

Friday, 27 June 1941

Iceberg sighted on the port bow! Great excitement! And, my goodness, it is cold enough for anything, but the sea has gone down a good deal since yesterday. By tea time there was a terrific gale blowing, and the ship was tossing violently. It was really impossible to walk about without falling over something or someone. There was a heavy list to port, and the ping-pong table and several chairs slid over the deck to the rails and stayed there. In the bar every now and again the ship would heave and down would go all the chairs (basket ones) and the tables, throwing all that was on them to the floor. It had been fairly rough all day, but at tea time it suddenly seemed to become very rough indeed. The boys had just finished laying the tables, when crash!—everything on the port side fell to the floor. Cakes scattered in all directions, plates, cups and saucers all mixed up together. But I think the thing that struck me most was the terrible waste of lump sugar strewn among the chairs, not to mention jam, butter and bread. When the passengers came down to tea, we sat on the starboard sides of the tables, holding onto our cups and plates as best we could. By dinnertime, however, they had kind of wooden trays fixed to the tables. They are actually wooden squares which lie along side each other all down the table, one square for each person. This is most uncomfortable, but infinitely better than having a plate of soup in the lap.

The waves were quite fascinating to watch; they were simply enormous. Great bottle-green cones whirled out of the sea and blown into spray by this terrific wind. It kept up steadily all the evening and into the night, but this morning, although it is still very cold, the sea is somewhat calmer. The sun has come out, making the sea that lovely dark, rich blue, but yesterday the decks were awash and it was all we could do to get from our cabins to the saloon. Unfortunately, we have to go on deck to get to the lounge, smoking room or dining saloon. There is no way other than that, which is all right in calm weather and when there is no wind. But when you have done your hair for dinner, there is little hope of arriving in that beautiful state, for you are usually blown to pieces before you can reach the entrance to the saloon. However, that is a minor detail, and I would much rather have a cabin on the boat deck than one down below. We are very lucky indeed.

I spent most of yesterday sitting, and as little of it as possible on my feet, with the result that I finished the back of my cardigan and am well advanced with the front. The cinema had to be postponed, owing to weather conditions, but I should think we will have it tonight if it still continues to keep fairly calm. It was rather disappointing, but we spent quite an amusing evening in the smoking room, and I turned in quite early. It was bitterly cold all night, and how we pitched and tossed! I did feel sorry for all those on watch.

Donald Wescotte has been writing home this afternoon, and he has asked his father to ring Uncle to say I am in good hands! It will be interesting to see who hears first, for we are both posting at Halifax. I am afraid that this lengthy journal of mine may be held up in the censor's office for weeks while he wades through it!

There was an unexpected lifeboat drill this morning. I happened to be in the Chief Steward's office when the officer came to remind him, so I was let into the secret. But the Klaxons were sounded very gently, not like they were the other day; there was no mistaking the urgency in the note that time.

Saturday, 28 June 1941

The icebergs caused great excitement yesterday. We saw several, and just before tea, the purser came in to ask me if I would like to see one through a telescope. It was a marvelous sight. They seemed quite near, and you could see the sea breaking over them. One that I saw through the telescope had three peaks, which stood up like the spire of a cathedral, appearing very white against the deep blue of the sea. The atmosphere was very cold, and there was a peculiar smell from the water, rather like the sort of smell there is on the beach at night—old boats, dead fish and the like.

After dinner we had the cinematograph show. I had always wanted to see *Dr. Syn*, having heard so much about it from Rosalind [a classmate and friend; I would be replacing her in Sumatra]. It was made on Romney Marsh—at least parts of it were—causing a great stir in the neighborhood. At the interval, Tony and I came out for a breather; it was getting dark by this time and the sun was beginning to set. I don't think I have seen anything more lovely than the sky last night. The sea was very calm and smooth with large shadows playing over it and the sky a deep, bright orange, not a scrap of red, but a heavenly yellow orange, with a bright crescent moon and the pole star. We came out later after the show to see the last of the sun disappearing behind the horizon.

This morning it is much warmer, and now it is quite hot in the sun. People are really beginning to talk of cotton frocks for the landing at Halifax. There is still no confirmation that we are to be allowed to land, but most people seem to think we will. Anyway, several dates have been made! So let's hope that the parties will not be disappointed!

We saw a whale this morning, at least, so it was stated, but I just missed it. However, I saw the icebergs and porpoises yesterday, and I am told there will be plenty of opportunities for seeing more whales later on in the Pacific. During the morning two planes of the Canadian Air Force circled round us, and later an American destroyer came alongside, turned and saluted, while we dipped the Red Ensign. Coming up the port side, she signaled to us, and I gather she is sending escort for the rest of the convoy, which we have not sighted since Monday. I do hope that they are all safe.

I attempted to type outside this morning, but it was too uncomfortable. Besides, a gramophone was playing jazz just close to me, not to mention my naval escort, so I am afraid that I was very easily persuaded to join in a game of deck tennis. However, I have got down here early, so shall have a chance to get some of my letters written before tea. It was arranged that I should type the news summary today. They have found a man who can take down shorthand notes during the news. He comes to dictate them to the purser, so I have been asked if I would care to do the typing in the future. Today, however, when I came down, I found they had already started, so I let them carry on and will do it tomorrow.

Yesterday Bunty told me that Penelope Pearcy, the girl that Mrs. Paton knows, had asked her to share a cabin with her or to try, if they could, to get a three-berth cabin for the three of us. But Bunty was not at all keen. When she told me, I said that I was not going to change my cabin in any circumstances. If she liked to go, I should be very sorry indeed, I said, but we had the best cabin on the ship. I was not going to change mine. Today she told Pen, and nothing more was said. Bunty is rather given to sudden decisions, but I find they are nearly always subject to alteration, so I did not place much importance on the whole affair.

I went down yesterday to the barber to get my photographs, but I am afraid they are disappointing. The one I took on Monday at the lifeboat stations has not come out at all. The light was too bad, and there was nowhere I could have steadied the camera sufficiently to take a brief time exposure, so they are all underexposed. Still, four of the eight have come out tolerably well. I will keep them until I get to Singapore and then send them home all together from there.

Sunday, 29 June, 1941

Yesterday evening was very cold, and I spent most of it in the smoking room, knitting and reading. Another horrible day today, with a thick mist settling upon the ship and a cold wind blowing round all the corners. It seems to be trying to clear up, but it is still very cold and miserable. I regret to say that I have caught a cold—I think it must have been on Monday, standing out in that bitter cold on the decks, and a heated game of deck tennis yesterday morning did it no good. However, it will run its course, and as soon as the hot weather comes to stay, I shall be all right. My throat is a bit sore, so shall stay inside again this afternoon. I spent the morning in the smoking room. There was a service held in the music room at eleven o'clock, which most people attended.

I counted up the pages of my journal yesterday, and I learned with horror that there are twelve, so it will cost a small fortune to post by airmail. Still, I expect I shall be able to cut off margins and reduce the weight a bit. Anyway, it is worth paying the extra and sending it airmail; otherwise, it will be ages before my family gets any news of me. How I am dying to get their letters at Singapore. Most people seem to think we shall not be there before the end of September! I don't mind!

Yesterday was great fun. I did so enjoy going ashore. We did not know until nearly tea time that we were to be allowed to land, so there was great rejoicing when the notice appeared saying that we could do so. We docked just before lunch. I was typing in my cabin when I looked through the porthole and was surprised to see blank wall, obviously the quayside. After lunch I went down to the saloon where two Imperial cable agents were coping with piles and piles of cables. I managed to get my two sent off, so I hope it will not be long before my family will have news of my safe arrival. They will be most surprised to get a letter with a Canadian postmark. I did not discover until too late that one could say "Arrived *Canada* safely." However, it does not really matter. The letter will tell them that, and I have sent it airmail.

Having sent the cables, I went up to the music room, where we had to take our passports in order to get a landing card. There was an enormous queue, so I decided to go up to the cabin to change first. It was a lovely sunny day, and many people were tempted into cotton frocks. I thought it a little too cold, especially as we were allowed leave until 11:30 in the evening when it would be sure to be cold. So instead, I wore my gray coat and skirt, which, as it turned out, was just the right thing. Once changed, I came to join the queue while Reggie Pike, the Sub. Lt. from Birmingham, got some money changed for me in the purser's office. We went ashore together.

Letters could be posted ashore, so the first thing we did was to find a post office, which closed at 6 o'clock. It is really the most impressive building in Halifax, in fact, one might almost say the only building, for the rest of the town is dud. Both of us were feeling in need of exercise, so we took a tram out to the Iron Bridge. From there we followed a road up through a kind of settlement, along a very stony path up to a tower. The houses were mostly wooden bungalows set up from the road, in some cases with quite a steep climb to the front door. The road seemed to be cut through a wooded hill, the houses on the left being set down in a dell, while those on the right were perched up the hillside. There were no railings or fences; each house stood by itself, but there was nothing to separate Mr. Jones from Mr. Smith. The idea was novel and, I think, an improvement on our rows of houses in England, each minute bit of garden enclosed and separated from the next.

The walk to the tower was really as much as our untrained muscles would allow! Having climbed to the top to observe the view, we decided to take the ferry across the lake and then catch a tram back to the town. This we did, and a friendly tram driver told us of a place where we could eat, namely the Green Lantern. This was a modern restaurant with a sandwich counter down one side and confectionery the other, with a restaurant at the back. Here the tables were arranged round the walls, somewhat like a dining car on the railway. There were similar ones in the center of the floor, and sitting at one of these, one could see the heads of the people in the next compartment but not observe what they were eating. The supervisor came round first, taking our orders and giving each person a chit. These were added up as we progressed through the meal, so that there was no waiting about at the end for a bill. It was about 8:15 when we had finished, so we set out to find the cinema we had decided upon. It was some way away, but a brisk walk soon got us there. The cinemas certainly did not come up to those at home, having only wooden tip-up seats! We were out of the cinema by eleven o'clock and made our way back to the Green Lantern, where I embarked upon a double sandwich. This double-decker sandwich was an enormous affair. Three slabs of toast spread with peanut butter, lettuce, red currant jelly, ham, stuck together with an orange stick [toothpick] and served with pickles! I was unable to cope with it all as it was then 11:25 and we were due back on board by 11:30. We walked back, however, and were not so late after all. Anyway, many arrived heaps later than we did!

Wednesday, 2 July 1941

Yesterday morning we slipped over to the other side of the harbor to fill up with oil and, by the afternoon, were away. Not long out, we ran into thick fog, and this has continued ever since the ship left. The foghorns have been going all night and most of today. It is not quite so dense now but still very thick.

I felt rotten last night, my cold having reached the heavy stage. I was persuaded to go to bed early with a hot whiskey and lemon with two Aspros. The result was excellent. I woke up this morning feeling much better, having slept soundly all night. I heard neither foghorns nor anything else until the stewardess arrived with the tea. I got up and had the first really hot bath since we left Glasgow! It is muggy today, and, I think, if only the fog would lift, it would be a really boiling day. The sun is trying to come through.

Yesterday morning it was really hot, and most of us sat out on deck getting slowly redder and redder. But by the afternoon and as we moved further out to sea, it became cooler, and the wind sprung up. With the first patch of sun, there was an outcrop of sunbathers and torsos! My goodness, what a sight! How people can make such exhibitions of themselves, I don't know. One party, in particular, had all eyes on them from the bridge downwards. I am rather afraid they are the people who are trying to get up onto our deck cabins as soon as the others get off at New

York, but that remains to be seen. I don't like them any-way! One of the crew, an old Laskar [Indian seaman], came by with an expression of disgust on his face. He went up the companionway, half turning round, and when he got to the top, he gave one look and just spat! I think Miss Collins and myself were the only two who saw him.

For the first time, the Captain—H. N. Edmondson—made an appearance, coming to all meals. He seems a jolly sort. He has disappeared again today, and we shall prob-ably not see much of him until after Panama.

We have a marvelous new supply of oranges since Halifax—lovely juicy ones and masses of fresh vegetables. Really, we are fed excellently; I eat so much butter that my cotton frocks will not fit me when it is time to wear them. How I wish my family could partake of all these good things.

After boat stations today we had a general meeting called for the purpose of proposing a committee for the organization of games and entertainment amongst the pas-sengers. It was rather a lengthy affair, but in the end, mat-ters were settled. Two women were proposed, the doctor and myself. She got it by one vote. There is a committee of six persons, and they are to run tournaments, etc., and ar-range an entertainment, the latter in one month's time. I have offered my services as typist, for the purser will be far too busy and there are sure to be notices to put up.

A piano has appeared on deck just by the dart board. It looks as if we shall be able to dance there after all, as soon as the weather becomes a little hotter! That is really the only place one can dance as the nursery is too small for any number.

Just before lunch I did some washing. It really is a prob-lem. I managed to use the tub in the bathroom and have taken the things down to the drying room. It was very full, so I could not spread things out at all. Still, it is better than having wet garments hanging about in the cabins. They take such ages to dry, apart from the fact that they take up so much room. A laundry has, however, been started on board. Of course, it is expensive, and I would rather save the money to spend on shore at the different ports of call.

Thursday, 3 July 1941

Well, we hope to be in New York by tomorrow. Who would ever have thought that I should see that city! Once again we are kept in suspense as to whether we shall be allowed to land. I do not think the captain knows until he docks. It rests with the authorities. All the Halifax passengers have had to come along to New York. They were not allowed to land after all and so had to have all the trunks carted back again to the cabins for these few days.

I have just come down from a concert meeting in the Fourth Officer's cabin. We have been trying to decide on a plan of campaign. But it is very difficult as no one really knows what talent we have on board as yet. I think it should be good. However, the chief difficulty at the moment is to get the thing going.

This morning I did some ironing, but it was very difficult. There are always so many wanting to use the iron at the same time. However, I did not have to wait long and got my little bits done! Then I went up to the cabin to re-pack my trunk. I arranged the warm things at the bottom and the summer frocks, etc. on top. I discovered, to my horror, that there is yet another bash on the bottom of the trunk. They were exceptionally rough with the baggage.

Clocks are still going back half-an-hour a day, so by now we are something like six hours back. I have a habit of forgetting to do it at night and find myself half-an-hour too soon for breakfast!

Sunday, 6 July 1941

The last two days have been so exciting and full of events that I hardly know where to begin. It is impossible to write on the days we go ashore. There is so little time, and the dining room is always full of immigration officers, etc. I have thought over this matter of sending the journal from Singapore. I think that perhaps it would be better to send a few sheets home at a time from the next port of call as they seem to be accumulating at a great rate. Today I shall start to look over the first sheets and sort them all out. Also, I must wash my hair and attempt to dry it on the boat deck.

Well, to go back to Thursday. We heard that we should be getting into New York about four o'clock in the morning, so several of us—Tony, Bunty, Donald, Reggie—decided to stay up all night in order to see the sky line as we approached the harbor in the morning. Accordingly, we installed ourselves in the Pig and Whistle [the bar] and prepared to wait for the morning. The night watchman supplied us at intervals with cups of hot coffee, and altogether we enjoyed the waiting very much. Earlier on in the evening we had an informal dance on deck. We were to have had it in the nursery, but later it was decided to hold it on the deck until it should get too dark. So we danced until a fairly late hour and had a drink in the smoke room. We then went down to the Chief Steward's cabin to hear the news, had a cup of tea and then up to the Pig and Whistle. It was great fun, but my word, I was sleepy next day!

Towards 2 a.m. we sighted lights from Long Island, which was a great thrill, and by 4 a.m. several others of the passengers appeared, looking sleepy. It was quite light by this time, and we all repaired to the deck. But imagine our horror and disgust to find a thick mist was fast coming down all round! For this we had waited up all night! I then went to bed in disgust, but not before I had persuaded myself that there was really nothing to see. Unfortunately, the adventure had a tragic ending. I was running round the corner of the deck when I slipped and fell, severely bruising my legs, hip and elbow. The decks were very slippery with mist and rain, and I still had on my high-heeled shoes from the dance. However, today, although I am still very stiff, my bruises are better, but I cannot lie on my left side.

I went up to the cabin and slept until the stewardess brought the tea at 7:15. I got up and had a most refreshing bath, got dressed and came on deck again. There was quite a crowd of people, but it was still very misty and pouring with rain, so we could not see very well. By this time we were steaming into the outer harbor where we dropped anchor. It appeared that we were to go further up later in the day. The breakfast gong rang. We went below very hungry and consumed a hearty breakfast. It seemed very uncertain that we should be allowed ashore anyway that day. Some reporters came aboard and took photographs of the survivors from the other ship, and later we saw them in the paper.

We could just faintly distinguish the skyscrapers in the distance through the mist. Straight ahead was the Statue of Liberty, but that was scarcely visible either. Later we moved on up the river, and by lunchtime we were really approaching the harbor. It was thrilling to see those vast buildings. I tried to take a photograph, but I am afraid the visibility was too bad. We steamed right up until we were

met by tugs, which came alongside and maneuvered us
into the berth. Ours was the pier next to the one where the
Normandie was. Goodness, what a huge ship she is! There
was so much to see—the harbor seemed so busy with ferry
boats and steamers. The lunch gong rang just as we were
coming alongside the pier.

Straight after lunch there were the formalities with the
immigration officials, passports to be stamped, etc. But nobody thought we should be allowed ashore until the next
day. So, after I had seen to my passport, I went up to the
cabin and went fast asleep. I was awakened by a loud
knocking at the door. It was Tony to say that we were to be
allowed ashore that afternoon and that I had to go down
to the saloon to get a pass. It was difficult knowing just
what to put on, for it was pouring with rain, but at the
same time very stuffy. I put my costume [suit] on in the
end, but left off the coat and wore my tweed coat over the
gray skirt. It was some protection against the rain, although
it was very hot.

We could not get any money changed on board, and of
course, being a holiday, all the banks were closed, so most
of us were penniless! However, Tony and I were lucky. We
were told of a hotel where they would change Canadian
money, so we set off straight away to find it. Everyone we
asked said, "Take a street car, or a taxi. It's about thirty
blocks away!" But, alas, we had not even money for that!
There was nothing for it but to walk. It was pouring with
rain most of the time, but we did not mind. It was so marvelous to be really in New York. Eventually we found the
said hotel, namely the Prince George, and there the cashier
very kindly changed our Canadian money. It was lucky
that we had some with us, instead of English money, for
the rate of exchange is very poor indeed, and we were
strongly advised not to change any English money if we
could possibly help it. The normal rate of exchange is $4.35,

I think, but it is not everywhere that one can get this. Some people only got $2 odd, which is terrible. We did quite well, however, with our Canadian money. The cashier was very nice to us and very helpful in giving information about the places to see and explaining the coinage to us. So, after a drink at the hotel, we came back to the ship for dinner. I then changed into a cooler frock, and we sallied forth once more to look at the sights.

The thing that thrilled us most, I think, was the lighting—it was truly marvelous. We wandered down Broadway, just dazed by all the lights. We saw so much that I can hardly remember what we did see. I do know that we went to Radio City, and afterwards to the Rockefeller Center. Elevators take you up the first 67 floors. You then get out and walk round to the next lift, which takes you up the remaining two floors onto the roof. My goodness, what a marvelous sight! The whole of the city lay spread out around us, twinkling lights outlining every street and avenue—we just sat and gazed at it all. By this time we were really very tired, having walked a good way in the afternoon in search of money. Not to mention the late hours we had kept the night before! So, we decided to come leisurely back to the ship and were in by 11:30 or so. We had coffee and sandwiches in the smoking room and then turned in so as to be up early the following morning for a shopping expedition.

We were up duly early the next morning. We could not get any breakfast until 9:00, as usual, but straight afterwards we went ashore. Bunty had decided to come with us but at the last moment changed her mind, so Arthur, Tony and I went alone. I wanted to get some stockings and a pair of shoes to wear with my cotton frocks, and in both these I was successful. First we took a taxi to 52nd Street and went in search of a shop where I could get my stockings. We wandered along 5th Avenue, but all the shops were closed, and besides, they looked very expensive. I asked a girl where I could buy stockings, and she told me they were the same price all over the town. She proceeded to direct us to 54th Street where she thought we would find a few shops open. We proceeded in that direction when I spotted a Kayser shop and went in, taking my escort with me. I bought three pairs of beautiful stockings for $2.30 plus tax, which was not so bad, and they are really very nice stockings indeed. The assistant then directed me to a shoe store just round the corner. By this time it was getting late. As we wanted to have an ice cream soda before getting back to the ship, I dashed into this shop and within five minutes came out with a super pair of canvas shoes. I have never bought a pair of shoes so quickly in my life! They are toeless and heelless, but very nice indeed, crepe rubber soles and very cool, which is the chief thing. Also, I can wash them with soap and water. They have already been much admired.

We came back to the ship in state. Really, the taxis are marvelous. They just whiz along and are so comfortable. When we climbed in, the driver at once turned on the wireless. The speaker under the back rear window was so loud that we could not hear ourselves speak, and in the end, we had to ask him to turn it off. I think he found it very hard to understand that we did not like it. People all have radios in their cars; in fact, it is the 'done' thing!

The pass was until midday, but it was nearly tea time before we were away. In fact, some people managed to slip ashore in the afternoon, but I don't think they dared to go very far. When we got aboard, they still had not loaded all the stores; some trucks had not even come to the dock. The Chief Steward was running round in circles, checking the things as they came on board.

By tea time we really moved off, and we crowded to the decks to catch a last glimpse of New York. I do hope that I shall have another chance of seeing it some time. I finished up my roll of films, but the light was not terribly good. Most of us turned in for an early night shortly after dinner to try to make up for the lost sleep.

Today it has been really hot, and most people have blossomed out into cotton frocks. It is a pity that we could not have had this weather in New York, but still we were lucky in having at least one fine morning.

The afternoon I spent on the boat deck sunbathing. It was lovely up there, and not many people knew of the haunt. I intended to wash my hair and then dry it in seclusion. I waited all afternoon, hoping that the hot fresh water would be turned on, but, alas, I was disappointed, and so had to go down to tea in a very hot and sticky state!

After tea I washed a few clothes; it is marvelous now how quickly they dry in our cabins, for I really think that the hot weather has come at last. About 9 o'clock I went up to the cabin, washed my hair and then dried it by moonlight! It was heavenly on the boat deck, a warm wind blowing all the time. Having dried it sufficiently, I returned to the cabin where I set it, and then, with a scarf round my head, repaired to the Pig and Whistle where I joined the rest of the party.

The hot weather today has brought out a rash of cotton frocks and shorts, a most ravishing sight, not to mention the number of breathtaking hairy legs and chests!

Whole group of Naval Reservists in whites

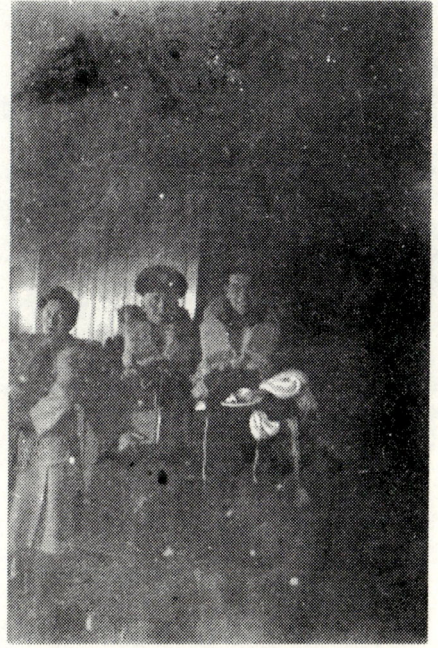

Boat stations the day we were attacked

My cabinmate Bunty Alston

Swimming suit bought in New York

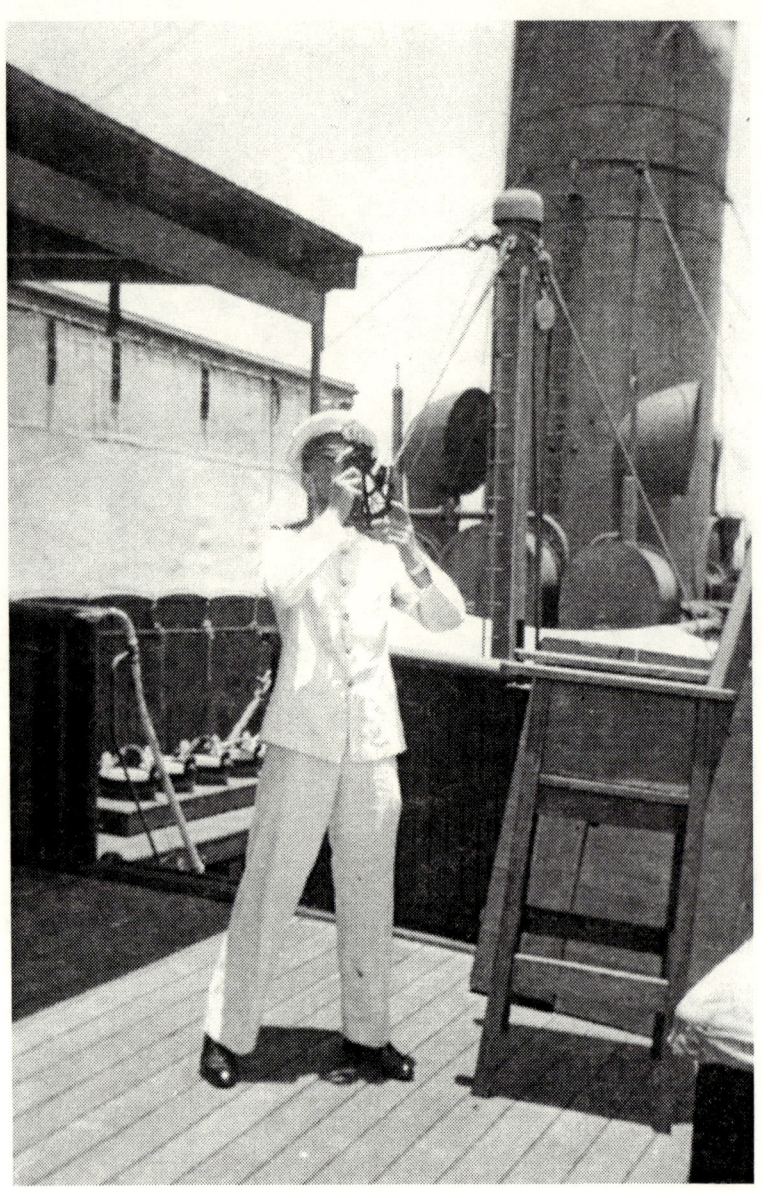

Tony taking a sight

Deck tennis court

Off to the races!

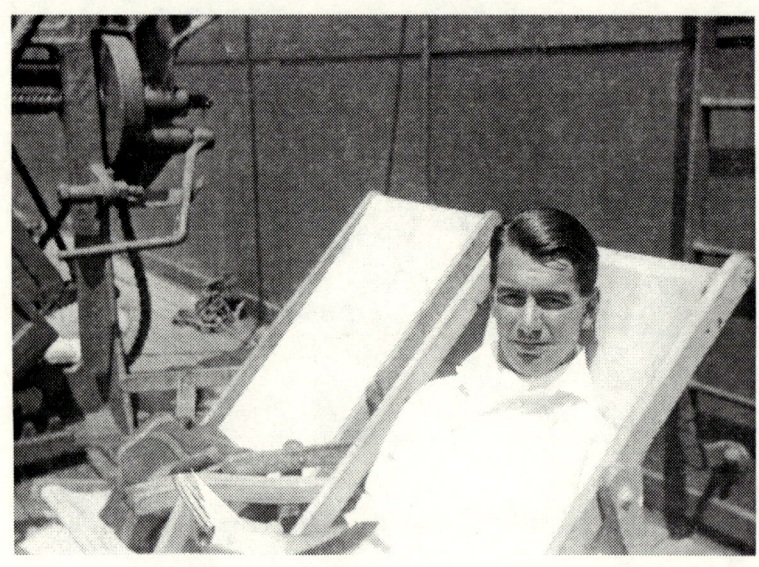

Tony in our special place on the boat deck

Margaret and Tony

P & O and British India Line

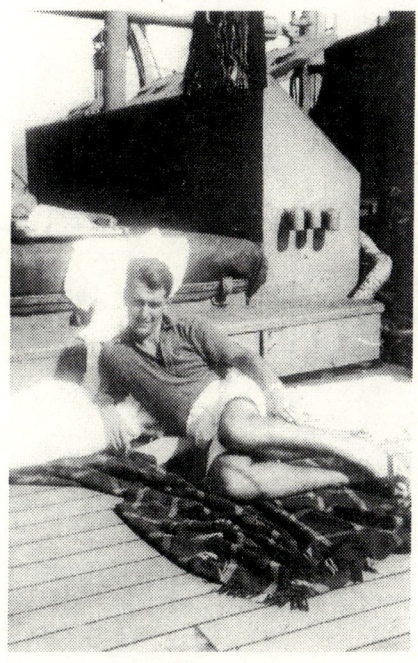

Tony relaxing on my rug

There is no mistaking where we are. I think I shall surely melt if it gets any hotter! Everyone assures me that it will! All the officers and men have today appeared in tropical kit, and very smart they look. The stewards and cabin boys, too, have their white suits; I thought they must find them just as hot as the blue ones, for these have high-necked collars. I put on my new blue cotton frock, the one with the white bands round the skirt; it is very cool and has been much admired. Also, I have taken to tying a ribbon round my head and then twisting the hair up round it; this is a very cool way of doing the hair and looks neat and tidy. But I find no way is really satisfactory for deck tennis. There always seems to be a wind, and it is quite impossible to keep the hair out of my eyes when playing. I have tried tying a scarf round my head, wearing a net, etc., but none of these ways seemed effective. I expect soon we shall get out of the winds, but then it will be hotter than ever!

I was up before breakfast playing deck tennis. It seems to be the best time of the day, for it gets so hot towards the middle of the day. Even after tea it is quite hot work, but I love it so. It is great fun. I have entered for the matches (tournaments), which, I think, start today and have to be played off by July 24th. It will be a lengthy business, as there are so many entries. I have entered for the women's singles, the mixed doubles, open, and the mixed doubles with a chosen partner.

I have started to learn Dutch, and I had my first lesson this morning in the smoke room. The girl who is instructing me, a Miss Tailleur, is going to Batavia to work for the Dutch government. I hope we shall see something of each other, for she is a very nice girl.

I find that most people seem to change into something in the evening as the majority of them are wearing sun suits and bathing costumes most of the day. One party appeared in housecoats that they had bought in New York, but I draw the line at that! Truly, they were so pretty, and we had never seen anything like them.

A whist drive had been arranged for the evening, but I did not take part. Instead, a party of us, Tony included, of course, found a nice cool spot on the promenade deck, and there we sat until 11 o'clock. I fell asleep there, and when I woke up, decided it was time to go to bed! Goodness, it was hot in the cabin and the fan had broken, so Bunty and I were really roasting. However, we turned out the light, opened the portholes and the door, and found it not so bad. But this morning the sun was shining full in through the open ports.

Tuesday, 8 July 1941

I wore my mauve frock this morning as today is the race meeting, and I was elected a "jockey" with mauve and purple as my colors. The meeting was held on the promenade deck. A straight course was marked out on the deck, divided into sections by rope, with a wooden horse on a stand at the end of each line. Attached to each horse was a string, which was carried up the course to the far end, under the stool and onto a wooden spool. The "jockeys" sat on the stools with their backs to the horses, and at the word "Go" started to wind as hard as they could. The handles were very tiny, which made it hard work, and most of us are suffering from blistered hands and fingers. The "vet" acted his part very well and was a great success, causing much amusement by his examination of the jockeys before they were allowed to enter the race! My efforts as a jockey were not very successful, I am afraid. It was quite fun, but a terrible waste of a good morning. I do so hate these organized entertainments but quite see that they are necessary on a trip of this length. I must say that the organizers deserve every praise.

A large drink of lemonade revived us before it was time to tidy up for lunch. It is still very hot indeed. There seems to be some kind of a gale blowing outside, and it is raining very hard.

It is still very hot today, but on deck there is a strong wind, which just saves us. Most of the sunbathers are now suffering from raw backs and arms. My own legs have caught it rather badly, and my ankles are very swollen. I am told that will wear off quite soon. I certainly hope so, for it is most painful. I am not playing any deck tennis for the time being until the swelling goes down a bit. It is really absurd to play in the middle of the day. Some seem to be at it all day, and this morning two of the women were playing off a singles match. It was too much for one of them. She finished up by doing a faint and is confined to her cabin for the next forty-eight hours.

After tea last night we had an informal dance on the promenade deck from 5 o'clock until 6:30. There was rather a swell, which made it difficult to do a slow foxtrot! Still, it was fun. At 6:30 I went up to have a cold shower and change for the cinema show in the evening. This was held out on the deck. Screens were put along the railing to shade the beam of light, but the experiment was not a very great success. The sound was not at all clear, and it was very hot. However, it was better than being in the lounge with the windows closed. That would have been unbearable. The film was *Crackerjack* with Tom Walls and Lilli Palmer—not very good, but then I was asleep most of the time.

I spent most of the morning rearranging my clothes,

clearing my winter things out of the wardrobe, and packing them into my trunk. It made me quite hot to look at
them—tweed coats in this weather! However, now there is
much more room in the wardrobe for our cotton frocks. It
was really terrible having to pull out a trunk or suitcase
every time we wanted a dress.

My Dutch instructress is not very well today, and she is
having a series of injections. I expect those will make her
feel rotten for the next day or so, especially in this heat. For
the time being the lessons are off, but I shall continue them
again as soon as she feels able. Also, I saw Mrs. Doig about
giving Sally lessons, and she is most pleased that I should. I
shall start tomorrow.

There is to be a dance on deck this evening, and I am in
two minds as to whether I shall go in my housecoat, as I
gather many of the others are. I am using it as a dressing
gown, but that need not matter. It is certainly as pretty, if
not prettier, than any of the others I have so far seen. But it
remains to be seen if I have the courage to wear it down to
dinner.

Goodness! It is even hotter than it was yesterday. I understand that we are in the Gulf of Mexico and that we should be in Panama within a few days. I am afraid that we shall not be allowed to keep our cameras. I think they are to be confiscated until after we are through the canal.

The dance last night was a great success. The only snag is that there are not enough women to go round! There are few really good dancers amongst the men, but still it is fun. We did not have lights as anticipated, but there was a very bright moon. We were able to dance until 11 o'clock without any difficulty. There was a strong breeze all the time, which made it very pleasant; otherwise, it would have been unbearably hot. How I shall manage on shore when it is hotter than this, I don't know! I suppose one must be dripping wet all the time. One gets used to these things, I assume.

This morning I have been asked to play off my first singles with a Mrs. Turral. How I dread the thought of it! I think she is very good, and it is sure to be very hot. However, we are not playing until 5:30 in the evening when it should be a little cooler. The sun will not be so strong by that time. My ankles are still very swollen, but I think they will go down in time and it will not hurt to play tonight.

I am having a Dutch lesson later on this afternoon. Miss Tailleur is coming down here to me in the dining saloon. It is much cooler here than anywhere else. The other Dutch girl has found a little phrase book that she had in England, which will be very useful to me.

They have been busy today erecting a swimming pool on the forward well deck. First, they put up iron girders to support the heavy wooden planks, and now I see they have fitted a kind of white waterproof bag into the square and are erecting diving boards all round it. There is a most sumptuous floor of marbled rubber. The whole thing is 6 feet deep, and roughly 7 feet square—a really marvelous effort. I should think we shall be able to use it before long but expect the only time one will be able to get a turn to swim will be in the early morning or late evening. Anyway, I think it is a jolly good show. I took a photo of the men erecting it, and I hope to get some of the bathers as soon as possible.

Friday, 11 July 1941

The match yesterday was great fun. It was a struggle all the way through and Mrs. Turral won 6-3, 4-6, 6-2. We both got soaking, although it was not as hot as I had expected. There was a good deal of wind and a heavy list on the ship, which made it difficult to stand. Still, we both enjoyed the game, and so, apparently, did the audience. They said it was the best women's singles so far. I am suffering today from a rather stiff hand, although my ankles are much better than they were yesterday.

In the morning I did a bit of washing and then went below to iron. Goodness, that is a hot job if ever there was one! Only one of the irons is working, and there are usually a good many people waiting for the precious remaining one. Two of the Subs—Donald and Percy—asked me to wash their cap covers, which I did and left them on my bunk while I was at breakfast. I returned to find them spattered with oil specks from the ship's funnel—at least, I suppose it must be from there since our cabin is on the boat deck. I thought at first it was the fan, but several people have complained of the same thing, and my bed is all spotted again today. I consulted my learned friend Donald, as well as Bob, who in peace time is also in the dry cleaning business, but neither of them was able to offer any suggestions. I acted upon Mrs. Griffiths' suggestion of peroxide, and it did the trick. I shall be wiser in the future. They are perfectly beastly things to iron anyway. I would infinitely rather do shirts!

Lotto was arranged for the evening in the music room, but it did not appeal to me very much. I spent the evening in the smoking room attempting to knit, but it was far too hot. I did very little; in fact, my knitting is getting on very slowly indeed. It just seems to stick to one's fingers, but I really must try to finish this cardigan of mine. I have been so long with it.

Cameras are to be taken up today by 5 o'clock, so I shall have to finish off my roll. I should think we shall be near Panama by Sunday.

I went along to Sally this morning, but she was not very well and so was not doing any lessons. Her mother has brought along a French book, an arithmetic and a geography book, so there will be quite a lot to work on. Anyway, I gather it is only occasional lessons she wants. The child amuses herself very well; she reads a great deal. It is a pity there are no other children of her own age on board.

The rest of the morning I spent on deck in a cool corner, learning my Dutch. I am slowly mastering the pronunciation, but goodness me, it is difficult.

After tea, I went to watch Tony play in the men's doubles. We all cheered him to victory. Really, deck tennis is a grand game; I have become quite an enthusiast. I have, at last, discovered my partner for the mixed doubles, a Mr. McIntyre. We arranged to play a practice game this morning before breakfast.

It was then 6 o'clock, so I went up, hoping to change while there was a little space in the cabin. In this hot weather, two in there seem two too many, both struggling to see in the mirror at the same time, and one's hands get so hot and sticky that it is almost impossible to do one's hair at all. All the same, I would much rather have this weather than the intense cold.

Now it gets dark almost before dinner, and it is so hot in the music or smoking room. Really, the only thing is to sit out on deck. Nearly everyone does. About 11 o'clock Tony and I wandered round to look at the moonlight bathers, and we were persuaded to join them. It was grand; the water was quite warm, and the pool is just large enough to dive in and finish up with a couple of strokes to the other side. I think bathing at that time will be very popular. In the daytime it will be very hot, as well as crowded.

I got up this morning and had another dip before playing two sets of deck tennis. Now one of the courts is completely covered by an awning, because at New York we took on board several Indians, survivors from another boat, who are traveling steerage, and they were assigned to sleep in the tennis court at night.

I got a very handsome watch strap from the barber the other day, a white one. It is much nicer as it can be washed. I find that the dye from the leather one comes off on my arm. I also got a bottle of calamine lotion for my legs, which, by now, are nearly normal. The ankles, too, have gone down considerably. Now I am suffering from that heat rash I used to get at home in the summer. It is just on the sole of my right foot. I have been advised to prick the blisters and smother them with iodine. I have taken the precaution always to wear socks and shoes. I notice some of the children are allowed to go about barefooted on the decks, which is a very dangerous thing, especially as one man has apparently got "Singapore foot" [athlete's foot]. Talking of infection, we have a further case of chicken pox. The children started it soon after we left, and now I hear that one of the Chinese boys has got the rash, so I suppose it will spread. In any case, it is not a very serious thing but most uncomfortable.

Last evening we had a dance, but it began to rain hard, and in spite of the screens, the wet came onto the deck and made it very slippery. French chalk was sprinkled, but that made it even worse. There was a terrific list, which made dancing uphill rather difficult! All the time we were dancing, there were blinding flashes of lightning, and before long we had run into the storm, which, however, did not last long. It was terribly hot, and none of us was feeling up to the mark, so very soon I snooped up to bed. Bunty decreed to sleep out and wanted to bring her mattress on deck, but I suggested that she should sleep in a deck chair with a pillow and blanket. Surprisingly, she acted on my suggestion. She appeared in the cabin this morning at 6 o'clock, opened the ports, which later let in all the rain, causing much trouble to the overworked staff. They are struggling desperately to get things in order, for today we are to go through the canal.

We were expected to arrive at Colon early this morning. I arranged to get up early to see the sights, but it was raining so hard that I thought better of it and did not appear until 7. There was some talk of a medical inspection before landing. In fact, I very much doubt if we shall be allowed to land this end of the canal.

Not until about 8 a.m. did we drop anchor in the harbor of Colon. By this time, I was up and dressed. I met some of the others wandering about, so we went down to the saloon. There we found a friendly steward who provided us with coffee. We took this out onto the lower deck from which select spot we could watch the shore activities. It is expected that we go through the canal and arrive at Balboa by 11 o'clock tonight. I shall certainly sit up!

I spent a very disturbed afternoon! First we arranged ourselves on the boat deck. Then it began to rain, so we moved under cover. Then the heat became so much that once more we moved out into the open, as the rain seemed to have stopped. About half an hour of peace, then down came the rain, this time in real earnest, so there was nothing for it but to pack up and go on to the lower deck.

Later: It appears that we are not going through the canal today. The town of Colon looks beautiful with all the twinkling lights. I have been watching them from our haunt on the boat deck. It seems incredible that we are half round the world and just about to cross a continent!

I got up early to play deck tennis. We have got quite a good four together, Tony and I playing Lt. Davies and Mrs. Turral. We had three hectic sets before breakfast while we were still outside Colon. The harbor seems encircled by a kind of reef with an opening to the Caribbean Sea, through which we must have come Saturday. It seemed that there was quite a lot of activity in the harbor. We saw an American destroyer going out, also three submarines, not to mention the various other ships passing to and fro.

At 10:30 we began to move off, so I rushed up to the cabin to inform Bunty. We didn't want to miss anything. A party of us went up to the boat deck from which we had an excellent view. For about an hour we crept slowly up to the lock entrance. We were terribly excited and kept rushing from one side of the ship to the other so as not to miss anything. At Colon, U.S. Marines came aboard, fully armed, to take over the ship officially whilst she came through the canal. They seemed to be everywhere, spending most of Sunday measuring the corridors and taking copious notes in large books. As the ship approached the canal entrance, we had our first glimpse of tropical vegetation, for the land came down to the water on each side of the ship, merging into swamps through thick undergrowth. Great excitement on our part in seeing the first coconut palm! In fact, there were a great many of them, some even growing out from the water. There were also bananas and sugar canes. Major Mummery pointed out all the things to us, but I am afraid I do not remember the names of all the others we saw—no doubt I shall see similar in Sumatra. The country, as far as we could see, was very hilly; it rolled back from the water in great wooded slopes, so very different from our wooded hills at home. They looked absolutely dense and dark as if one could not put a pin between the trees.

It was stiflingly hot up there on the boat deck, although the sun was not shining. I brought my rug, and we sat on it for a time, eating apples and drinking lemonade, but one could not sit for long for fear of missing something!

At last we came through the first lock—the Gatun Lock—in fact, there are really two here. On either side of the lock, or quay, run railway lines. These continue the whole length of the locks and are for the peculiar beetle-like engines, which pull the ship through. They move, of course, both backwards and forwards. Attached to the center of each is a strong wire cable connected to the side of the ship, three on each side. These act as a drag, rather than actually pulling, I should imagine. In this way we were towed into the first lock and raised some several feet, then again pulled further into the second where we were raised to the level of Balboa Lake. It was all most exciting. By this time it was lunch, and so we had to go below to the saloon. When we came up again, we were just pulling out of the second lock, so we had not missed much.

We found a comparatively cool spot on deck, and from deck chairs we watched the beautiful scenery as we plowed our way slowly through the lake. It was so smooth and calm, thick towering vegetation all round, with most lovely cloud effects.

After tea, I was asked to play off my mixed doubles tournament. I was not feeling at all like playing, nor had I ever played with my partner before—Mr. McIntyre, whom

I have been trying to track down for some time. However, there was nothing for it but to play. There was a large audience, and I played very badly indeed. So did he, with the result that we lost heavily. Tony and I hope to do better in the open mixed doubles. We have been practicing hard together.

Through two further locks, the Pedro Miguel and the Pacific Lock, bringing us down to the level of the Pacific Ocean. By 7:30 it was dark, but we had no blackout, and the docks were a blaze of lights. It was wonderful! We had a drink before dinner, standing out on deck watching the activities ashore where they immediately started to take on supplies. We speculated as to whether we should be allowed ashore the following day and thought probably not!

After dinner, I was on deck watching the lights, when suddenly Tony came rushing up to say we were going ashore until 2 a.m. and I was to get my passport! I simply didn't believe him and was only convinced when I actually saw other people with passes. I, then, went to my cabin, put on another pair of shoes and got my edge-to-edge coat [it had no buttons, but the sides met at center front], for I gathered it would be quite late by the time I returned to the ship. About 9 o'clock we set foot in Balboa. It was rather exciting. No one on ship had much money—some none at all, others a little left over from New York. We had $5, but what an evening we had on that!

Along the docks and through the barriers and we were out in the town. The thing that struck me most was the high-pitched hum of insects. I have heard Auntie speak of them in Singapore so often, and now I have really heard them for myself. We caught a bus into Panama City. An American sailor told us where to get out, and we were just standing on the curb wondering which way to go next, when two Yanks—a man and his wife—drove up in a car. They asked us the way to some nightclub. They were most interested to learn that we were English. They at once insisted on our coming along with them. So we all packed into the front of the car and drove off to Kelley's Night Club. It was great fun, but, my goodness, what a dump! We had a table right by the dance floor. They were most anxious for us to see the floor show, which, however, later proved to be very poor. Our host and hostess, John and Phil, were grand sports and gave us a marvelous evening. As I said, we had only $5 American money, and they would not accept English money at the nightclub. Apart from one round of drinks, we were absolutely unable to repay their kindness. Luckily, we had some English cigarettes, and they asked for the matchboxes as souvenirs! All drinks were served with ice—we ordered gin and tonic. First a glass of ice, with a little tumbler of gin, which you pour in yourself, filling up with tonic. John and Phil had never heard of this drink before—they stuck to Canadian Club and Coca Cola. Later we were persuaded to have a devastating drink known as Planter's Punch. I thought it might lay me out, but I survived two more gins *AND* still sober!

By this time, there were other parties from the ship joining us, including the Captain, Chief Officer and several more. They were very merry indeed. The Captain was terribly amusing—he did not appear at all the next day! We were due back on board by 2 a.m., and it was then nearly 3:00, but as the Skipper's party had not left, we took our tip from them. Tony and I wandered down the High Street to cool off. We were amazed to see that several of the shops were still open—I don't think they ever close. On our way back we met a policeman in plain clothes who had been on the quay when the ship docked. He had recognized us and asked Tony if he and his wife (!) would like to come for a drive out to old Panama City. We thought it a grand idea and so returned to consult the Captain. He was a great sport, and we said we should be back by 6:00. I found Phil and said goodbye to her. I think it was just as well we went, for she and John were in the middle of a domestic upset, and there were arguments and tears!

Having said our farewells, Tony and I went outside where we were conducted to a marvelous car and were driven all round the countryside. Unfortunately, it was still rather too dark to see much in the way of scenery, but we drove out to the ruins of old Panama City, a drive of about fifteen miles or so. Funnily enough, in the Canal Zone they have the left hand drive as we do in England. We visited several other night haunts on the way where we drank quantities of beer. It got light about 5:00, but we thought it best to be getting back to the ship. We came back through Balboa, hoping to see the church with the golden altar, but it was closed. After another short spin round, we landed up at the dock gates. They would not allow the car inside, so we got out, thanked our host for a very pleasant morning, and hoping we were not the last aboard, crept back rather sheepishly to the ship, thankful to find her still there.

We went down to the saloon where a kindly steward gave us a pot of tea, and we talked to the stewardess who was preparing the early morning trays. Much revived and feeling very wide awake, I went up to the cabin to change into my bathing costume for a swim. It was really the officers' time, but only one of them appeared, and he did not mind our being there. The water was very dirty, or looked so. Canal water. But it was one of the best swims I have had! Afterwards, I went up to change and returned on deck where we sat in deck chairs until breakfast. I was terribly sleepy by this time and thought I should never get through breakfast, but I simply couldn't give in at that stage. However, after breakfast I found a quiet spot on the lower deck, and there we slept soundly until lunchtime. Several people came to rouse us, and it was just as well. I know I should have just turned round and slept again had I not been bullied into getting up! I managed to rouse myself sufficiently to get through lunch and then straight afterwards went to my cabin where I continued my sleep. It was a quarter to five when next I regained consciousness, to discover Bunty with a tray of tea for me. I ate some cakes and drank a cup of tea and then did not know anything else until it was time to change for dinner. What a day! Needless to say, I had an early night and by Wednesday morning was completely recovered, not a bit the worse for the outing. Everyone seems to have had a marvelous time ashore. We found remarkable hospitality everywhere and a most friendly feeling towards the English, although they realize they cannot possibly understand what the war means to us in England— they are so far away. It is just as war in Europe seemed to us until we became involved in it ourselves.

Wednesday morning I went to inquire if Sally wanted any lessons, but she was already engaged, and so I am to have her some tomorrow. I returned to my cabin and did copious washing. Unfortunately, Bunty had also decreed to wash, so our cabin was hung with sundry articles of underwear belonging to both sexes! A truly demoralizing sight! The water in the tap is so warm that I never bother these days to get any hot, for my Lux lathers in cold, and I find it "ackles" just as well. We have erected a line across the cabin from the porthole to the door, and with the fan on, things dry very quickly indeed. In a few hours they are ready to roll up for ironing. I tried the washhouse one afternoon, but it was really too stifling for words. The drying room is even worse, whereas the present system is most workable and easy.

This morning Sally and I had great fun. We started with writing and dictation, and then I showed her how to make patterns with letters, coloring them with my crayons. I am so glad I slipped them in at the last minute. Also, my Penguin Poetry book that I got in the Woolworth's in Glasgow. She is learning "The Walrus and the Carpenter."

I finished with Sally about 11 o'clock, and after a cup of iced beef tea, which we have every morning at that time, I went up to the cabin, intending to get my journal up to date. About twenty minutes to one, Tony put his head round the door, and we went down for a drink of lemonade before lunch.

A party of us spent the afternoon on the boat deck, knitting and reading. I have, at last, started my bathing costume, but it is very hot to knit. The wool seems just to stick to one's fingers. However, I trust I shall have it finished before long.

I see they have erected a paddling pool for the children, a white canvas one with painted fishes and crabs on the bottom. I saw the ship's black cat the other morning, walking round the edge of our pool, just like Kutching round the edge of the bath at home.

There was a cinema show in the evening—*Oh, Daddy!*, with Leslie Henson Frances Day and Robertson Hare—very amusing indeed.

Friday, 18 July 1941

With a great effort I dragged myself out of bed this morning to play deck tennis. I went out on deck and found Reggie waiting, but a four was already on the court. Davies joined us shortly. We found a fourth and had a very good set. A rule has been made that as long as there are players waiting to go onto the court, not more than one set may be played. As it was rather late, we did not wait for another. I walked round the deck a few times to cool off. I watched the black cat perilously walking round the children's pool, getting his nose wet every time the ship rolled and the water came up the side.

Sally and I did sums after breakfast for about ten minutes and then her favorite "patterns." She really is a sweet child and most intelligent for her age. We get on very well together; in fact, she came rushing to me straight after her breakfast to say that she had all the things ready and would I come!

I spent the rest of the morning writing my journal.

We had great fun last night when a scavenger hunt was organized. We had a list of nineteen things to get before ten o'clock, some of them causing a great deal of fun, especially the pair of ladies' pink cami-knickers [undergarment]. There appeared to be a dearth of such articles, but the substitutes that were produced! Tony and I managed to get seventeen out of the nineteen required. We were stuck over a banana and a 1909 penny. There were about two bananas on the ship. We have not had them for several days, and of course, they would not open the "fridge." Two other pairs each got eighteen, and the first one to go before the judges won the prize. I have no idea what it was. Tony and I were among the first to get through. We then cleared off to a cooler spot as it was terribly hot in the smoke room where the judging was going on.

There is a dance again tonight, and I have been bullied into promising to wear my housecoat. I shall alter the shoulders this afternoon and press it. Then I shall have sufficient courage to appear in it tonight! I have also acquired a marvelous little sunbathing garment, red and white striped, with a white frill round the edge! Miss Wilson bought it in New York in a great hurry and found it did not fit her. I am going to appear—in private—in it this afternoon!

We had boat stations this morning, the first in a very long time. Goodness, how those life belts hurt when you have few clothes on! They were bad enough with thick winter coats and jumpers, but with only cotton frocks, they are terrible!

I then discovered Sally in the smoke room, busily engaged in tracing a map of the world, upon which she is going to mark the route. So I left her at it and told Mrs. Doig that I would do something with her tomorrow instead. Mrs. D. remembered that it was Sunday and said that I should have a holiday! She is a dear. There are some very nice people on this ship, a group, in particular, who are going to Singapore or Kuala Lumpur. One of the party is an inspector of police in Singapore, a youngish, rather fat man, but I have yet to learn his name. He speaks good Malay and is very friendly with this Malayan prince.

There have been many changes at table since New York. It has been rather amusing to watch. The couples that were so terribly thick during the first week at sea have separated and paired off elsewhere, resulting in much speculation and gossip on the part of the other passengers. For the last few days there has been an empty place next to me—nothing to do with me, I am sure! The headwaiter asked the Captain what he should do about it. There is also another empty place two away from the Skipper, but he said to leave them, as he thought we would settle it amongst ourselves. So this morning, having slept on the question all night, I asked him if he would mind if I invited a friend of mine to sit at his table. He was much amused and said, "Of course not," so at lunchtime, amidst loud comments, Tony filled the place!

Well, I have promised to rest this afternoon and so had better do so!

Sunday, 20 July 1941

The sunbathing suit was a great success. Apparently several people saw it and highly approved, so I shall have courage to wear it again today. A bathing costume is really too hot to wear for sitting about in the afternoon, and anyway, I always hated wearing one. But this garment is both cool and comfortable. It is, of course, just blown together, but I shall take a pattern from it and have another made for future use. Another thing, it will probably run the first time it is washed. I shall have to get another bathing costume as soon as I arrive, for these woolen ones take so long to dry.

The dance was quite good fun, but it was terribly hot and there was not much breeze. I did not come down in my housecoat after all. It is really not quite suitable, I think, and one is really much cooler in a short frock. People seem to have taken to dressing much more in the evening than at the beginning. Some of the lunch 'get-ups' are too frightful: one man yesterday appeared in a singlet and braces! The headwaiter reported him. The Captain sent his compliments and requested that he go up and dress!

It being Sunday, Sally had no lessons, so I took the opportunity of ironing in the morning. It is so much better than in the evening just before dinner when there is always a great rush. I am becoming quite an expert in the art of ironing shirts!

It is ten to one, so I shall do my hair and have a drink of lemon squash before lunch. Afterwards, I intend to wash my hair and spend a lazy afternoon in the shade on the boat deck. I am so enjoying this trip—it is really grand to be going round the world. I think we should be in port by about Tuesday. I shall try to cable from there and also send these last few pages.

Yesterday was terribly hot. We sat in deck chairs on the promenade deck after dinner, and I managed to get a good deal done to my knitting. Unfortunately, I did not pack a pair of 11 needles and so had to scrounge around among the women passengers to find a pair. The only ones I could get were a pair of those bendy kind from the doctor. Last night I broke the tip of one and had to re-sharpen it this morning with a nail file. I have since learned that the barber has some. I shall have to visit him and see what he can produce.

The first part of the morning I sat with Mrs. Doig in the music room. I think she wanted Sally to do some lessons, but she was quite happy writing an account of the voyage to her father, which is to accompany this famous map. I sat and talked to her mother instead and did my knitting until 11 o'clock when I had to go for my Dutch lesson. It is some days now since I had a lesson, but on Saturday I studied quite hard. I do so wish I had brought a really good grammar book with me, for it is such a marvelous opportunity to learn; still, I must see what I can find at the next port.

After sitting out again on the boat deck this afternoon and sunbathing for a little while, Miss Wilson, Tony and I found a cool place under the awning where some slept and some knitted! After tea I went below to iron some things for the boys. Goodness, what a job those white shorts are, to be sure! They are pleated at the waist, which makes it difficult to iron them flat, and then the crease must be just so! Still, I enjoy doing them. Yesterday, as I was ironing, I was called away to see a whale out on the starboard quarter. It was sending up great spurts of water every now and again. Someone lent me a pair of glasses, and I saw the spouts quite plainly.

The captain has just asked me if I would join a party to play deck tennis tomorrow morning at 7:30, so I shall have to be up betimes and not be late!

Tuesday, 22 July 1941

The stewardess called about 7 o'clock this morning, and I got up for our game of deck tennis. It was fun, although Tony and I did not manage to win. But we shall have another chance tomorrow when it has been arranged that we play at 1:15.

After breakfast I found Sally, and we did some lessons together, first sums and then writing. She made a rhyme sheet with a border of letters, colored with crayons, and wrote Tennyson's "Eagle," which was her own choice, from my *Penguin Book of Poems*. I think tomorrow we shall probably do some French. Teaching her is really great fun. After this, I went to the boat deck where I studied Dutch for about an hour. By that time it was getting on for 1 o'clock.

The boat deck is certainly the best place in the afternoon. Several of us congregate there and sunbathe for about half to three-quarters of an hour and then spend the rest of the afternoon in the shade under the awning. Today I got quite a lot of knitting done. Tony spent part of the afternoon on the bridge taking sights and working out our position. They all do a certain amount of this, as it is a marvelous opportunity to put into practice all they have learnt in their brief three months' training as officers.

Wednesday, 23 July 1941

Deck tennis again before breakfast. We had an amusing game with Wilson and the Captain. He is a grand sport, very popular, I should imagine, with his officers and men, but not one to be crossed. I should think slackers have a very thin time of it!

Sally was having lessons with Mr. Gardner, so I went off to study my Dutch on the boat deck. But, alas, I was thwarted! Young Richard came up for a chat. He is a perfectly sweet child, aged about three, I think. He has recently been isolated for chicken pox and is just beginning to mix with people again. All the time he was covered with spots, he was just as cheerful and happy as ever. Mrs. Turral has brought him up so beautifully. I had just got rid of Richard after about twenty minutes when up rolled two of the subs. In the end, I gave up all hope of serious study and abandoned myself to knitting, which needs no thought nor concentration.

The boat deck has become our special haunt. It is usually quiet up there, and few of the passengers use it. In fact, there is only room for a very few. The for'd end is reserved for the officers, the little bit after for the engineers. This leaves the length each side of the cabins, a little more than a corridor, which the passengers may use. Over this, an awning has been erected, which makes it very nice and cool.

There has been a bit of trouble today as a group of passengers has started this silly business of note writing. I am afraid that Sylvia is at the bottom of it. I gather that yesterday she and a man I loath composed a very unkind menu, which was put on the Friend's table where Bunty is now sitting. It contained many hurtful insinuations about non-fighting, etc., all of which was in very bad taste, and the whole thing was a pretty poor joke. These people are conscientious objectors, you see, but I think everyone thought it was a horrible thing to have done. The Captain was most annoyed, so I hope that something is said. All day at every meal foolish notes appeared on our places, with anonymous signatures. Really, it is too silly and 'third gradish'! Mrs. Griffiths and I have decided to ignore them absolutely. I think the trouble is that people are beginning to find the trip rather long and tedious! I, personally, am enjoying every moment of it. It is all such fun to be going around the world. I only hope we eventually get to our destinations. The news today does not seem very good, but I am not really worrying.

Thursday, 24 July 1941

After tea I took my inflated raft down to the bathing pool. There is a puncture in it, and one of the engineers has promised to mend it for me if I find the hole! In return, I have promised it to him for an afternoon's sunbathing! Accordingly, I took it down to the pool. Percival was in there, and he climbed on top of it, eventually finding the weak spot. There is a line where it must have been folded at some time, just under the pillow. A small patch will remedy it.

Yesterday morning Tony and Percival were on the bridge taking sights. When they came down, they let me take one through the sextant. First you have to get the horizon as one clear line; this is done by twiddling a little knob. Looking through the lens, you see a round glass, divided into two, one half being a mirror on to which the sun is reflected through a filter. Through the clear half, you can see the horizon. Then by holding it towards the sun, you can see it reflected onto this mirror, and by twiddling another knob you bring the lower lip of the sun onto the line of the horizon. This is not so easy to do. After this, there are lengthy mathematical calculations to make. I am going to watch Tony working them out today and see what I can gather. They take two sights and then work out the latitude and longitude, thus finding the ship's exact position—all very complicated!

Tony and I had a drink with Mrs. Griffiths, Mrs. Turral and Lt. Davies before dinner. There was a dance last night, but we did not feel like going and so played cards instead. It was a change and we enjoyed it very much. Mr. Spragg, who sits at our table, offered to bring down his game of "Tripoli." We played until 10:30, when, dropping with sleep, I went up to bed.

I got up bright and early again this morning and played with Tony against the Captain and Wilson. We managed to beat them in a close set. It was not a serious game at all. We were laughing far too much, but it certainly was fun. We cannot play tomorrow as we shall be getting into port and the captain will not be free. Still, maybe the others will play.

Sally is again occupied, and to tell the truth, I am not sorry. It will give me a chance to get my letters done in the morning, which is always a good thing. I have a Dutch lesson at 12 o'clock. I went down to the smoke room this morning before breakfast to do a little study. I did not get very far, as one of the passengers came up to me and said, "I hear you are from Handcross!" [my hometown]. This bloke comes from Horsham and knows Handcross quite well. Mr. Burst, his brother, owns the garage in South Road and also the draper's on the corner where I got that scarf— at least, I think that must be the place. I shall probably hear more about it later on!

We had boat drill this morning. Goodness, how hard those life belts feel next to sunburn! Richard has just put his head in at my cabin door. He announced to Tony that he wanted to go to see his (Tony's) "mother," as he will persist in calling me! Tony is alluded to as either my father or my man!!

Sunday, 27th JULY 1941

(Well, we are certainly getting about and seeing places! Nearly two whole days and a night in Los Angeles and Hollywood. One cannot write sense after being up all night, and I have come to the conclusion that it is foolish to try. It is now Monday, and I must go back to Friday morning in order to tell of the marvelous time I had ashore.)

Having sat up rather late on Thursday night, we decided against a game of deck tennis the next morning. We had a late morning in bed—that means getting up just in time for breakfast! The night before, we had a coffee party on the stairs outside the saloon. About eight of us congregated and imbibed coffee or tea, with the result that it was late by the time we got up to bed.

I got up about 7 o'clock and looked out of the porthole. A range of reddish-looking mountains was in sight, looking singularly bare against the blue sky; there seemed to be not a tree growing on them. Yesterday, too, we saw land in the distance, which must have been part of the California peninsula, and by this time we were steaming up the coast to San Pedro, the port of Los Angeles. It was estimated that we should dock somewhere about noon, but once again it was not known if we should be allowed to land. Anyway, we made preparations in the hopes that we should.

I revived my spirits at lunch with a curry. Those dry curries are so nice; this is only the second one we have had on this voyage. After lunch we were asked to assemble in the smoke room with our passports in order to get the shore pass. Great rejoicing at the news of going ashore! There was a rush, so I thought it best to wait until the crowd thinned out somewhat. We had docked by this time, and they were beginning to take on supplies. One could not really go far, or sleep, and so I brought my letters down to the music room and sat there, finishing them while waiting to get my pass. Having done this, I wandered into the smoke room and joined the others. We hung about until nearly 3:30 when at last my name was called. Once I had my pass, I went up to my cabin, had a leisurely bath and changed in time to have tea before going ashore. On my way down, I met Richard and Mrs. Turral. She was trying to get hold of the vice-consul to arrange about money and was having some difficulty, so I took Richard into tea with me. This question of money is terribly difficult. They won't change any for us on board, although, of course, the crew are paid in dollars. The Subs, too, were supposed to be able to get a certain amount, but there seemed some hitch. We were kept hanging about until nearly 5 o'clock, when Tony and I decided to go ashore and risk getting some of our English money changed. There was, in fact, no alternative as the other money did not turn up. A *free* trip had been arranged by the British actors in Hollywood to take a party from the ship to Hollywood for dinner. Accordingly, we put down our names on the list, and having ascertained that they would be leaving sometime before dinner, we set off by ourselves.

Once off the ship, we walked along the quay to the barrier, and there we had to first go into an office and sign a book. Then we were allowed out into the street—through an electrically controlled door! Really, we do have good luck—we had not been out two seconds, when a car came along and offered us a lift. The man was something to do with the customs, I think. He offered to take us into Long Beach. He said he would be coming back about 9 o'clock, and if he saw us, he would pick us up again. But we really intended to get back to the ship in time to see if our names had been drawn for this trip to Hollywood. We were able to get some money changed, and we were undecided anyway. We would see Long Beach first and then decide if we should stay there or not!

It was a grand drive all through the San Pedro oilfields. I have never seen anything like it! Great iron derricks are erected whilst the boring is in progress. But once the oil has been reached and the pump is in action, these great iron structures are of no further use. I suppose the cost of labor in taking them down again is not worth it and so they are left, until the whole place now resembles some fantastic and unreal forest of iron trees. They are everywhere, just as far as the eye can see. Approaching this harbor as we did earlier on in the morning, we could see these spikes clearly visible, making a jagged skyline and giving rather a misty effect to the landscape. We saw men working on one derrick as we passed. Our companion told us that they had been working on it for some weeks now.

After about half an hour's drive, we arrived at Long Beach and were dropped outside the Hilton Hotel where we hoped to change some money. All the banks were closed at this time of the day; they close at 2 p.m. This is the hotel with the famous sky room. We did not know that until later. The cashier was very nice, but, although he made several inquiries by phone, he was not able to find out the exact rate of exchange and would not change our money. Tony had travelers' cheques, and I think he would have changed those had we stayed the night there and been able to call in next morning when the banks were open. But we wanted the money then and there, so off we went in search of another hotel. No luck at the next one, but at the third we asked to see the manager. Although he could not change travelers' cheques, he consented to exchange two of my pound notes at the very good rate of $4.30. It is a shame to be visiting all these places that we may never see again and not have any money to spend. I have about 3 pounds left now, but I am not worrying, as nearly everyone is in the same boat. I shall probably cable to Singapore for a little as we have a very long way to go yet. And there is yet a possibility of our being put on another ship. No one really knows, and anyway, I am not worrying.

Feeling very rich with $8.40 in our pockets, we decided to go back to see if our party had left the ship. If they had, we would have dinner on the ship and come out to Long Beach again later on. We made our way to the streetcar stop, but a fruit shop arrested our attention on the way. Goodness, what masses of lovely fruit! How I wish I could have sent some home. Peaches at less than sixpence a pound! We bought some to munch on the way home. The streetcar took us to the ferry, for we had docked on an island. We met several of the passengers and learned from them that 50 out of the list of those wishing to go to Hollywood had been chosen. There were too many for us all to go. We rushed back to see if our names were on the list. We met Mrs. Doig and Sally on the ferry, and we munched peaches together. As we got to the barrier, we saw most of the party assembled and almost ready to start. We raced back to the ship and were somewhat relieved to see that we had not been chosen. By this time we had other plans!

We went to the smoke room and cooled off with a Pink Gin, a navy drink—gin and bitters—to celebrate the evening. There were very few of the passengers on board for dinner. Tony and I, feeling superior, had a table to ourselves! Mrs. Turral and Lt. Davies came down later and sat not far from us. We decided to join forces after dinner and repair to the Hilton Hotel at Long Beach to dance on the roof. We arranged all to meet in the smoke room for a drink before starting.

When Tony and I got down, however, it appeared that there was some hitch. These two had previously arranged to go out with the vice-consul, who had offered to take them round. But this was at 7 o'clock, and it was now nearly 8:30. They thought that he had forgotten all about it; however, then he turned up. We at once offered to go off on our own, but Mrs. Turral would not hear of that and very much wanted us all to go together. Transport was the chief difficulty as the vice-consul only had a small car. (Surely the only one in America!) Finally, it was arranged that he should ring up a friend of his, who would possibly come along, too, with wife. He, however, was not very keen; being an editor, his work was just starting. The little vice-consul ran off again and phoned for a taxi. He came back to say that the car would be at the barrier in a quarter of an hour, and he had told the man to ask for a Mr. and Mrs. Jones. He did not know our name and that was the first one that came into his head. Anyway, he thought Tony and I were married, so "Mrs. Jones" I was for the rest of the evening! By this time, we were at the bottom of the gangway, and our party was joined by John Tura, the Third Officer. He is a grand lad with a red beard! We repaired to the barrier to await the taxi, which was to convey John, Tony and me to Hollywood to meet the others. Our first port of call was the Tropicana, a nightclub in the center of Hollywood. It was a grand drive. I nearly went to sleep in the car; however, as soon as I stepped out, I became wide awake!

The others had not yet arrived. We went in and ordered a table. John very sweetly bought me a gardenia. What heavenly flowers they are! I pinned it onto my dress. A few minutes after we had settled ourselves, the others arrived.

It was quite a small place, a dancing floor in the center, with the band and tables arranged all round amongst imitation palm trees, and with dim lighting—the effect was most pleasing. We had an alcove to ourselves, right opposite the band, with a good view of the floorshow. The two naval beards of our party caused quite a sensation. Much to our embarrassment, the announcer drew attention to the fact that they were honored in having as guests, officers of the British Navy, and forthwith played the "Lambeth Walk!" All very embarrassing! We were dancing at the time, so there was no chance of escape. However, I trust it did no harm, and it certainly shows the friendly feeling America has for us—and our cause. Just before the floorshow, a girl photographer came up and asked us if we would like a photo souvenir. We got into a huddle in the middle of the seat and tried to look dignified! The result was really very good indeed, so much so that we all had copies. I do hope that I am allowed to send mine home at some future date, but I shall wait until I arrive in Singapore and post it from there.

After the floorshow, which was not very good, we moved on to another place, namely N.T.G.'s Florentine Gardens. This was a little way away, so our friend the vice-consul took John, Tony and me there first and then went back for Pamela and Charles. This place was very much better than the Tropicana. It was a huge place with a vast domed roof and concealed blue lighting, much more restful than the dim lighting of the other place. Right in the center was a very large dance floor, with a dance band on a stage at the back and steps going up each side to the dressing rooms behind. The tables were arranged in little compartments on raised tiers going right back to the walls, so that those sitting at back tables could see the floor show quite easily, in spite of the crowd in front. We had a table about half way up the first tier. We had settled ourselves and the floorshow had just begun when the others arrived. It was a very good show—for those who like that kind of entertainment! In particular, there were two very clever dancers and a conjuror, the rest of the show being mainly a parade of glamour girls! The whole thing lasted for about an hour and ten minutes. Just before the end, the commentator went round picking out celebrities or people of interest who were there. For instance, there was a 21st party, a wedding party, a birthday party for the manager of a big hotel in Long Beach, and each of these was singled out by the spotlight. Imagine our horror when the spotlight was swung round to our table! While the commentator jab-jabbed about the honor of having amongst them officers of the finest Navy in the world—the British Navy, he reminded them and spoke at length of Nelson, Drake, etc. Everyone clapped, and we all looked foolish. It was all very difficult because the Subs are not supposed to go ashore in uniform, America being a neutral country. But the authorities permitted them to do so, which was why we were anxious not to be too conspicuous. It was the last straw when he even sent two of the glamour girls down to our table to fetch the poor things onto the floor, but at that they drew the line. Davies explained to him afterwards that they were not allowed to do so in uniform. We were very glad when the next turn came on!

The show finished about 1:30, which left about half an hour for dancing before the place closed at 2 o'clock. Accordingly, we danced until then and had to pack up. We decided to go back to the ship and continue the party in the 3rd's cabin, so we hailed a taxi. John, Tony and I climbed in, leaving the others to follow in the car. On the way back, we felt very hungry and proposed to stop at one of these many sandwich bars that one finds along the roads. We went in and had a drink while ordering large quantities of hot dogs and hamburgers to take back to the ship. It was great fun. They are lovely things, though goodness knows what is in them! Lettuce, pickles, mince and garlic, I should imagine, but, oh boy, they are sure good!

About half an hour later, we staggered out with large parcels of food and continued our way back to the ship. A few minutes after we arrived, we all assembled in John's cabin where the others imbibed whiskey. I am afraid I could not face any and munched my hamburger and sipped lime juice instead. Unfortunately, the other two were overcome on the way back by hunger and had stopped at the sandwich bar where they had also consumed masses of hot dogs and hamburgers. They were not in a fit state to eat those we had brought! However, we ate what we wanted and later the rest were given to the quartermaster, who knows how to rid of them! It was about 4:30 by this time, and the party broke up. John, Tony and I were, however, still wide awake, so we stood for'd on the boat deck just under the bridge and watched the latecomers arrive on board. It was not long before the skipper's party arrived. He and Bill (Miss Wilson) joined us, so the party started all over again! About 5:45 it was decided that we should all go ashore in search of breakfast, and the suggestion was hailed with enthusiasm. We each repaired to our cabins to wash and change, with strict instructions to meet in ten minutes and no longer! I went to my cabin, finding Bunty fast asleep. I managed to wash and change without waking her. I put on a cotton dress, and taking my coat, I made my way to the rendezvous.

At the barrier, we had once more to sign our names and there we met Sheppherd and his friend just coming back. We persuaded them to join us. Leaving their purchases with the officials, we all set off for the ferry. Coming off the ferry, we met yet another gay party returning to the ship, complete with flowers in the hair, colored paper ropes round their necks, their arms loaded with souvenirs and waving branches of palms! Once across the ferry, we ordered two taxis to take us to Long Beach where we proposed to have breakfast. We called at the Hilton Hotel, but they would not serve breakfast until 7:30—it was then about 7 o'clock. We went across the road to a snack bar, and there sitting up to the counter on high stools, we partook of waffles, fried eggs, and coffee. At least, I did; the others indulged in various fruit juices, fried potatoes, bacon and eggs, etc. I found it difficult enough to struggle through my waffles, though, really, they were delicious. I was a bit too tired to enjoy them.

After breakfast I felt considerably revived, and we all ambled forth down to the beach. None of the shops were open at that time, but we wandered down the arcades. Most of the shops here are Japanese. At the end of the arcade, we came to the fair ground, but that, of course, was quite dead. We eventually came to a sweet shop that was just opening, and there Bill and I were presented with large bundles of popcorn, which we clutched all the way back to the ship. A few doors along, in front of a shop was one of those automatic cameras—a kind of box, in which you sit facing a glass, having drawn the curtains around you. You slip a 5 cent piece into the slot and a bright light appears, this indicating that the lens is exposed. Then, in about four minutes, the finished photo appears, complete with frame, from a little slit. Bill and I had ours taken, each trying to look as foolish as possible. Mine is quite a masterpiece. I hope to send it home one of these days.

The tide was out when we were there, leaving a marvelous expanse of soft yellow sand, quite different from our pebbly beaches at home. It stretched out for what seemed to be miles, before reaching the sea. The colors were wonderful, for by this time the sun was quite strong, and the sky and sea appeared very blue against the glare of the sand and white buildings. From the sea, the beach runs back to a concrete promenade, behind which are white buildings, some shops, such as one sees on any beach in England, fruit shops, nicknacks, sweet shops, etc. Others are private residences or hotels, which run the whole length of the beach. The gardens on front of these buildings are quite fantastic, with weird palm trees and cactus plants, and in some places along the promenade there are patches of grass with beds of these plants laid out and palm trees growing in the sand.

It was nearly 9 o'clock by this time, and I think most of us were a little footsore and weary. We inquired where we could catch a streetcar back to San Pedro. Luckily, we were not far from a stop, and before long the said streetcar arrived. We tumbled in, still feeling very hilarious, in spite of tired feet! At San Pedro we separated to make last minute purchases, Tony and I going off in search of postcards. We tramped about the town for some time looking for non-colored postcards and at long last, found some. Then we staggered up to the post office to get stamps. It is a magnificent building. A lift took us to the actual post office section on the first floor. I sent off the second part of my journal and also various postcards.

Prior to this, we had made large purchases at a fruit shop; the fruit here is so cheap that we bought an enormous bag of it—peaches, melons, plums and I don't know what else! We intended to sit and gorge ourselves on the boat deck in the afternoon. We had just come out of the post office and were debating whether or not to take a taxi when a car drew up beside us and asked if we would like a lift back to the ship. A little taken aback, we asked how he knew the ship, to which he replied, "I should. I was working on her all last night!" It was a grand ride all round the oilfields, across the bridge and right back to the barrier gates. Once more we signed our names in the book. We came aboard and wrote our postcards in the music room before dinner.

There was a notice on the board to the effect that the ship was not sailing until 4 o'clock, so once more we wandered ashore to post our cards. This we were able to do just outside the barrier. But it was such a nice afternoon that we decided to cross by the ferry and have a last wander round the shops. Tony's Navy shorts and blazer caused a minor sensation. I don't think anything like them has ever been seen here before! Everyone stared and seemed much amused, but, really, the folks here are so very nice and friendly and so anxious for us to know that America is with us.

We got back to the ship for the last time just before tea. A cup of tea was most welcome and so was a deck chair on the boat deck immediately afterwards. We were joined by Pamela, Charles and Richard, so we produced our bag of fruit, and we sat and devoured peaches and bathed ourselves in melon.

It had turned quite cold by this time, so wrapping myself up in a rug, I went fast asleep until 7 o'clock. I woke up to find myself very cold. I went in, changed for dinner and had an early night.

Back to Sunday: I did not get up early for deck tennis, but had a lazy morning in bed thinking about the fun I'd had the night before and how incredible it is to be half way around the world.

After lunch, I went down to the saloon and had a session with the typewriter down there and made good progress. After tea, Tony and I made a four with Bill and Arthur and had a very good game of deck tennis before the matches started.

At 7 o'clock we had arranged to have a party before dinner and had invited Bill, Pamela and Charles. They are such nice people. Pamela is sweet and unsophisticated, a perfectly charming person. In spite of our early date, we still arrived a quarter of an hour late for dinner.

Tuesday, 29 July 1941

I got up this morning to play with Tony against Bill and the skipper. We had a very good set and nearly managed to beat them! It was 6-5, so not too bad. Later on I had another set just before breakfast. After tea, Tony and I went up to see Sally, who is confined to her cabin on account of a cold. It has been such changeable weather, and with this cold spell, everyone was either in the smoke room or the music room. Mrs. D. thought it wiser for Sally to stay away. We found her sitting out on the boat deck in a chair. She was very pleased when we offered to play a game with her.

Wednesday, 30 July 1941

It turned out to be a heavenly morning, so I sat on the boat deck most of the time, until about 11:45, when Tony went up on the bridge to take a sight. Then we both went down to the smoke room where he worked it out, while I sat by trying to look intelligent. Later, Arthur came and joined us, and we all had a drink before lunch.

A select party of Bill, Arthur, Tony and I sat on the boat deck all afternoon. John Turk came along during the course of the afternoon and lent me his sextant, but the sun was too far over for me to take a sight from the port side. I shall try tomorrow.

A cinema show has been arranged for the evening, and I think we shall try to go. It is the *Great Barrier*, which does not sound up to much, but it is always rather a novelty to be at the cinema at sea!

Thursday, 31 July 1941

The cinema show last night was a washout as far as we were concerned. We had seats right at the back, so could only see the top of the screen. After about half an hour of straining and stretching, I fell asleep, or nearly so, and was removed at the end of the first reel. We revived in the smoke room with a Shandy!

Later on, we assembled in Mrs. Griffith's cabin and ate oranges until 11:45 when I went next door and found Bunty asleep with her glasses on her nose, her book in her hand, and the light still on. I removed both glasses and book, then switched on my light and switched off hers. She did not stir. It was not long before I was in bed myself and asleep. This morning I went down to see Uncle Bill, as the Chief Steward is called by everyone. I wanted a piece of cardboard to make a Ludo board for Sally. She has no games at all, besides the one Snakes and Ladders, and I am getting a little tired of it!

It started to rain after breakfast, so we were not able to sit on deck. I retired to my cabin where I started to write this, while Tony took a sight. Then we both repaired to the smoke room where we attempted to work out the sight. They are really rather fun to do, although I cannot really pretend to understand them. Logs and Natural Haversines are little more than just tables to me. Still, I get a lot of fun out of it.

The sun has been shining most of the afternoon, but it has been raining all the time. Sitting out on the boat deck was impossible. Instead, we found a quiet spot in the music room and spent the afternoon reading and sleeping. At least, Tony slept. I sat and read until I could not bear the hard seat any longer. I retired to my cabin, leaving the sleeping babe!

Now I must go and iron before dinner; then, I shall come up and change in good time. There is a dance tonight, and I think I shall go this time.

I have seen the headwaiter, who had promised me that cardboard. He has given me two large folders, which I shall be able to convert into board games for Sally. One I shall make into a Ludo board, and the other I think I shall make into Snakes and Ladders!

Yesterday the bridge was thrown open to the passengers, but I was promised a private session this morning. At 10:30, Tony nipped up to see the Captain first and then came down for me, and I spent a very instructive hour and a half up there. John Turk was on watch, and he showed me round. First, I was allowed to try my hand at the wheel. It is infinitely more difficult than one imagines. The course was 56 degrees. I managed to keep her steady fairly well, but once or twice she slipped a few miles out! Lying just in front of the wheel is a compass, and you have to keep your eye on the magnified section. A thick line indicates the degree of the course you are keeping. The whole art, of course, lies in judging just how much to pull the wheel round and just when to release it so that a steady course is kept. The quartermaster does a trick (a watch or a turn) of about two hours at a stretch. It must be terribly boring, I should think, and for the first time most alarming. I am sure I should be in a flat spin, left to myself!

After this, I was shown the chart room and saw various positions plotted. It is all most complicated and interesting. How the R.N.V.R.'s learn it all in their very short course is quite amazing, for they do have a terrific amount to cram in. I was, then, shown various instruments, which I do not pretend to understand, one for finding depth, by which a charge is sent down and, hitting the bottom of the seabed, the echo is returned and recorded on an indicator in fathoms. The other was a radio apparatus for finding position by sound waves, or something equally complicated. Next, I climbed up to see the dry compass, which is above the bridge on Monkey's Perch. The compass here is different from the one by the wheel. This one is not in liquid, but is suspended on iron rings, with two gimbals on each ring, thus enabling it to move both forward and backward, as well as sideways, and allowing it to remain stable on a horizontal plane. Standing on the glass top is an instrument containing a prism, through which you could sight the sun and, at the same time, see the magnified chart of the compass indicating the position. By altering the position of the prism, one could see, in the same way, positions of objects ashore. The whole was covered by a metal cowel against weather. I went down onto the bridge again and tried to take a sight with John's sextant, but the sun was, by this time, almost vertical. It was very trying, holding the sextant up so high. Having found the sun through the lens and nearly broken one's neck in the process, the next thing to do was to bring the sextant slowly to bear on the horizon, at the same time keeping the sun reflected on that mirror. This is very difficult for the beginner!

By that time, it was nearly 12 o'clock, and I had to go, but there was just two minutes to spare. I hastily got my camera and managed to get one or two photographs. I do hope they are successful. I am keeping all my films until I get to Singapore, as the barber does them so badly and charges terrific prices.

Saturday, 2nd August 1941

A shocking game of deck tennis this morning. Really, I must go to bed earlier or else give up playing deck tennis! We spent an exhausting morning on the boat deck working out sights that Tony had taken before breakfast. Really, it is great fun. I did the writing today, while he looked up the logs and tables. Tomorrow I shall try to work one alone, although it will probably take me all morning! It started to rain heavily in the middle, so we were forced to take cover under the awning. Just before lunch, we were joined by John as he came off watch, and we had a drink together up on deck. As a third officer, John was not allowed in the public rooms with the passengers, nor was he supposed to sit on the promenade deck or lower deck, so Tony went down for the drinks and we had them up on the boat deck.

After tea, I was asked to join a team of six ladies to enter for the skittles competition. I don't think any of us have played before. However, we are to have a practice match with the Second Malaya team, so we shall see!

A most tragic event happened this afternoon when Mrs. Groves, one of the passengers who sits at our table and who is traveling to Singapore to join her husband, gave birth to her baby. I don't know if it was a boy or a girl, but the child only lived five minutes. And it was so terribly wanted. How very sad it is!

The game of skittles was quite successful, but we shall

have to practice a little more before our match if we are to win through the first round. A match was already in progress when we arrived for our game, so we were terribly late in starting, which made us late in changing for dinner. I do hate having to rush over this, as it is hot and one simply cannot do it in comfort. The dance was canceled. I don't think many of us felt like it—we were all a little subdued by the sad news this afternoon.

Sunday, 3 August 1941

It is terribly hot today; there is not a breath of air. Now I see that it is again raining hard, so am forced to have the portholes open. If I have the fan on, all these papers will blow about, so what is a poor soul to do!

Arthur, Tony and I went up onto the fo'c'sle head this morning during the church service and took some photographs. Once docked on Oahu, I understand we will have to hand in our cameras once more. This is very disappointing as I should have liked some snapshots ashore. I think we can just sight land on the port quarter, but it is very indistinct. I understand that we are to get in some time this evening. There are various rumors about the time of our arrival, so I don't know what to believe.

Later: We had just docked but did not know if we would be allowed ashore. I thought it rather improbable, considering how late it was; still, it was late at Balboa when we heard, so there was still hope.

Sunday, 3rd August 1941

Today we spent the entire afternoon on the boat deck, watching the ship approach the island of Oahu, of which Honolulu is the port. Earlier on in the day, just before lunchtime, we sighted land, but only in the distance and very faintly visible on the horizon. By three o'clock, great rugged mountains came clearly into view as we rounded the southern tip of the island. These mountains are of volcanic origin; in fact, most of the peaks are craters of extinct volcanoes. Looking at them as we steamed slowly past, one could almost image the reddish-brown spurs of land to be still molten as they steamed down the sides, to end in a jumbled mass of huge rocks at the water's edge. The green breakers hurled themselves to white spray as they dashed against them. It was a truly marvelous sight! I am afraid my idea of a south sea island was sandy beaches and palm trees. I had no idea that there would be such impressive scenery as this. Clustered just off the promontory known as Diamond Head were several little islands, some not more than mere rock, looking very bleak and bare as the waves broke over them.

Slowly we worked round into the bay, still keeping not far from the coast. There were, in fact, one or two smaller vessels between us and the coast, but, nevertheless, it was quite possible, with the aid of glasses, to see people on the cliffs. Even with the naked eye, one could distinguish cars

as they crept along the coast road where later we, ourselves, were to drive. The bay was full of white-sailed
yachts, twisting and twirling in the strong wind; some came
quite near to the ship, and we waved as they passed. A
beautiful beach of yellow sand could just be seen—the famous Waikiki Beach. Shallow breakers were rolling inland,
and we strained our eyes to see the surf bathers. Pamela
and Charles were standing next to us, and there and then
we made up our minds to go ashore early next morning
and see if we could get any surfing. Behind the beach stood
a cluster of white buildings, and behind these again rose
the hills ending in rugged peaks, some of which were hidden by patches of white mist. The hillside came down in
spurs of land and on these spurs were grouped the white
houses of the inhabitants.

By this time it was tea, so we went below to the saloon.
After a hasty drink and a biscuit or two, we returned to the
boat deck where we were joined by Arthur and Bill. We
had come right across the bay and were nosing our way
up to the quayside. This took a bit of doing. All the passengers crowded to the side to throw pennies to the group of
very dark skinned boys with dark curly hair, who were
diving for coins. Like lightning, they swooped down on
every coin that was thrown, the lucky finders putting them
carefully into their mouths. After a time, their mouths became so full that they were obliged to come out of the water and transfer the loot to little bags reserved for the purpose, which they kept tucked in the tops of their swimming trunks.

Hearing that we were to assemble in the smoke room
with our passports, I made my way down. The smoke room
was already crowded, but they had not started to call the
names. It was rumored that they would call them this time
in alphabetical order. At Halifax, when our names were
first entered, they put them on three large sheets according

to destination and not in alphabetical order, which accounted every time for the delay in getting passes. This time, however, we were all through in less than no time. It appeared that we had leave until Wednesday morning or Tuesday evening. There was excitement over the news!

The officers had to go ashore in white duck suits, so there was a good deal of scrounging among them all before everyone was fitted out. Many of them wisely did not get much kit in London as they will be able to get it much more cheaply in India; nevertheless, it was a good thing some of them did! Tony and I went ashore together. We just wandered along into the town, looking at what shop windows were open and getting the layout of the town. The place seemed full of American sailors. Many of them saluted the British officers, but I doubt if any of them were in a fit state to recognize the uniform!

In the course of our wanderings, we came across Storer (Sub. Lt.) and Mrs. Toyne, and we all joined up to go in search of a drink. This proved to be somewhat of a difficulty as nearly all the places were closed, it's being the Sabbath evening. We managed, however, to find a hotel and were shown into the "garden." It hardly seemed that we were in the open, for the palms and tropical plants under which the tables were set grew up so high that they almost shut out the sky. It could have been made a very charming place, but it was very badly arranged and could, really, be in no sense called a garden, but just a sort of backyard. However, we were glad to find some place open, and most of the others were filled with the American Navy. We were shown to a table for four and proceded to consume bottles of rather inferior Hawaiian beer! After a further wander round, we returned to the ship where I inquired if there was a Catholic church anywhere near. I was told it was about five blocks away, so once more we set out to find it and to see what time the service was in the morning. Having found out that there was a Mass at 8 o'clock, we returned to the ship and after a drink of coffee, retired to bed.

Monday, 4th August 1941

I got up when the stewardess bought the tea at 7 o'clock. After a bath and leisurely dressing, I met Tony in the smoke room and we proceeded ashore together. The church was very large and cool but rather ornate. There had been two previous Masses, which probably accounted for the emptiness of the 8 o'clock. I should think there were only about half a dozen of us in the church. It was nice to get to Mass after all this time. We were out by about 8:30 and made our way back to the ship. We had not got very far before we met Percival, who persuaded us to come with him to buy a pair of American shorts and a shirt. We went into the shop and were shown a marvelous assortment of highly-colored shirts, with Honolulu and Hawaii written all over them. He purchased a green one with huge white flowers sprawled over it, truly a marvelous effort! Oh, the comments later on when he appeared in it, together with a later effort in the way of orange trunks!

The evening before, Pamela and Charles had a lift in a car and had learned that at Fort de Russy there was a beach reserved for the families of officers. Provided he and Tony went in uniform, there should be no difficulty about our getting in. We decided to collect our bathing things, do a little shopping, chiefly to get sunhats, and then proceed to the beach. We had really planned to shop the next day, but both Pamela and I wanted a sunhat, and so did her little

Richard. We dived into the first suitable shop—it might have been Selfridge's large store in London at sale time. I never saw such a scram—a melee of people trying to grab things! I think Tony and Charles were the only men in there. The counters were just packed with women struggling to pick up bargains. I was very tempted to get another swimsuit. They do have marvelous ones here, but most of them were $5 and $8, which, with the present rate of exchange, is rather a lot. We were not very successful about the hats. We did manage to get one for Richard but thought possibly we should do better on the beach itself, so we made our way to the bus stop.

A ride of about half an hour along the coast road that we saw yesterday brought us to Fort de Russy, which is just before you come to Waikiki. We wandered slowly along until we came to the fort entrance, and there Charles went up to the sentry to find out to whom we had to apply in order to get permission to go onto the beach. He let us through and directed us through the camp. We changed into swimming kit straight away, planning to have a swim before lunch and then find a spot on the beach where Richard could dig and the rest of us sunbathe. The tide does not go very far out at this point, and when we arrived, it was right up. There was a wooden building at the back which contained dressing compartments and in front of this, a car park. Most of the swimming and diving was done from the clubhouse, which was built right out over the water. As you entered from the roadway, there were diving boards on one side, a covered-in place with a counter where valuables could be left, and to the left was the club-house itself. The water, so we were told, was about 18 ft., so one had no fear of diving from the very edge. There were also three rafts: one quite near, the second about 50 yds. out, and, I should think, the farthest was about 200 yds. The water was deliciously warm, and we took it in turns to be with Richard while the others swam out to these rafts and sunbathed on them. The joy was that one could sit without getting frozen, as one does in England, even on quite a hot day when there always seems to be a wind. Here it was quite perfect.

Before we went into the water and while we were waiting just outside the club, two girls came up to talk to us and asked, seeing that we were English, if they could do anything for us. We asked them where we could get sunhats. They said they knew of a place in Waikiki and at once offered to go and get them for us. Off they went and later returned with the most marvelous hats made of palm leaves. I will have my photograph taken in mine. They—Alice and Julia—joined us for a bathe, and then we all went in search of eats. We were led to a kind of sandwich bar where we sat in the open on a beach. We consumed large quantities of hot dogs, hamburgers, and beer, then returned to the beach, where Pamela settled herself down with Richard for an afternoon's paddling and digging! The rest of us dumped our belongings with her and went off to Waikiki to buy Tony a pair of sandals. We took off our shoes and walked along the beach, paddling in the water as we went. It really is the most lovely stretch of beach imaginable, soft yellow sands, on one hand, the sea, with low, green breakers, rolling onto the beach, and on the other, palm trees standing up at hundreds of different angles, making the whole scene seem fantastically unreal. Groups of houses and hotels come right down to the edge of the sand, in some cases just a wooden railing dividing them from the rest of the beach. In front of the buildings, some tropical gardens were laid out, and in front of one of the hotels was the most enormous banyan tree. It was planted in a huge courtyard overlooking the sea. It literally filled the whole area, its branches spreading out and taking root. Instead of one tree, it looked like a small forest! Tables and chairs were arranged under its branches, where the residents of the hotel could sit and have their drinks.

This part of the beach was very crowded indeed. We saw several of the passengers and were thankful we had found another spot! Here we turned in towards the street and padded along the hot pavements, which were almost unbearable to our feet, unaccustomed as we were to walking about with bare feet on board. It was a perfect paradise of gift shops packed with Hawaiian souvenirs. Going into the first one that we came to and looking at postcards, we were greeted by a group of my erstwhile convoy! We exchanged greetings and then proceeded to rummage for a pair of sandals. In this, however, we were not altogether successful, for they had not the right size, and so we came out once more and continued our stroll along the street.

It was very hot, and after our long walk, we were all feeling somewhat thirsty, so the suggestion of an ice cream was very welcome. Accordingly, we went in search of a soda fountain or drug store, which is one and the same thing. There is usually one to be found on the corner of the street, and sure enough there was one, so in we all trouped and clambered onto the stools at the counter with the assurance of American citizens! I had the most wonderful "sundae", called "Black and White," vanilla ice cream with chocolate sauce and nuts. Refreshed by our ices, we climbed down and went over to look at postcards. We found a pair of sandals for Tony. It was getting on for 4:30 by this time, and we said that we would only be about half and hour! So we bethought ourselves to get back as quickly as possible, in case Pamela wanted to get home with Richard. Leaving the roadway, we came onto the beach once more and walked back to Fort de Russy where we had left the others.

On the way back, as we passed Alice's house, she went in for her movie camera and took several shots of us all on the beach. I had my camera, also. At the last minute we heard that we would be allowed to take them ashore with us after all, so I determined to take as many snaps as I could. I do hope they are a success.

Richard was still digging happily; Pamela and Charles had been bathing and seemed not to mind being left all the afternoon! Pamela thought she would be getting slowly back to the ship and put Richard to bed. The rest of us wanted to have another bathe, so, as Alice was going to drive us back, we took the basket and bag and went back to the clubhouse. The water was still deliciously warm. We swam out to the furthest raft and sat there for some time. Even at that hour of late afternoon, it was still not cold. This raft was on a coral reef, and several people were diving for bits of coral. You could get a kind of glass mask, which covered the upper part of the face, including the nose, and this enabled you to see clearly underwater. I did not try, but Tony did. He got a large piece of coral up, but it was too difficult to break. I did swim ashore with a little bit, but I am afraid that I left it behind!

On our way back from Waikiki in the afternoon, we all arranged to go out in the evening to a dance somewhere. Alice and Julia had to go home to get Mother's permission! They were such nice girls, not at all sophisticated, but somehow they gave the impression of being very much older than they were. Later we learnt that they were still at school and were graduating next year! But one would have taken them, at first sight, to be at least 25!

Time was getting on, so we dived into the water once more and swam ashore. We dressed and then went with Alice to meet Mother! She proved to be a very nice person indeed. We sat on the grass outside her house and drank Coca Cola—at least, I did. Mrs. Allen had been to England during the last war and knew London a little. She consented to let Alice come out with us, on condition that we did not keep her out too late! She then offered to drive us all back to the ship, so we went back to the clubhouse in search of Alice's brother, who had the car. We were invited into the clubhouse to meet some American soldiers. There, to our surprise, we found Pamela, Charles and Richard in a group of officers and their wives. We were asked to join them for a drink before getting back to the ship. Alice's brother, however, could not be found. We got a lift in one of the officers' cars, having first arranged to pick up the girls at a quarter to nine.

Once back in the ship, I rushed up to my cabin and changed before dinner into my new frock. Storer and Nancy were also going out to Waikiki that evening, and we decided to share a taxi with them. At half past eight, we met on the quay outside the barrier and summoned a taxi. There were five of us, with two more to pick up, and the drivers were not supposed to take more than four at a time. But we persuaded him to take us. No, there were six of us, for we had asked one of the engineers to make up the party. We all squeezed in and off we went. Later we picked up the girls, and they packed in, too!

Our first port of call at Waikiki was the famous Chinese restaurant known as Lau Yee Chai. Here there was an open-air dance floor with a beautiful waterfall at one end, where the water came trickling down over the rock face amongst all kinds of tropical plants. The whole was floodlit and looked most spectacular. We all trooped in and were shown to a table quite near the dance floor. We sat down and ordered drinks. Tony and I tried one known as Hawaiian Collins, and it was quite good. We learnt that there was to be no floorshow that evening. As it was very hot in there, after a few drinks, we decided to move on to another place, the South Seas. We understood that there was a floorshow there of hula-hula dancing.

The South Seas proved to be very much smaller and

was packed with our ship's passengers. However, we went in, and all they could offer us was a table right at the back where we should have seen nothing of the show. It appeared there was hardly anywhere else to go. Monday was not a good night to have chosen! Either Saturday or Wednesday is best when the boat comes in from the mainland. After much talking, it was thought best to make for the last hope, the Hawaiian Village, but this closed at midnight and was not likely to be much of a show. We were really rather tired by this time and were feeling it foolish to have left Lau Yee Chai's.

The Hawaiian Village was not a great success, I am afraid to say, but after a good deal of bargaining with the man at the door over cover charges, we all went in. It was packed and terribly dim and dark, with only a tiny dance floor. The whole was made to look like an old Hawaiian hut, the walls being made of plaited palm leaves, such as those used to make my hat, mentioned earlier. The tables were polished surf boards. The small dance band was nearly blowing the roof off—we could hardly hear ourselves speak, and as for ordering drinks, it was almost an impossibility. Tony and I had half a dance and then gave it up as a bad job. The entertainment at Hawaiian Village was provided by the patrons themselves, various members of the audience getting up and doing steps of the hula-hula dance. I must say, the Hawaiian music was rather fascinating. I should have liked to see genuine hula-hula dancing, which is still possible up in the hills where there is a village. Four of us went out for air, and we watched a bit from the doorway. We were trying to decide where to go next and what to do. By this time, nearly everywhere was closing down.

Maurice and Nancy decided to hitchhike home, while the rest of us made our way back rather disconsolately to a bus stop. We caught a bus to the beach where we had been this morning. None of us felt like bathing—I, for one, did not, being dressed up for dancing and not feeling that I could cope with wet hair and a borrowed bathing costume, and then having to struggle into my clothes again. However, we took off our shoes and walked along the sands back to Alice's house. There we sat for a bit on the beach in their small palm garden. It was beautifully cool and fresh, sitting there in the moonlight! We sat there talking until nearly 1:30 a.m. when Mrs. Dutton drove us back to the ship and invited us to come over the next day.

I got up at 7:00 and went to church with Bunty, who was most anxious to accompany me. We arranged last night that John and Tony should come to meet us at 8:30 when we came out of Mass.

We were out in good time and were wandering down the street looking at the shops when we met the others. We had one or two purchases to get and then thought it would be fun to have an American breakfast at a drug store, instead of going back to the ship. First we went into a shoe store to get Tony a pair of tennis shoes. I discovered that he, too, had been up early shopping, for he presented me with the sweetest cigarette case, enameled at the back with a little map of the Hawaiian Islands beautifully painted on the front. It really is a lovely little thing, and I was so pleased with it.

We all had breakfast, sitting up to the counter of the nearest drug store. I started with papaya and then had boiled eggs. Here they serve them, not in a shell, but broken into a small bowl with quite a week's ration of butter! They were simply delicious, and we finished up with butter and toast and lovely coffee. After breakfast, we went over to the cosmetic counter and made several purchases, and then wandered out and into a kind of glorified Woolworth's, known as Kress. It was a perfect heaven of a place, and one could have spent hours there. We bought some postcards and then thought it better to split up as we each had shopping to do. Tony and I did not want to get back to the ship too late because of meeting Nancy and Storer, so we went off together in search of a bathing costume for me. I am sorry to say that, after seeing the lovely ones yesterday on the beach, I felt that I just must have one! We made our way into Liberty Hall where we had been the day before, and I was lucky enough to come across the same assistant. She was most helpful, and by a stroke of luck, it appeared that there was, just that day, a reduction in swimsuits. I was able to get a really lovely one for #3.65. It is white, with a flared skirt of some sort of elastic material. I was some time choosing this. I met Pamela, so we tried on bathing costumes together. I could not stay, however, to see what she finally purchased as I did not want to keep Tony waiting any longer. The poor thing had been waiting patiently among a crowd of excited shoppers while I tried on costumes!

We returned to the ship, and, finding a note in Tony's cabin to the effect that Maurice and Nancy had gone shopping and would be back, we went into the smoke room and proceeded to write our postcards and letters. Soon afterwards, first Storer appeared and then Nancy, having completed their various shoppings. So we collected our bathing things, etc., putting them in the black bag. I decided today not to be bothered with a handbag, as well as the black one. All you really need is your money and the pass.

A taxi was found, and the men bargained for the price to be paid. These taxi men will have you all ways up if you are not careful, but they seem to come round if once there is someone to argue with them. Finally a rate was decided upon and we all four settled ourselves and the junk into the back. We intended to take the coast road round the island until we came to the Sacred Falls, and there we would have lunch and trust to getting a lift either further on or back.

First we had to call at a house where Maurice and Nancy had been the evening before because she had left her sunglasses there. Thus, we had an opportunity of seeing something of the residential district. It really was rather nice; all the houses were different, each set in its own garden, but not railed or fenced off. Some of them were so pretty; I should have liked to see inside. The gardens, too, were lovely, with the huge palm trees and the masses of flowering shrubs. All the flowers seemed so brilliant and huge.

Leaving the town behind us, we took the main road that runs across the southern tip of the island through the mountains. What a wonderful drive it was, and how I wish I could describe it all! We climbed up and up, through the most wonderful country—quite tropical, I understand, but without the intense damp heat of a tropical climate. A range of high, rugged mountains known as the Koolau Range runs down the eastern side of the island, and our road cut right through this range. Majestic scenery lay before us as we reached the highest point. Here there was an open space through which the wind just whistled with terrific force. Before us lay the sea of Kaneohe Bay, while all around us rose the mountain peaks, the highest ones half hidden in the mists. To our left, Suicide Peak stood out ominously against the sky. Here, we were told, in days gone by, the invader drove the reigning Hawaiian King and his army in retreat up the steep sides, and rather than surrender, they pushed on to the summit and jumped over. The road took a winding course down the *Pali*, or precipice. It was a thrill descending this road, which zigzagged in great bends all the way to the bottom. There seemed to be a constant stream of cars both up and down the road, and it was quite hairraising the way we seemed to take the bends. Once at the foot, we followed the road along the coast. In some places the sea was only just a few feet away. We continued along until we came to Kahana Bay. We got out, paid the taxi, and found a suitable spot in the sands where we could eat the fruit lunch we had bought in Honolulu. There were a few houses within sight, but absolutely no one for miles—it was glorious! Unfortunately the sun had gone in and did not show much prospect of coming out again. However, it was getting on for 2 o'clock by this time, and we were somewhat hungry. It was no wonder that we consumed the whole of two pineapples among the four of us! We cut them in chunks and just sat and munched, dripping into the sand! I have never enjoyed a pineapple so much.

Just as we finished, it came on to rain. We were obliged to take shelter under a palm tree. It did not last long, however, and we came out once more. This time Tony and I thought a walk along the beach would do us good after the filling lunch.

We ambled along the beach until we came to a place called Hauula, and there we spent the rest of the afternoon just lazing. Unfortunately it was too cold to bathe, but it was lovely to sit wiggling one's toes in the soft sand and enjoying the feeling of peace and quiet away from the ship's passengers for a short time! Funnily enough, just before we reached this place, we were walking along the road, remarking how far away the ship seemed and all its passengers, when just at that moment a car drew up, and who should be in it but the deck steward and the bar steward! They were being driven round by two of the embarkation officials from the port. They gave us a few bananas and then drove on, much amused at seeing us!

Nancy and Maurice had stayed on the beach at Kahana and were going up to the Sacred Falls later on in the afternoon. They said they would look out for us, but by this time we had wandered too far along and were really too tired to go back. I am rather sorry we did not all go up there first as it was rather a lovely sight, so they told us afterwards. Still, one cannot see everything, and it had been a lovely drive in the morning.

It began to get dark rather early, chiefly, I suppose, because it had been a rather dull day and very over-clouded. Anyway, it was nearly 6:00 by this time. We thought we had better make moves for home as we were than over 30 miles away and we intended to hitchhike. The first car was only going to the store at the next village, but they took us as far as that. We were glad to take shelter there for a little while as it was raining rather fast by this time. We went in and bought a supply of biscuits of local manufacture, and very good they were, too. We were a little hungry by this time, having had only fruit for lunch, so we were glad of the eats. The rain stopped and we once more took to the road, eating as we went and taking it in turns to hail the passing cars, which, I might say, were not so frequent at this hour. Tony bet me that we should need five lifts to get back to Honolulu; I bet two. As a matter of fact, we were terribly lucky, for the next car that we stopped was going right back to Honolulu and they were only too pleased to take us. They were two very nice men of Portuguese origin but had lived on the island all their lives. In fact, they told us that they had never been outside the island, not even over to the mainland. One had a herd of cattle up in the mountains, and he had been along to look at them; his friend was a butcher. They were most interesting and told us a great deal about the island and the people. On the way back they stopped the car outside a fruit shack on the road and bought quantities of bananas, which they insisted on our sharing. We produced our biscuits and English cigarettes, and so the party was complete.

We came home by the same route across the mountain pass, and while we were slowly coming up the *Pali*, they switched on the news on the car radio. It was from a station in Honolulu, so I understand. Oh, how one misses the news here, on the ship, I mean! It is either too indistinct on the radio or else one can get nothing at all; it is chiefly because all the fans are going at the moment during this hot weather.

We were anxious to find a fruit shop in order to get a pineapple for Mrs. Groves. Our friends insisted on driving in search of one, waiting while we bought it and then driving us right back to the port, which was very nice of them indeed. Really, people *have* been kind to us.

It was about 8 o'clock by this time, so we were a little late for dinner. But we were able to get some all the same, and afterwards we sallied forth once more, this time in search of a post office and possibly to end up at the flicks. It was still raining, so we took a taxi to the Soldiers' and Sailors' Y.M.C.A., where I was given to understand that letters could be weighed and stamped. All this time I had been carrying Mummy's letter about with me and never seemed able to get it posted. However, I got it done successfully, at least Tony did for me, and then we went in search of a picture house. In this last effort we were not so successful. It appears that here in the evening, one has to book in advance. This we had not known, and all the seats were sold. We were both rather tired and I was not feeling too good. It was probably overtiredness and perhaps a little too much car driving. Anyway, we decided to return to the ship and have a drink on the boat deck. We must have been tired, for we both fell fast asleep and woke up at 12:30! Still half asleep, I staggered to my cabin and fell into bed!

I woke about 7:00 to find we were just off, so I woke Bunty and we thrust our heads out of the ports to catch a last glimpse of Oahu. Suddenly the thought struck me: why not have tea outside? In a flash we had put on dressing gowns, and grabbing the rug and the tea tray, we sped outside. It was lovely sitting there on the boat deck in the morning sun. A huge white Matson liner lay outside the harbor waiting to berth where we had been, and as we pulled out we saw her slip in. About 7:30 we had to move; the deck was about to be washed, so we went in to bathe and dress before breakfast.

On Monday morning, I had taken two rolls of film to be developed at a Kodak shop in Honolulu, and they were ready by Tuesday evening; someone had kindly collected them for me, and I got them the next morning at breakfast. On the whole they are very good! I shall have copies made when I get to Singapore, and I hope to be able to send them home. I also took a good many ashore. The light was bad the day we went round the island; however, I was using one of my Panatomic films, so I have every hope of getting some successes.

It was a messy morning; we had dropped anchor just outside the harbor and did not get under way until 11 o'clock or thereabouts. I spent most of the morning wandering about the ship, comparing notes with the others, and watching the activities on the harbor. I ended up in the smoke room until lunch. Straight afterwards, I washed and set my hair, which was terribly sticky from bathing at Fort de Russy, and then I sat on the boat deck in my new costume, which appears to have been a success! At four o'clock the tea gong rang, and Tony spoilt me by bringing a tray up on deck.

Thursday, 7th August 1941

To think that I have really visited the Hawaiian Islands and have spent nearly three whole days in Honolulu! It sounds quite fantastic! What a wonderful place it is and how kind and hospitable are the people! We had a grand time there, and I think everyone was really sorry to leave.

I spent the rest of the afternoon on the boat deck yesterday making notes of the stay in Honolulu so that I could get my account typed out at leisure. I find that is the best way, for while one is in port, it is not really possible to type every day.

After breakfast, I went up to the boat deck and sat on the starboard side out of the sun and wind. There, after much arrangement of my *barang-barang* [Malay term for possessions, or junk], I eventually settled in a deck chair with the typewriter on the footrest. It was not altogether comfortable, but the best I could do, for it was too hot to be in any of the rooms. I was getting on very nicely when Richard came along and showed interest in the typewriter. I persuaded him to go back to his Mummy, who was sitting a little further along, but in a few moments back he came. However, in spite of these interruptions, I managed to get a good bit done. Just before lunch Tony and I had a lemonade with Pamela.

In the afternoon I put on my new bathing costume and sunbathed on the boat deck. Really, that rug of mine has been so useful; I should be lost without it. I am so glad that Mummy darling made me buy it!

A race meeting has been arranged for Saturday morning, and the auction of horses and jockeys took place in the music room this evening. It was very amusing. Shears dressed himself up as the auctioneer, in a tailed coat over breeches, with a huge red tie at his throat, powered hair, and a very red nose. His drooping mustache came off in the excitement, but it was very fine to start with! One of the Chinese boys made a very good clerk. A rostrum was erected in the music room, and wielding a large hammer, Shears conducted the auction from the raised position. He did it extremely well, keeping up a flow of conversation all the time. At first the bidding was slow and rather careful, but as the evening progressed, it leaped up in farthings to as much as 6 shillings and 7 shillings a horse, and the jockeys fetched even more. Bill was bought for 35 shillings, and later sold in bits! I learnt later that Donald had bought me for 7 shillings 6 pence. We did not stay to see it all as it was terribly hot, but taking a couple of glasses of beer, we retired to chairs on deck. There was a super moon. I must try to take some photographs tomorrow night; I should think a time exposure would be all right.

Friday, 8th August 1941

In the afternoon I sunbathed again, at least, only for a little while, and then we found a cool spot on the port side and slept peacefully until tea. We had arranged a game of deck tennis with Bentley and Donald after tea, and it proved to be good fun. Mr. Yardley has offered to lend me his tripod, and so I must try to get a silhouette photograph by moonlight tonight.

Saturday, 9th August 1941

It was still very hot about 10 o'clock last night, and we were sitting out on deck as Bunty came past. I hailed her and suggested that we should sleep out together. She thought it an excellent suggestion, so we went to make the bed. I must have got another puncture in my Lilo, for still it will not keep up. However, I used it as a ground sheet, spread my rug over that, and put the bedclothes on top. It was, thus, not quite so hard as the bare deck. Having completed these arrangements, Tony and I thought that a moonlight bathe would be rather nice. We could not persuade the others to join us, so off we went. We promised to come and tell them when we were ready, and we would all go down for a coffee before turning in. It was a grand bathe, quite a number in the pool. It really is quite marvelous bathing by moonlight. We came out, and attired in dressing gowns and housecoats, the party descended to the saloon where we sat, as usual, on the floor outside the Chief Steward's cabin. Quite a crowd of us had collected by this time, and Uncle Bill sportingly supplied biscuits from his cupboard. Someone—Arthur, I think—suggested taking flash photos! So a couple of cameras were produced, and several groups were taken.

It was late when we eventually retired to our hard bed! It was grand to feel the wind blowing over one all night, but the deck was rather too hard to be really comfortable. I woke up each time I turned over. However, I saw the sun rise, and about 8:30 I thought I would go in for a sleep before getting up for deck tennis! So waking Bunty, I got up, and we both struggled in with our bedclothes and were asleep again in two seconds.

At breakfast we found our race cards on our plates, with designated colors for each jockey. I found that I was "running" in the third race and should not be wanted much before 11:30. After breakfast I went below to iron until the racing started, and then I brought my typewriter and papers along to the smoke room and sat there typing until it was time to go out for the race.

This time the jockeys sat the other end of the course, so that we got a little more air than last time. I could not, of course, see what was happening, but I understand that for the first part I was in the lead. But my hand slipped, and I came in third, which was a pity for Donald. After the race, Tony and I joined Bill and Bentley for a drink of lemonade in the smoke room, and soon it was time for lunch. Rather a wasted morning again, I am afraid.

It was very hot on the starboard side in the afternoon, so our particular place on the port side of the boat deck was rather crowded. I do hope that this does not mean that these people are always going to be there. It is mostly only the passengers with cabins up there that know of the haunt, but several "strangers" appeared today. However, it cannot be helped; they have as much right to be there as we have.

I had left my things in the smoke room all afternoon. After tea I returned and typed until it was time to change for dinner. Once again we took glasses of lemonade onto the boat deck to watch the sunset. Bunty's friend Michael is having a birthday tomorrow, and we were invited to a cocktail party this evening in the Pig and Whistle. About twenty-two of us sat round in a large circle in the Pig and

Whistle. After dinner we went on deck, intending to wait until it was time for the dance. Soon after it started, Pamela and Charles came up, too, and it was no good. There was too much of a list. It was not really worth going down, so we stayed up in the cool.

Sunday, 10 August 1941

A slightly better game of deck tennis this morning. I think, given time, we may beat them! After breakfast I sat in the smoke room with Mrs. Griffiths and looked at a Dutch grammar that I have been lent by a Mr. Sheppard, who, by the way, is going to Singapore and knows Sumatra. In fact, he spent his honeymoon at Kaban Djahe [my destination]! I have made a resolution to study Dutch every morning after deck tennis and before breakfast in the morning.

We arranged to go for a swim before tea, but it was still pouring very hard. I did go out and walked round the deserted decks down to the swimming pool, but somehow I just missed Tony. Not seeing him and not wanting to stand out in the rain, I returned to my cabin and made myself ready for tea.

I spent an uneventful evening. It was terribly hot, so I cooled off with a glass of Bass (!) [stout] and went to bed.

Monday, 11 August 1941

Deck tennis as usual, after which I was made to keep
my resolution of studying Dutch. I did not feel in the least
like doing so. Somehow I feel just limp in this hot weather
and seem to lack energy. Of course, it may be the late night!

After breakfast I found Sally, and we did some lessons
in the smoke room. It is some time since I did any with her.
Now that we are once more at sea, I think it is a good thing
to start them again. Accordingly, we did English for about
half an hour. Then I showed her how to make a Ludo board,
and we spent the rest of the morning doing it. Tony and
Bentley had been playing deck tennis. They came and
found me and asked me to join them in a drink before lunch,
so we sat out on the promenade deck and drank our lemonades. It was very windy. I was obliged to go up to the
cabins and do my hair again. Really, this wind is terrible
for the hair; one simply cannot keep it tidy. I have resorted
to the bandage! I understand it is typical doldrum weather.

A skittles match had been arranged at 5:15, but it had
to be scratched because it was too windy. Great excitement
was caused after tea by gunnery practice. We had all been
warned previously that it was to take place, so we were
ready for the bangs. Everyone crowded to the rails, and we
went aft to see the target put over the side. It consisted of a
raft, with a sail attached to two masts and a bar to steady
it, rather like an outrigger canoe. This was lowered over

the side, and the wind carried it out on the starboard quarter. As soon as it was a little distance out, they opened fire with the small stuff first and later with the larger. It was very thrilling to watch, although the noise was terrific. What must it be in a man-o-war with all guns blazing, I cannot imagine! As soon as the target was out of range, they sent up a kite, such as they had used earlier in the voyage, to act as a sort of barrage—this was a particularly beautiful one, with Hitler painted on the lower surface! We had a good view of all this from the boat deck. We stood under cover of a roof that is part of the engineer's quarters.

After dinner we were sitting out on deck. Suddenly there was a great banging and shouting as Father Neptune came aboard, demanding particulars of the passengers. He called up to the bridge from the well deck, and information was returned from the bridge. We rushed to the rails but could see nothing. I suppose, had we crossed the Line earlier in the day, they would have held some sort of ceremony. However, I see that there is a list up of all those who want certificates, so I have extravagantly put my name down.

Tuesday, 12 August 1941

After breakfast I took Sally for a few lessons in the music room; at least, I set some work for her, as at that time she was busy finishing a game of chess. After waiting for a little bit, I went down to iron. Sally came down to me to tell me that she had a surprise, and would I come? As soon as I had finished my ironing, I went up to the smoke room where she showed me the finished Ludo board with the name beautifully printed on the cover.

Wednesday, 13th August 1941

After tea yesterday, I took my Lilo into the children's swimming pool in order to find where this puncture is, but I was unsuccessful in doing so. Although I submerged it and tested it on both sides, I was unable to find the hole. I shall have to try in fresh water, which I understand is better than salt. Most of the children were in, and they all had rides in turn until it was time to go to bed. It was getting dark, and I could not see any longer to find the puncture. I came in and spread the Lilo on the deck to dry.

In the evening there was a showing of the film *The Great Barrier*. The sound was very bad, and although this time we had front seats, we could not gather much of the story. It was rather like watching an old silent film, only without the captions!

After breakfast this morning, I had Sally again for lessons, and afterwards she started to make a kind of Snakes and Ladders board. I left her after about an hour, still hard at it, while I went up to my cabin to write. Our afternoon was rather a mess, chiefly owing to weather conditions! We went out to our haunt on the boat deck but had to come in as the rain simply fell down in buckets. We came down to the smoke room where we stayed until tea.

Thursday, 14th August 1941

It cleared up sufficiently to spend last evening out on deck. With the blackout, it is quite unbearable inside on these evenings. Our skittles match had been put off until this morning. We had attempted to play yesterday afternoon but were driven in by the rain. The team was sheltered under a tarpaulin screen. We did at least manage to keep dry but got very dirty in the attempt. However, this morning we were more successful and got to the end of the match without any rain. We were playing the "Kitson Kittens", our team being the "Amazons". They beat us by about ten points; however, it was a good match. We hope to do better in the subsequent matches, for we have to play all the games.

I wrote for part of the evening in the smoke room and then went to change for dinner. I attempted to wear my new dress but had to take it off. I was simply boiled. I think I shall have to leave off wearing it until I get to Sumatra, for it is impossible in this weather.

Saturday, 16th August 1941

Please note we have missed a day, owing to crossing the Date Line. We went to bed on Thursday evening and did not get up until Saturday morning! Sounds a bit like a hangover, I must admit!

Another skittles match this morning, so I had to give Sally a miss. This time we were playing "The Rovers." We were winning easily for the first two innings, and then the men caught up beautifully, which made the end of the match most exciting. We both wanted two points, and the match went to the team who could knock the two skittles down in the least number of balls. We went first and got a skittle for each ball, which made us sure that we had lost; however, there was great excitement when the men missed their first ball. The second ball brought down three skittles, thus making the match a draw.

The lunch gong sounded. I went up to make myself respectable. It has been a lovely day, very bright and sunny, but with still this wind.

Sunday, 17th August 1941

After lunch we found our same spot on the boat deck and spent the afternoon there. Mrs. Toyne had lent us "The White Cliffs", by Alice Duer Miller, and Tony and I read it aloud together. It really is rather a lovely poem, and I couldn't put it down until I had finished it.

There was a dance yesterday evening, but we did not stay for much of it. As always when we are getting into port, there is a list on the ship as cargo is shifted. Last night it seemed particularly bad; however, we had one or two dances and then came away.

No deck tennis this morning. Nevertheless, I got up at 7:30 and was down in the smoke room by 8 o'clock studying my Dutch. It is really a most suitable time in which to study. I find I get quite a lot done. We played again after church service. I came off the court like a dripping rag and went straight up to have a shower, consequently arriving somewhat late for lunch.

This afternoon I washed my hair and sat out on the boat deck in the hopes of drying it. Thank goodness, the wind had dropped, and there is a bit of hot sun in which to sit. By tea time my hair was still not dry. Tony went down for a tray of tea, and we had it out there on the rug, which was very pleasant indeed. Afterwards, I got some washing done, amongst other things a cotton frock to wear tomorrow, for it is estimated that we land on Fiji at 6:15 a.m. We shall not be there very long, although it remains to be seen whether we shall be allowed to land. Having washed, I later went below to iron. Just before 7 o'clock, Pamela and Charles invited us to have a drink in her cabin. I scored with Richard by playing "Trit trot to market" with his teddy. It was after 7 o'clock before we were able to get away to change, and we had invited them to have a drink with us before dinner.

Wednesday, 20th August 1941

Twelve hours in Fiji: it seemed so short after our long stay in Honolulu, but how very different a place, so much more primitive, and the country so much wilder than anything we saw in Hawaii. The Fijians are certainly a fine race of people, most striking in their appearance, due, no doubt, to the carnivorous appetites of their ancestors! The men are very tall and beautifully straight, with a great mop of thick, fuzzy, black hair, brown eyes, large flat noses, and thick, dark lips. The women seem to be tall and well built, with the same mop of black hair, which, from time to time, they plaster with mud to set it. Some try to dye it a browny color, but on the whole the black fuzz looks best!

I think the policemen attracted everyone's attention and admiration. They were quite marvelous! They wore a blue uniform jacket over a white skirt (most of the men wear skirts) cut in scalloped points, and, of course, bare feet. One came on board with the emigration officer to stamp the passports. There was one at the foot of the gangway and another at the barrier to inspect the passports as we came in and out.

We got our passes before breakfast. I came down quite early and found the officials already installed in the smoke room. Several of the passengers were there in dressing gowns, so I joined the queue and before long got my passport stamped. Then we went down to breakfast. We had not docked but had only dropped anchor in the harbor outside. I went down to iron a dress for going ashore, and by the time I came up, we were moving slowly to the berth alongside an Australian ship. Most of the passengers went ashore at once. We, however, did not, but wrote our post-cards and finished off letters, and then we wandered ashore. It was nearly lunchtime. We made for the post office and cable office with the intention of coming back to the ship for lunch and then going off somewhere in the afternoon. We had leave until 10 a.m. the following day.

We posted a wad of letters and postcards, and I sent a cable to Mummy. The one I proposed to send to Singapore they would not accept at the post office, but they directed us to the cable office. We thought we would go there after lunch, and as we had met two of the ship's passengers who were also going back for lunch, we shared a taxi with them back to the ship.

Straight after lunch, we made for the cable office, and there I was able to send a cable to Auntie and Uncle telling them that I had arrived safely in Fiji! Then we went to the Tourist Agency of the Bank of Australia, where we were able to get several pamphlets about the island. We were told that there was not much to see, which was a little damp-ing. However, nothing daunted, we consulted the booklet of tours and decided to hire a car and go for a short ride into the country. There are only two roads—King's Road and Queen's Road—which skirt the island. To go the com-plete round takes about three days! These are, of course, the main roads. There are others round Suva, but the cen-ter of the island is very mountainous, thickly covered with tropical vegetation and only accessible along bullock tracks, which merge into jungle.

Hailing a taxi, we went back to the ship to see if there were any stragglers who would like to join us, but there were none. So we set off by ourselves, having first fixed upon a price with the Indian driver. It was a grand drive and very well worth the money. First, we went up to the reservoir above the town and had a splendid view out across the bay. Behind us the mountains rose up tall and green into the rather dull sky. A keen wind was blowing, and after the stifling heat on board, I actually felt cold!

Getting into the car again, we continued our way up into the mountains over a very stony road. The country could not be described as beautiful in the way that Honolulu was. Here the mountainsides seemed untidy, with straggling growths of trees and the creeping undergrowth. Dotted about the countryside were the most awful tin shacks, red-roofed with corrugated tin! Some of them looked the most terrible hovels!! Soon we came to a native village, so called; it was certainly a collection of rush huts. The driver stopped the car, and natives crowded round trying to persuade us to go inside. We did not stop, however, but went on further up past other similar settlements. Several times we stopped the car and got out to look at the view. The mountains were thickly covered with trees, but still we could not get away from the tin huts! At another point we saw a mandarin tree. The fruits were still quite green, but the driver managed to get one down for us, and I brought it back to the ship. On the way we passed a group of the passengers on bicycles, but I should think it must have been hard going on those stony roads.

We came down to the Waimanu river, rounded a bend in the road to the Methodist Mission. We stopped to inquire if a friend of Tony's mother were still there. The minister's house was perched on the top of a rocky piece of ground, overlooking the roadway. Leading down from the house were stone steps winding in and out through groups of tropical shrubs. At the bottom was a little lawn over which some bare-footed little Indian children were scampering, amongst them Alison, the eldest of Mr. Blacker's three children. They were a charming Australian family. Mr. Blacker came down and invited us to tea and then showed us all round the mission, which was most interesting. We sat in a mosquito-proof room and drank tea and ate tomato sandwiches. Then Mr. B. sent over to the mission for two of the Indian students. They climbed up a coconut palm and got down two coconuts for us, striking them with a long handled knife [machete] peculiar to the Fijians. Apparently, they always carry this weapon, which is most useful for cutting their way through the jungle. These boys were very agile, and I could not resist the temptation of trying to climb a palm myself. I clambered down the bank, and taking my shoes off, I tried but with very little success, I am afraid! It is most frightfully difficult. Still it was great fun to try. Alison, of course, had to try too, and then we both climbed back up the steep bank to the lawn. There the boys neatly chopped off the top of the coconut, and we drank the milk as best we could. It was delicious, but we had to be careful not to get it on our clothes as I understand it stains badly. These were not the kopra nut. Since they are usually gathered solely for the milk, they are not allowed to reach maturity, so that the flesh is very thin and soft. The boys chopped them open when we had as much of the milk as we wanted, and then we ate the flesh with a spoon. The two smaller children, Muriel and Margaret, were greatly excited and thought it all a great joke.

By this time it was beginning to get dark, and we had to take a lamp in order to see round the mission. It is both a home and a school for the Indian children, as there are a lot of Indians on the island. The tiny ones were just going to bed, and the matron was giving the baby his bottle. It was the sweetest little thing. Then we went over to the school building and saw the classrooms. The Australian educational system is in force all over the island, and Australian books are used. The lessons are given in English, but the children also have to learn Hindi, which is the recognized dialect for the Indians and is taught by these Indian student teachers. By this time it was quite dark, but the playground was still full of children running about and playing on the swings.

Leaving the mission, we came down to the gate and there said our farewells. Mr. Blacker had arranged for the taxi to wait for us, and we found him there at the gate, so, getting in, we drove back to Suva. We thought it would be nice to go to the pictures as there was no dancing to be had. Besides, it was some time since either of us had been to a cinema, so we stopped at one of two cinemas and booked seats. We did not intend to be disappointed this time! In fact, we did ourselves proud and booked the Governor's box! Once more we got into the taxi and drove back to the ship, where we went straight down to the saloon for dinner. We only had half an hour as we had ordered the same taxi to pick us up at ten to eight.

We hurried out and found the taxi there waiting for us. We arrived at the cinema in good time and were conducted in state to the box, which was in the very center of the cinema, over the staircase. There we sat in basket chairs, with piles of cushions! It was rather fun! The film was *The Valley of the Giants*, but the thing that struck us most was the ancientness of the news. They were actually showing pictures of the Maginot Line and French women working in munitions factories, as if it were yesterday's news!

Back on the ship, we were just in time to have coffee, for now we cannot get tea or coffee after 11 o'clock, which has put a stop to our evening staircase parties. However, we were just in time and took our cups up to the music room.

I got up early intending to go to Mass at the church not far from the ship, but when I got there for an 8 o'clock mass, I discovered that the only one had been at 6:30. I wandered up to the convent to make further inquiries and there met a most charming nun who was from Winchester and had been on the island for six years. We had a long chat together, and then it was time for me to be getting back to the ship. We only had until 10 o'clock, and we wanted to do some shopping before we sailed. Just at the barrier I met Tony, and together we returned to the town and found a milk bar where we could get some sort of breakfast. As it turned out, we had a very good one consisting of waffles, syrup and coffee. Then we set off in search of souvenirs. Tony bought me the sweetest little outrigger canoe with a basket sail; he also bought me one of the long-toothed wooden native combs and a basketwork fan. I bought him an elephant carved out of coconut—it was rather sweet, with the trunk thrown over the back. We had great fun going round the shops and choosing the things. On our way back to the ship, we met women with strings of beads on their arms, which they were trying to sell to the passers-by. These strings were very pretty indeed, made from the seeds of the various fruits that grow in the island; some, also, were made with shells threaded between the beads. We stopped and were immediately surrounded by a chattering mob. They held up string after string and tried to put them on our arms. In the end, we chose two, and giving them a coin, we left them to fight it out by themselves.

We were quite tired by this time, so we sat in the smoke room, and had a lemonade while we wrote our postcards. Soon we began to move, so we rushed out on deck to see what there was to be seen. There was a great excitement among the Indians in the well deck, for two of them had been left behind! However, it turned out later that we were not really off but only drawing away from the berth. We had to wait for the *doebe* laundry. Nevertheless, it caused much anxiety and not a little amusement, especially to the passengers, who all crowded to the after rail and watched the launch bring the Indians aboard. A wooden rung rope ladder was thrown over the starboard side. The launch came alongside and they climbed up onto the well deck. I took two photos of the event!

Just before lunch, I met Mrs. Doig, who gave me a little tortoise shell broach—a present from Sally. I had bought Sally a little elephant, which I gave her as I was going down to lunch; she was very pleased with the addition to her collection of animals.

After lunch we took our afternoon rest on the boat deck. Coming back to the ship in the morning, we had passed a shop where they were selling coconuts, and we bought six for threepence. We did rather well on the exchange, as there were 25[?] to the Fijian dollar, so we felt quite rich! We ate one of our many coconuts, first banging a hole in the top and drinking the milk in turns, and then smashing it open and eating the flesh—or as much if it as we reasonably could without hurt or harm.

Wednesday, 20th August, 1941

Breakfast was followed by a very exciting skittles match—the Amazons against Singapore, which I am pleased to say we won. After the match I typed in the smoke room until lunch.

All week on the boat deck, the Lascars have been working at the davits, which hold the lifeboats. These were sadly in need of paint, so all week they have been up there, chipping the paint off the ironwork. Imagine the noise! In addition, there has been a strong wind all the time, so that bits of paint and red lead seem to be all over the place. I see with horror that they have come over to the port side today. We shall have to endure the horrors of chipping from now onwards. It is a curse having the portholes closed all the time, but it is better than having the bunks covered with this dust. We have had to keep the ports closed most nights lately, for it has been so cold, but I am told it is quite seasonable and right and proper for the Southeast Trades. All the same, I wish it would get hot again. We had a comparatively peaceful rest this afternoon but were rudely awakened at four o'clock by the Lascars coming to start work. We were compelled to come down to tea in time, for once.

After tea we again played deck tennis with Sylvia and Russell and then once more had a swim before changing for dinner. We came into the smoke room and were hailed by Pamela and John Brakes, who asked us to join them in a drink, which we did, and stayed until Charles had finished his rehearsal. Every evening from 7:30 until 8:00, the dance band, formed from among the passengers, rehearses for the coming concert, and from the sounds that issue from the music room, it should be a rather a good show. They have a piano, a violin, a saxophone, a drum, and a uku-lele—it really is rather a good noise. I was asked if I would join with my fiddle, but I did not feel equal to it. Besides, Mr. Gardner is a very good violinist, although he has not played for some time.

I got up reasonably early this morning and ironed a blouse to wear with my slacks; it is so bitterly cold. Yesterday I had a great washing and tried my hand at starching. I only had time to iron one blouse before breakfast, and that appeared to be quite successful. In future, I shall have courage to use starch. We can get boiling water from the steam tap in the bathroom, and if only a little water is turned on—and as much steam as possible, one can get the water as nearly boiling as possible. Anyway, it seems to work, and that is the chief thing. I had borrowed a blouse of Bunty's in which to come down to iron, so I slipped into the bathroom and changed into the newly ironed one before the breakfast gong rang—a most successful operation!

I have been asked to take part in a charade sometime this week. After lunch our party held a meeting in the smoke room to decide on the word and the scenes to be acted, a scene for each syllable. The party consists of Sylvia, Newbolt, Morris, Shears, Sheppherd and myself. The words chosen are "pain-stay-king" and "tor-pe-do." After this, I went up to the boat deck, where we spent a very blowy afternoon. Tea was at 3:30 on account of the arrival of Father Neptune and his retinue, which is timed for 4 o'clock.

After tea the passengers packed themselves along the rails overlooking the for'd well deck. We had quite a good stand on the gangway, from which place I was able to get some photos, but again I am afraid that the light was not good. It was a dull day and rather cold, not at all what one would imagine crossing the line. However, it was a panotomic film, so they may be all right. Neptune's throne was arranged on the tennis court, facing the swimming pool, with a plank leading up to the side. A proclamation had been issued earlier in the day and posted on the notice board to the effect that Father Neptune and his Queen would come aboard at 4 o'clock and that four of the most villainous passengers were to be brought before the court for trial. Of course, there was much speculation as to who the victims would be.

Accordingly, at four o'clock the procession slowly emerged form the depths of the fo'c's'le. They proceeded to the foot of the gangway, where the First Officer was there to meet them. (The Captain is suffering from a strained back, the result of a fall whilst ashore at Fiji.) The procession then mounted the tennis court and took their places. Their Oceanic Majesties then greeted the ship and called for the four most villainous passengers to be brought to trial. The guards went in search of the first victim. They had, of course, been warned and were suitably clad in bathing trunks. Arthur appeared and led them a chase up onto the fo'c's'le head, on to the winch cover and was finally caught and brought before the judges. After paying enforced homage to the King and Queen, the charges were read out. He was dragged off to the doctor for an inspection to prove that he was fit to undergo the punishment meted out by the court for the crimes of which he was accused. Arthur put up a very good show indeed and gave his guards a very strenuous time trying to hold him. Twice he escaped and had to be caught. Many of the passengers took part in the performance. Shears made a superb barber, shaving the culprit's head and getting ducked several times in the process. In fact, nearly all the players got pushed in before the ceremony was over. Arthur managed to push several of his guards in before he finally went, and even then they had a job to duck him. The next victim was Donald, then Morris, and last Allen. They kept it entirely to the Sub. Lts., which, in a way, was a pity, but the Captain only allowed the ceremony on the understanding that the passengers remained spectators. I understand that in the past there had been serious accidents, for which the Company gets the blame, so the victims had to be chosen carefully. Anyway, it was a very good show indeed, and I think everyone enjoyed watching it. Few envied the hapless victims.

Friday, 22nd August 1941

We arranged last night to get up early and do some ironing before breakfast, and this we did most successfully! My efforts at starching have been rewarded, and the shirts look quite well laundered!

There was a final meeting after lunch for the charade; we intended to act Stanley Holloway's poem "Albert and the Lion." After much thought and concentration, several of the passengers managed to get most of the verses down. If it was not absolutely correct word for word, it was very near. I went up to the cabin to make typewritten copies of it and spent most of the afternoon messing about, getting ready for the charade.

The charade in the evening was a great success. I think most of the ship's passengers were there assembled in the music room. I did not see the first charade. It was just between two people sitting at a table and talking. We came on second. Our first scene was Mr. and Mrs. Ramsbottom at the zoo with Albert. I was Mrs. Ramsbottom wearing my gray skirt, a silk blouse, gym shoes, and a brown straw hat of Bunty's stuck on with a knitting needle, and my hair screwed up into a bun. The rest of the company were animals behind a length of tennis net. Albert was duly eaten by Wallace in a most skillful manner, falling over the net and being at the same time covered with a rug. The next scene was before the magistrate, and Newbolt and I were the same as Mr. and Mrs. R. Shears made a super policeman. The third scene was a skittles match between the Non-Benders and the Non-Entities. The final scene, bringing in the whole word, was a meeting of the German cabinet, Morris making a wonderful Hitler. We had a grand time, acting this charade, and really enjoyed ourselves very much. I understand that we are to do another one some time next week. We are keeping the same team. The last charade was acted without words. The actors did very little dressing up, which is, in itself, an amusement to the onlookers. However, it made variety.

After lunch Tony and I went up to the boat deck, and

bagged a patch in the sun. There we were joined by Johnny Turk, and the three of us slept most of the afternoon. We had all had a drink together in Turk's cabin before lunch, hence the party afterwards.

We spent a most pleasant and interesting evening. Mr. Spragg, who sits at our table and is going back to Kuala Lumpur, has a cine Kodak on board and has taken several rolls. He was able to get one colored film developed in Honolulu, and together with several others that he already had of the trip home and ones taken at his home in K.L., he gave us a private showing. We went down to the soldier's mess and had the projector there. He has some wonderful films.

Sunday, 24th August 1941

Tony had bought a pair of bathing shorts in Honolulu and they did not fit, so this morning I unpicked the side seams and tacked them up, altering the band. In the afternoon I went to Mrs. Banks' cabin and borrowed her machine; the result is most successful and the said shorts now fit. Mrs. Griffiths came and sat with us for a little, and then, finding it too hot, retired below, where she very sweetly ordered two lemonades and had them sent up to us.

Just before lunch we decided to go in for a bathe. Turk signaled from the bridge that the bath had been filled up with a change of water, so we went down. But, alas, others had the same idea as ourselves, and after one or two dives we came out, there being too much of a crowd. We returned to the boat deck and there dried off in the sun before changing for lunch.

Monday, 25th August 1941

I managed to get in a little Dutch this morning before breakfast; it is a few days since I did any, but must pull my socks up now and try to get some done every day.

After breakfast I found Sally, and we did some English together in the music room. I set her a few exercises and then started looking over my letter; as soon as she had finished, we started on the Snakes and Ladders board. At 12 o'clock, I left her, and Tony and I went on the boat deck for a little sun-bathing before lunch. We were rather tempted to bathe but left it for the afternoon. The lunch gong sounded, and I retired to put a dress on over my bathing costume. Then down to the saloon, where I was fortified with a bean curry. Once again we staggered up to our haunt on the boat deck. This time we had secured a spot, and just as well, for there was quite a crowd.

Bunty and I retired to make starch and finally disposed of our washing on the line in the cabin and on towels spread over the deck in the sun. Then I settled down to go over my letters, as we are due into Cairns on Wednesday. However, several people came up from the pool, saying how marvelous it was, so we were persuaded to go in for a swim. Johnny came down again with us. The pool was beautifully cool and clear, and we had a wonderful bathe. There was a game of deck tennis going on at the same time. We watched for a little and then thought it would be rather nice to come on after the game was finished, and so we put on tennis shoes and came down to take our turn. We got Sylvia and Allen to play again with us, and we had a very good game indeed! At the finish we were so hot that we had to go in again to cool off! Then, in a dripping state, we descended to the saloon to ask the headwaiter for a tray of tea, which we took on the boat deck.

Pamela was playing in a skittles match, so she had asked me to look after Richard. He sat with us on the rug and had tea. Then we went down to the children's pool where he paddled about until Pamela was ready. We then all sat on the hatch behind the tennis court and watched the men's final deck tennis match. It was a most thrilling game between Charles and Hu, one of the Chinese boys. Charles won after a strenuous struggle.

A wonderful sky, the water very dark against the sunset, and on the port side a storm coming up, so we have just rushed up to the boat deck to gather in the washing and rug, only just in time, too.

Tuesday, 26th August, 1941

A notice was on the board to the effect that Mr. Spragg would be showing his films in the music room last night after dinner, but, as we had already seen them, we sat out on deck. There was a very brief shot of Bunty, Donald, Tony and me playing deck tennis in the early days. My green tweed coat and slacks have come out very well in the color film.

This morning there was a very loud knock on my door, and Tony's cabin boy appeared with a note asking me to come out for a swim. I went out to find the pool both clear and full of fresh water, but, goodness, it was cold! We had to do some strenuous swimming to get warm. Now I am in the smoke room where everyone seems to be hastily writing letters for the mail today. In the corner there is a Chinese lesson in progress!

Wednesday, 27th August 1941

Well, what a disappointment, our not being allowed ashore after all! Apart from anything else, I wanted to get another typewriter ribbon, for this is nearly dead. I have another ribbon, but it is in the ship's hold in my trunk. I never dreamt that I should use one completely before the end of the voyage, but then who thought I should be making a world tour?

After finishing my letters yesterday, I had a game of deck tennis before lunch and then down to the saloon. In the morning, land was sighted, ranges of distant mountains, very high and green. We had some ironing to do before going ashore (as we thought!), and so after lunch we made straight for the iron. The shirt and shorts that I had starched for Tony the day before were a great success. It is much more fun ironing starched things, as they seem worthwhile when finished; shirts crease so easily without starch and look like nothing on earth after being worn for a few hours. I also ironed two of my frocks and a blouse, so I had a busy afternoon.

The pilot of Cairns harbor came aboard, bringing a suitcase labeled Thursday Island. He would be guiding us along the treacherous coral reef for three days. It did not look as if we were to be allowed to land. We had anchored just before lunch, within sight of Cairns Harbor. We had planned to have a wonderful day on the beaches, which looked so exciting through the binoculars. As we approached, the passengers crowded to the rails on the starboard side to watch the Quartermaster heaving the lead. The R.I.N.V.Rs. were a little scornful, but, nevertheless, he was rather good at it. Anyway, we all enjoyed watching him! Apparently, soundings had to be taken every few minutes. The anchor was dropped just before the gong rang for lunch. A great deal of sand was stirred up, which was an indication of the depth in which we were.

There was, alas, no doubt about the truth of the rumor that we should not land, for no sooner had the pilot climbed up the side than we were away again. It was certainly rather disappointing as we had been looking forward to a lovely day on the beach. By that time it would have been too late to have gone far, even had we been allowed to land, and I don't suppose the night life in Cairns would have been up to much. Still, it would have been fun to have set foot in Australia.

After my ironing, I did a little typing on concert programs and then went out to join Tony on the boat deck. We spent the rest of the afternoon sunbathing. In the evening we had a hilarious party. At first, it was just a crowd of us having a drink before dinner, but feeling we must make the most of the evening aboard, we decided to congregate again after dinner and continue the good work. Bob, Arthur, Bentley, Donald, Maurice, Nancy, Tony and I foregathered in the Pig and Whistle, and there did we have a party? I think the least said about that the better! I certainly expected a hangover this morning, but not a bit of it; I even felt roused to take a swim before breakfast. Yes—Bunty and I went down to the pool. I went along to Tony's port, banged on the side and finally persuaded him to join us. It was very cold indeed, but worth the effort.

At breakfast, still feeling sprightly, we thought a game of deck tennis was indicated. Tony nipped out to "bag" the court, as you now have to book the court by putting your name down on the blackboard that is beside the court. In this way you reserve the court for twenty minutes. Bob, Bill, Tony and I played in the end. After the game, I was asked by Mr. Morris and Co. if I would like to take part in the forthcoming concert. They have written a collection of topical verse, and they intend to work it into a sort of skit. For this purpose we all met in the smoke room and discussed the matter. It is really going to be rather fun.

All morning we had been passing the most fascinating little islands, some quite tiny indeed, others quite a considerable size, with trees growing on them and the most lovely sandy beaches, making us so envious. One reef we passed seemed to consist of a circle of coral, enclosing a small island with a little green vegetation on it. The water within the reef was as calm as a mill pond and very sandy and brown compared with the heavenly blue and green of the sea outside. The sea is really the most wonderful color I have ever seen. One can just stand looking at it for hours without getting tired.

Thursday, 28th August 1941

What happened to the ship last night, I do not know. It all started with a party in the smoke room before dinner. About eight of them had a special table arranged in the saloon. I understand it was a farewell party! "Hell's bells!" said the Skipper, "We haven't got there yet!" They had a good deal to drink before dinner, several bottles of Hock during dinner, and, I should think, several gins during the course of the evening. It had the effect of rousing many of the other passengers, and there was far too much drinking and unpleasantness generally. The stewards closed the bars at 10:30. I understand the Captain was not too pleased today and has threatened to close them altogether if there is anymore such behavior. There was supposed to be a dance. We went up to the boat deck before it began and there met Maurice and Nancy, so we thought we must go down to have a "look see." We had one or two dances but came away in disgust; it was really impossible to dance. Tony and I went to the Pig and Whistle for a lemonade. Dancing had started in there, but it had to be stopped, as the Chief Steward came up and said it was forbidden. After a few drinks with the crowd, we departed to a quieter place!

This morning the air was thick with rumors of last night and what happened! I see a notice has gone up on the board, reminding passengers that dancing in the Cafe Lounge is forbidden! I played the last Skittles match, and again, I regret to say, we were beaten. Afterwards, I went to my cabin, where I typed most of the morning.

We had arranged a rehearsal after tea. Newbolt, Morris, Shears and myself went up to the boat deck, where we managed to find a quiet spot in which we could run over our parts for this concert tomorrow. We have been invited to Mr. Morriss's party tonight before dinner. I understand it is his daughter's birthday.

Friday, 29th August 1941

We had such a nice party last night. They are such pleasant folk. The party included Mrs. Griffiths, Mr. Flemming,
Pamela and Charles, Bill and the Captain. Mr. Flemming's
daughter went to Miss Griffith-Jones' school at Cameron
Highlands in Singapore. He has asked Tony and me to go
up for a drink on Saturday evening. About 8 o'clock we all
went down for dinner, and there we found a wine glass in
each place, with a little note underneath saying, "With the
compliments of Diana Pamela Morriss. Born 28th August,
1928."

Straight after breakfast, I went below to the saloon again
and asked the Chief Steward if I could borrow his typewriter again. I used it last night for a bit, as I was typing
out some nursery rhymes for the concert. Accordingly, I
installed myself outside the saloon and spent most of the
morning there. I have hopes of being able to get at my baggage tomorrow, in which case I may be able to get my new
typewriter ribbon. It was only yesterday that I learnt that
the baggage marked "Not Wanted" had been put in the
baggage room. I understood it was all in the hold. Tomorrow, when the Fourth Officer is not so busy, I shall go down
and see if it is possible to get at it.

At 11:30 we again met for a rehearsal but could not
find anywhere in which to rehearse. After wandering about
for some time, we decided to give it up until after tea when

there is usually a quiet place on the boat deck. There has been great activity on deck this morning as they are erecting a stage for the concert this afternoon. They are using two of the rafts covered with plywood and have draped flags and curtains round the back of the stage and across the front. It should look very grand. I am afraid it will be terribly difficult making ourselves heard; it is bad enough to hear the cinema, and that is amplified.

Saturday, 30th August 1941

The concert in the evening went off quite well, all things considered, but it was rather a moldy show, I thought. The sound effects were not bad. The cadets had rigged up awning all along the side of the deck and one across the passageway. Once the seats were filled up, sound was not so bad; nevertheless, we simply had to shout from the stage. I don't think our items were altogether a success; the worst of topical verse is that it only appeals to a certain section of the audience. However, that is over now, and we must, alas, think about packing and that sort of thing.

This morning I intended to have a swim but found the pool empty. I returned, got dressed, and came down to the smoke room where I studied Dutch with great vigor until the breakfast gong rang. After breakfast, I typed in the smoke room until 11 o'clock when Tony and I went down to the baggage room to see what could be seen of my suitcase containing the records. I found the suitcase. I was much relieved to find the phonograph records were intact and not broken, as I had feared. I did not attempt to get at any of the other things, that trunk, for instance, for I should never be able to get it packed up again. I did, however, bring up the records and the photograph. There is plenty of room in that suitcase, and I shall re-pack it with all my books and odd stuff that I have amassed during the voyage. I noted with grief that the lid has also received a bash—

however, not so bad as the trunk. It really was a wonder that the records inside were not broken.

In the afternoon, we all repaired to the boat deck, where we had arranged to have tea and listen to some of my records. At 5 o'clock I had to go, as I was playing in a skittles match—the very last one, thank goodness! I understand we get to Macassar on Tuesday. After that, the next days will be filled up with packing and the like, so there will not be time for deck games.

After the match, we went below to iron in readiness for the Skipper's party. Tony and I have been invited up to the Bridge, together with Bill, Mrs. G., Morriss and Fleming, so we must look our best!

Sunday, 31st August 1941

The last day of August, and we sailed in June! We *did* have a nice party last night. What a nice crowd they all are—quite the nicest on board, to my way of thinking. Mr. Morriss was telling me that he knows Miss Griffith-Jones very well and that on several occasions he has had her teachers to stay on their way up to Camerons, up in the mountains of Singapore. Two of his daughters are now at Wycombe Abbey but were for a time at Camerons. One, I understand, is having a birthday on Friday, and we have all been asked to celebrate! Tony and I feel we should do something about it and so are throwing a party on Monday. We have had several drinks at their expense from time to time, so feel that a party is indicated. When I told Mrs. Griffiths, she was very sweet and wanted to come in with us; however, we have been very moderate in our drinking all the voyage and feel we can afford the little extravagance. One cannot continually accept invitations without returning the hospitality in some way, although I don't think it is expected of us in any way.

There was a dance last night, and we fully intended to go; however, first we went to cool off on the boat deck. There we sat most romantically in the moonlight and both fell fast asleep! We woke up from time to time, saying that we must go down to dance, but went to sleep again almost at once! Finally at 9:30 we thought it best to go to bed and really sleep! I crawled to my cabin and got into bed almost before I knew it. Not long afterwards Bunty came in and was surprised to find me in bed first, so she had to wake me up to ask if there was anything the matter! Being fully satisfied that I was just sleepy, she left me. I went to sleep again and didn't wake up until she came up to bed, but even then not for long; I was sound asleep again before she turned out the light.

I got up this morning, intending again to have a swim, but alas! the pool was empty. I again returned to my cabin, had a bath, got dressed, and then came down to the smoke room, where I studied Dutch hard until the breakfast gong rang. After breakfast Tony and I went for a bathe and sat for a while on the fo'c'sle head in the sun until it was time for me to have my Dutch lesson. I met Margaret on the promenade deck while the rest of the passengers were at church, and there we had our lesson. Really and truly, it is not worthwhile studying too hard, as one cannot learn much more than phrases without a proper Dutch Grammar; however, it keeps the brain active. It's nearly nine months since I did any work; I shall not like it when I start, I fear.

After the lesson, I met Tony and Bob. We took a glass of beer each and went up to the boat deck, where I sat until lunchtime, the other two going down for a swim before lunch.

I saw Mac, the bar steward, with whom I had arranged to play my records on his electric gramophone. First it was to be in the afternoon, and then it was changed to the evening. I think that is the final arrangement.

Monday, 1st September 1941

We spent a most pleasant evening on the promenade deck last night, listening to the Beethoven Concerto. Unfortunately, the slow movement was rather lost in the swish of the sea, but I think most of the rest of it was heard. At any rate, there were quite a lot of people sitting out there listening. It was very hot everywhere, and I should think it will be very hot ashore tomorrow. I must see to it that I have a clean cotton flock ironed.

Goodness! what heat! But how nice to have it back again. Straight after breakfast, I washed out a cotton frock against tomorrow, starched it, and hung it out on the line on the boat deck. I have just been up to see, and as it is now dry enough to iron, I shall try to do so before lunch. I also gave Sally some lessons in the interval of writing this. She is having a birthday party on Saturday, and I have been invited.

A minor sensation was caused this morning when activities were apparent on the fo'c'sle head. There were a couple of officers looking important and masses of Lascars. The cause of the activities soon became apparent when the derricks were swung out each side and the paravanes were suspended over the water. I was just in time to see the port cutter splash into the sea. I rushed up for my camera and came down to the promenade deck, where I think I was lucky enough to get the starboard cutter just as it touched the water. I had to be so quick that it will be more luck than good photography if it does come out.

I must now type out some Hindustani for Tony and then finish off my hair in the sun. Some reports say that we shall be in to Macassar today by 3 o'clock. It is officially reported, straight from the horse's mouth, that we shall not dock until 7 o'clock at the earliest! In any case, I shall have my letters in order and shall have a suitable cotton frock in readiness, against the possibility of an early arrival.

Later: By the time I had typed out the Hindustani, it was time for lunch. I did not get my hair dry after all. It was terribly hot in the afternoon, and hardly a spot of shade on the boat deck. Straight after lunch, however, I went up there in the hopes of getting two deck chairs and a spot of shade, if any. In the former I was partially successful, in that I managed to get a deck chair—and a straight up one. The deck chair later gave way, but we had the rug, so that did not matter very much. In the matter of the shade, I was not quite so successful. First I put the chairs on the port side, but as there was a list to port, it was not long before the pipe which runs along the side just above the portholes started to leak. When that happens, it just pours down and makes the deck quite uninhabitable! I hastily took the chairs round to the other side. There in a minute spot of shade afforded by the davits (lifeboat stays), we spent the rest of the afternoon. I am still altering Mrs. G's black evening dress, and I got a good deal done to that.

At tea time, we got tickets for the cinema in the evening. After tea, I went below to iron a few things before dinner. It is surprising how the time flies down there. It certainly was a little time before I could get the iron, but almost before I knew where I was, it was time to go and change before our party.

The party was very pleasant and most successful, I think. After dinner we came up to the music room, where the cinema was being shown. They were showing Will Hay in *O, Mr. Porter*. I had not seen it before and very much enjoyed it. They also showed a film that had been taken some years ago on this ship; it looked most smart in its peacetime color.

Tony has a bad cold, but I could not persuade him to go to bed before the film. Afterwards, however, I administered hot rum and lemon and, with a couple of aspirins, tucked him up in bed, issuing strict instructions not to get up for breakfast in the morning. I have just visited the patient, and his cold still seems rather heavy. But I know nothing will keep him in bed tonight, if we are allowed ashore.

Reading the dry compass

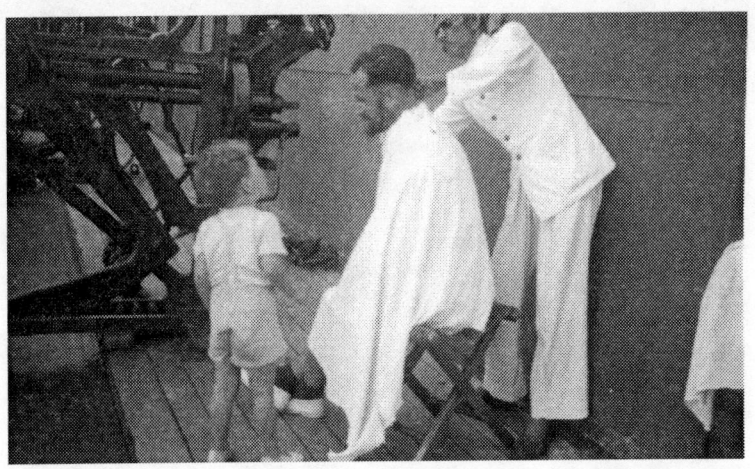

Little Richard entranced by the barber

*Father Neptune comes aboard to
celebrate crossing the equator*

Wrapped in the sarong I bought Tony

Diamond Head, Waikiki Beach on Oahu

Officers' beach house at Fort de Russy

Sally's birthday party

Sally Doig, aged five

At the fo'c'sle head

Fiji policeman in uniform, who stamped our passports

Tuesday, 2nd September 1941

Oh, how sad to think that we are on the last lap of the journey! At least, I am, although, I suppose, the Indian passengers still have a little way to go! It is now quite definite that we are going direct to Penang. From there I shall be able to post letters and 'phone Uncle in Singapore, or telegraph him. I understand that a 'phone call costs something like $ 2 1/2, but that it is cheaper after 7 o'clock and cheaper still after 9 o'clock. I don't suppose I shall be in bed by that time! What a thrill it will be to talk to them! It is estimated that we get in by Tuesday morning—today week; I expect most of the week will be taken up with sorting and packing!

Tony spent all the morning and afternoon in bed in hopes of getting rid of this wretched cold. I sat with him, correcting my letter until nearly tea time when he got up and came down to tea. Then we went on deck to see what there was to be seen. By this time we were within sight of Macassar; it looked very flat because the mists were blocking out the distant mountains. It looked a neat, tidy little place with spotless wharves; we watched from the side and saw the lead being heaved as before we entered Suva.

As we got nearer, we rushed up to the boat deck, from which vantage point one has the best view. The pilot came aboard, and we slowly approached the quayside. The sun was just going down over the water, and from the star-

board side several little fishing vessels were to be seen glid-
ing as silhouettes across the calm water. These were, apparently, native boats, with curious square-shaped sails,
which seemed to lie suspended across the boat as the wind
caught them and filled out. I took a chance of snapping
one of these as it sailed past, but I am a little doubtful of the
result as I only had a pair of sunglasses as a filter and the
sunlight across the water was very dazzling. This was my
last film and the last picture on the film. It was only after
this that I learned that all cameras were to be handed in;
the notice must have gone up while we were up on deck.
However, I hastily emptied the camera and stuck it in the
wardrobe; there was really no need to give it in, for we
should not be allowed to take them ashore.

By this time we were quite near the berth, and everyone was hanging over the port side rails, trying to see behind the tall quayside buildings. These were spotless and
as orderly as one could wish. As we tied up, we could just
see through a space in the buildings, and here we caught a
glimpse of the streets behind crowded with Malays in bright
magenta sarongs; in fact, this was the only bright color
amongst the white. This really seemed a bit of the East. We
were thrilled with the idea of spending a few hours there.
At the barrier there were a group of Dutch soldiers in their
greenish-khaki uniforms with the turned-up hats, breached
and with black riding boots. Very fine they looked! Pres-
ently, the new guard arrived to take over duties, and we
were entertained with some very smart drilling.

Officials came on board, and we went below to the
music room where the inspection of passports was in
progress. It was learned that all naval personnel were to be
allowed ashore—but none of the passengers. I met
Sheppherd, who said he had managed to wrangle a pass
on some paper he had. It was then that I suddenly remembered that I had a Dutch visa for Sumatra and determined

to try if this would get me ashore. I flew up for my passport and returned to the music room. After a little while, I approached the immigration officer. He looked at my passport and at length said it would do. I nearly threw my arms round his neck! Anyway, after a few more questions, he stamped my passport, and I was free to land just as soon as I wanted. I then went up to have a bath and change into something as cool as possible.

I came down to find that a general pass had been granted. Officials had telephoned to Batavia and had received permission to land passengers, so everyone was happy. The chief difficulty was money, for we were not allowed to take any currency ashore other than Dutch guilders, and there were only a limited number of these coming on board. It was rumored that they would accept American dollars ashore, but not English pounds, so Tony rushed round trying to get hold of dollars. We managed to get about $20 in the end, but still there was no chance of getting them changed into guilders. Everyone was hanging about, and few had been ashore. Gardener went, but he had to put all his money in an envelope and was not allowed to post letters. So, after a walk round the town, he had returned with this information.

The rest of us hung about the smoke room, and finally quite a large party collected. It appeared that some of them had been asked to dinner at the Grand Hotel where the President was allowing dancing in our honor, and Tony and I were asked to join the party. None of us having any money, we thought it best to start off this way, at any rate. So, hearing that drink was very expensive ashore, we had a drink in the smoke room before going. The dinner gong rang, but still the party sat and absorbed drink. Maurice, Nancy, Tony and I were impatient to be off because, after all, one can sit in the smoke room and drink any evening, but we only had 24 hours ashore. We wanted to make the most of them. After a little while we could stick it no longer. We would make a start and then meet at the hotel. Accordingly, we set off.

There were many formalities at the barrier. Nancy and I were taken in turn behind a curtain and searched by a most charming girl! However, no notes were found on our persons, and we were allowed to proceed though the barrier into the street. We were immediately surrounded by a crowd of excitable Malays, each trying to make us take THEIR rickshaw. These are most fascinating: the boy stands behind and peddles furiously. It struck me as so typically Dutch to have bicycle rickshaws! But they were most comfortable and an excellent method of seeing the town because they didn't go too quickly and, above all, they were quiet. I think that was the thing we noticed most about the town—the exceptional quietness. There were very few motorcars indeed, and nearly everyone went about in these bicycle rickshaws.

After much argument we picked two of these rickshaws and arranged for them to take us to the Grand Hotel for 25¢ the two of us. So off we went. Oh, it was thrilling! By this time, of course, it was quite dark, and there was only the street lighting, so we were not able to see much of the town itself until next day. However, we went through the main street, past the Malayan and Chinese shops. These were quite open and, I should imagine, very similar to those in Singapore and Sumatra in the native quarters. But here in Macassar there were no European shops at all, or very few; they were nearly all open-fronted bazaars. As we passed we saw groups of Malays sitting round under the dim light of an oil lamp. Business appeared to be over for the most part, but still they sat and talked, and many waved as we passed. The streets were still busy with rickshaw traffic.

On through the town, until we came to the Grand Hotel. This was a really wonderful building, so clean and tidy. At the side of the hotel there was a large open-air cafe, a huge area bordered by flowering shrubs and a low brick wall. Inside this and all round the edge of the dancing space in the center were tables and the most comfortable basket chairs. In the center was a very nice dance floor with a tall arc lamp suspended from a pole in the very center. This shed a not-too-glaring light over the floor and to the edge of the tables arranged under the trees. Indeed, little light would have been needed, for the moon was very large and bright.

We stayed here until the others arrived. Then, after a drink with them, we moved off, for they were rather merry, and anyway, we did not much want to stay with them. Prior to their arrival, we had some very nice dances on this floor. There was a radiogram at one end, and they insisted on playing English records in our honor! Somehow, wherever we go, we always hear "There'll always be an England"—I am really sick of the tune! We were able to get a few dollars changed at the hotel on the condition that we spent a percentage at the hotel itself. This we did and probably would have spent the whole evening there, had not the other party rather spoilt things. Anyway, we moved off and found our two boys waiting at the entrance. It appears that they are hired at 25¢ an hour, and not just for the ride, as we had supposed. This we learned from the hotel manager, and very useful it proved, as we had them until a very late hour! Our boy was called Malan. We kept him for the whole of our stay, he and his friend. No, I think they were brothers.

We then set off in these bicycle rickshaws, and the boys rode us round the town. On the way we passed a Malay market, or collection of food stalls, set out on a stretch of grass common. We insisted on stopping and having a "look-see." At the hotel we had *sate*, but they looked much more

exciting here on the stall. We bargained with the stall keeper,
and at last he took a great handful of these *sate*, and we
helped to cook them over the hot cinders—at least, I took a
turn at fanning the fire! *Sate*, by the way, seems to be little
pieces of meat on a stick of bamboo. I understand the meat
can be anything from beef to goat. I should not like to say
what these were. These sticks are laid on a bar over a grill
of hot cinders, and oil is poured over them as they grill.
Finally, they were ready. We retired to a table on the grass,
and together with the two boys and the whole crowd of
Malay boys of all ages, we started our meal. The *sate* were
served with a hot peppery sauce in a dish, with a glass of
iced water, and a neat little packet of what we supposed to
be rice. It was white and rather glutinous, neatly wrapped
up in dried palm leaves. We could not manage many of
these, but there was no difficulty in getting rid of the remaining *sate*. I am sure Auntie and Uncle will remember
them, but I am not sure of the correct spelling. Anyway, it
sounds something like *sah-tee* , and they were very good.

Having finished our meal and again argued over the
price originally decided upon, we moved off with the crowd
to see round the other stalls. One old man in particular
attracted our attention. He was making large omelets—at
least, that is what they looked like. First he took a piece of
dough, and by a most skillful twist of the hands, he pulled
it until it was as thin as a piece of skin. Into it he broke a
small egg and sprinkled chopped garlic into it. Then, with
a few deft movements of the hand, he folded the edges
over and scooped the whole thing onto a hot plate. The
finished article looked very tempting indeed, but we had
eaten so many *sate* that, alas, we could not face an omelet.

So, amid much shouting and hand waving, we got into
our rickshaws, and we were driven on round the native
quarters. The boys pointed out the real Macassar houses;
they were made of bamboo, with carvings on the front and

roofs that rise to a point at each end. It was at this point that we came to another group of stalls and again got out to inspect. This time we sampled banana fritters; they were very good indeed. Once more we moved on, this time Tony and Maurice trying their hands at riding. I, too, had to have a turn; they are quite hard to steer. It was too hot to go on for long, and soon we gave up and handed the machines over to their owners!

In our tour we passed Malan's house, and we had to stop and go in to meet his brothers and sisters, of which he appeared to have many! This was not a genuine Macassar house, but one of the Dutch design. Through the doors we entered the living room, which had a table and four basket chairs, the only other piece of furniture in the room being a large bed hung round with red curtains. The wall was stuck with pictures of Shirley Temple! and photographs of Malan with his bicycle. We were all asked to sit down, and we exchanged greetings with the family. They served us with coffee, and white bread and sugar; we, in return, distributed our American cigarettes. After a time we thought we could tactfully bid them farewell and go!

Amid further wavings, we took our departures and instructed the boys to take us to the other place we had heard of, where there was dancing, namely the Harmonic Club. Malan and his brother again seemed quite amenable to wait until it pleased us to go home to the ship, so in we went. The place was packed with ship's passengers. We recognized two of the Dutch officials who had been on board in the afternoon, and together with two of the Sub. Lts., we joined them. The whole party sat below in the open in basket chairs. Here the dance floor was under cover, one side being open. It was on a raised terrace and there was a dance band. Coming off the dance floor, one descended two steps and then out into an open air space where there were tables and chairs. We sat with this party, drinking Dutch beer, and then went up for a dance. It was a lovely dance floor and Tony and I really enjoyed our dance; in fact, we had several. But we did not think much of the party in which we were; one or two had quite enough to drink, and so we thought we would tactfully make an exit. This we did, and Malan and his brother drove us to the remaining hotel. But all was quiet there, and there was no dancing, so we drove round for a little. We returned to the Harmonic Club, where we made our own party and there spent a very enjoyable evening. Soon afterwards Maurice and Nancy left, and Tony and I remained for a little. We were so much enjoying the dancing and each other's company. It was lovely to dance on a steady floor, and one without a list! About three o'clock we thought it best to go, as the band had closed down. There were one or two fights in progress and a good deal of broken glass!

We went outside and there found Malan, who drove us back to the ship. We were very sleepy indeed by this time. At the barrier a Dutch officer came up, hearing our argument with Malan over the price to be paid. It was quite friendly. They seem to enjoy bargaining and are usually quite happy with the result. However, the officer would not let us pay more than a certain sum (I forget how much), and he insisted on lending us the required amount, as we could not change a 5 guilder note. We had previously arranged with the boys to be at the barrier in the morning to take us shopping, and then we had thought of going out to the country to get some bathing. We then crept on board, and it was not long before I was in bed and asleep.

Wednesday, 3 September 1941

I got up early and went down to the smoke room, where I had a letter to type out for one of the passengers; I had forgotten about it until then. I met Tony, who said that we were starting before breakfast time, and was I ready? I hastily typed the letter, and we all went down to ask the Chief Steward if it would be possible to get breakfast early. This, he said, was not possible, but that if we would come down just before the gong rang, he would tell them to bring us something at once. This we did, and by the time the gong rang, we were half through bacon and fried egg!

Taking my black bag stuffed with bathing things, we set off and once more had to undergo a search at the barrier. This time we were allowed to take American money, provided we declared what we wanted to change at the barrier, where we were given a form for that amount. First, Tony settled with our Dutch friend of the night before, whom, you remember, had lent us the money to pay the rickshaw. He was able to tell us of a place where we could bathe in the sea. He rang up a car for us and arranged about the price. We then went outside the barrier and were at once besieged by boys. With a lordly air, however, we waved them aside and sought Malan and his brother, with whom we had arranged to go shopping the night before. They came running up the moment they saw us, and in we got and made straight for the town.

Our first port of call was the bank, but here we were able to change only the amount that we had declared and not a penny more! However, we had enough. Next, we set off in search of hats and made various purchases at souvenir shops. Sally's birthday will be this coming Saturday, so we were anxious to find something suitable for her. In the end we went to a Malay shop in one of the back streets and there found hats, pottery and all sorts of wonderful things! Nancy bought her a pottery doll, and I got her a fan. Clutching our precious purchases, we climbed once more into the rickshaw and went back to the other shops. There were, of course, heaps of these silver filigree shops, and Tony bought me the sweetest bracelet, which I have worn a lot with my silk dresses. Finally, we bought lots of fruit and then made our way back to the ship. The car was waiting to take us to Barombong, where we understood we could get some sea bathing.

It turned out to be a most beautiful drive of about 25 miles. We set off through the town, and once again we were greatly impressed with the orderliness and cleanliness of the place. It was so beautifully set out, and the buildings all looked so clean and white. The residential houses were most beautifully planned and set out with gardens, not in quite so free a style as in Honolulu, but more in rows, but nevertheless with equal individuality. Once again we saw the beautiful flowering shrubs. There were very few cars on the road, mostly bicycles. It seemed that nearly everyone rode one—the Malays, with their brightly colored sarongs, white shirts, and black velvet caps, some barefooted, some with shoes; then again, the Chinese and Dutch in their European white suits.

Soon we left the town, and our road cut straight through a veritable jungle of banana trees and bamboo trees. On either side of the road, among the trees were the neatest pile dwellings of the island natives. They were all made of bamboo, typical pile dwellings, I suppose, the walls made of woven bamboo or palm leaves, the roof of rushes, and the whole supported on thick bamboo posts. In some cases the fronts of the houses were carved and painted, but for the most part they were plain. But all the way along, even right far out in the country, the houses were still neat and so very different from the shacks, half native, half European that we saw in Fiji.

I mentioned earlier that the drive was beautiful, but I think that is not quite the most suitable adjective to apply. It was more interesting than beautiful, for the countryside was quite dry and parched, and there were no brightly colored flowers as we had seen in Macassar itself. The fields were laid out in squares, with a raised path between each patch, and these patches were then quite hard and cracked. In some places, we saw water buffalo wallowing in the mud, and in others, ox carts being drawn over the hard ground. Once, as we crossed a bridge, we saw two native drivers wading through the water, waist deep.

Soon we came to a village, and here we stopped to buy fruit and to look round the market. Our presence caused quite a sensation and not a little amusement, I have no doubt. We bought a huge papaya and several oranges, some soap, and the men bought some tobacco! We also saw curious looking balls of something being wrapped up in leaves and then bound with what looked like strips of bamboo. We learned that this was molasses and so bought three of these things, which we hung up in the car. I later gave one to Sally, and Nancy had one. I packed the other in Tony's trunk a few days later.

Once more we got into the car and drove off. Soon we left the road and turned off along a lane, and did we leave a trail of dust! I have never seen anything like it. All the native children that we passed stared as long as they could and then were obliged to hide their heads in their sarongs to avoid the dust. Before long we came to the sea, and the car drew up at the entrance to a bathing place where there were changing huts. But we wanted just beach, and although there was no one else there, we decided to leave the car here and go along the beach a bit further in hopes of finding a secluded spot. So, leaving strict instructions for the horn to be blown at 2:30, we set off, carrying our coconuts, papaya, hats, and bathing things. We had not bargained for an audience. But that is a thing, I understand, one is always liable to get in these parts, and after a time one does not take any notice of it. We found a spot and sat down. Our audience, too, squatted a respectable distance away!

Well, we spent the most wonderful two hours there, *manging* our fruit, swimming in the warm water, and lazing on the beach. Alas! it was, all too soon, time for us to pack up and make for the car. However, we dared not be late, for we were some way out and we had instructions that the ship would sail at 3 o'clock. So, reluctantly we dressed and made our way back to the car. The ride home was over the same route, and of course, we did not stop, so we were back in just under half an hour. First, we called at the post office for stamps for our letters, which we had been obliged to leave at the barrier. I did not attempt to send a cable, for it was very expensive and I knew that I should soon be in Sumatra.

We got back to the ship at about 3:30 to find that shore leave had been extended to 4:30. In a way it was a pity that we could not have known this sooner, for we could have done with another hour on that lovely beach. On the other hand, it gave us time to have another look round the town. So Tony and I set off again after we had been aboard with our purchases and had tidied up a bit. I was very windswept and not a little sunburnt. We found Malan again, and he drove us to the shops. I was anxious to get something for Tony, and eventually we found a brightly colored sarong and came away with this. If he does not use it to sleep in at night, as I believe many people do in the hot weather, he can use it as a bunk cover when he is at sea. After a last look round the shops, we came back to the ship. It was not long after that we untied and drew away from the berth.

We, of course, rushed up to the boat deck. By this time the sun was setting, and the harbor was full of the loveliest fishing boats. I took several photos, and then we sat and watched the sun sink behind the sea. It was amazing how quickly it disappeared, all within the space of a few minutes, and then it was quite dark. We all sat there for a little, and then went to change for dinner.

Thursday, 4 September 1941

We had a wonderful 24 hours in Macassar; it was a novelty calling at a foreign port, although I was not able to air much of my Dutch. All the islanders, other than the Dutch, spoke Malay, and I should think it is similar to that spoken in Sumatra. I recognized several Dutch words.

The morning was wasted. I sat on the boat deck after breakfast. Then we went down to Tony's cabin to do some washing, but everyone congregated there and we did nothing but talk! Later we met Nancy and Maurice, and the four of us took ginger beer up to the boat deck, where we sat in the sun and felt very lazy. Just as we were about to sit down, we noticed a sudden change of course, with a terrific wake on the port side. Sure enough, the ship was turning right round, and we appeared to be going straight back to Macassar. There seemed great excitement for'd under the bridge, and Tony went up to inquire what it was all about. It appeared that one of the Lascars had spotted something on the horizon and thought it was a boat in distress. There was a fairly high sea and rockets had gone up, so this seemed feasible. The Skipper ordered the ship to go back to have a look. In the meantime, wild rumors spread through the ship as to what this speck could be. Some said it was a submarine, some a raft. Others were certain it was a piece of fuselage and we would probably pick up an airman!

It was really too tantalizing, but the lunch gong rang, and we had to go down to the saloon. On the way down, I met "Uncle Bill," and he let me look through his binoculars. By this time it could certainly be distinguished as a fishing craft, but whether it was in distress or not remained to be seen; she was certainly tossing about a good bit. We were halfway through lunch when we came alongside, and there, sure enough, was a fishing boat—happily fishing! We just turned round and came away. Imagine all that excitement for nothing. No wonder that I slept all afternoon on the boat deck. Reaction, no doubt. Anyway, I did not wake up until 4:30 when I was aware of Tony's rattling teacups. He had crept down and brought up a tray of tea for us both.

In the evening there was a charade and a general knowledge bee. I attended the former but went before the latter began. We came away after the charade and sat on the boat deck. I turned in early, rather out, for I slept on the boat deck outside our cabin.

Friday, 5 September 1941

I woke up this morning at 6 o'clock and thought it time to come in, for they would soon be washing the decks. I got up, collected my bedclothes, and slipped in without Bunty hearing me.

I spent the morning wandering around. Tony went up to the bridge to take a sight. He came down with a message from the Skipper to tell Margaret that Sumatra could be sighted and would she like to come up to the bridge to have a look at charts and see through the telescope? Accordingly, I went up and spent the rest of the morning there. Several islands could be sighted. Tony and I went up to Monkey Island [above the bridge] and took bearings from the compass there.

Bunty spent the day packing, so I was best out of the way. The cabin was a mess. Still, the only thing to do is clean it up, and I shall have to do it myself as soon as I begin to pack.

A mock prizegiving has been arranged for tomorrow evening. I have been asked to read a report in the capacity of Miss D.A.M. Prim, Suspecter of Morals. I shall have to think about it. I went down and found Gardener, who is also reading one, and we consulted together. I shall write mine out tomorrow morning.

Saturday, 6th September 1941

Most of the morning was spent in composing the speech for this prize giving. In the end I went out to Mr. Morriss for some help. We were soon joined by Mrs. Griffiths and Mrs. Flemming, so we all repaired to the Pig and Whistle for a drink before lunch. There was still some time to go before lunch, so I excused myself from the party and went to type some of the speech. The rest I finished on the boat deck after lunch. We had settled ourselves nicely on the rug under the awing. At last, we got up and went in search of some sun on the port side, and there I went to sleep until tea time. I then went to my cabin to change for Sally's party at 5 o'clock. Having changed, I slipped down with her presents and went on deck until the children's tea bell rang. They were all at a cinema show in the music room.

Sally had a grand party—paper hats, blowers, streamers, etc. All the children were there and quite a few grownups. After an enormous tea, we all went on deck for photos and played games. Tony and I thought we would have a drink in the Pig and Whistle for a change. No sooner were we in than we were hailed by Mrs. Griffiths and party and were asked to join them. The skipper was there with Morriss and Flemming. They are a nice crowd, and I must say that we feel very honored that two such "youngsters" as ourselves should be invited amongst them so often!

After dinner I had to rush and change into my costume, which consisted of Mrs. G's black evening skirt, my old gym blouse, a tie of Tony's, and a pair of gloves. I had my hair screwed up into a bun and my flowered hat perched on the top of my head. I think I managed to look really prim and certainly a schoolmarm! We had one of the rafts in the music room as a dais, and on this we arranged ourselves, while the "children" sat in front facing us and "parents" behind. The whole thing could have been very funny indeed, but it was far too long. At the interval, I disappeared, thinking it was all over, but when I came down again I found they were all in there again. So I had to make myself small and apologize the next day!

Sunday, 7th September 1941

I spent the morning helping Tony to pack. Goodness, was I tired at the end! It is so tiring trying to fold suits under a bunk, for down there they have bunks one above the other and only one porthole, which does not give much light. However, by using Maurice's cabin as well, we got the job done.

After lunch I went down to finish off the packing, and there I found Donald struggling with suits, so I gave him a hand.

In the evening I got Mac, the bar steward, to play my records on his electric gramophone. Tony and I sat on the promenade deck and listened to them. Afterwards I went up to the boat deck where I again slept out.

Monday, 8th September 1941

Alas! I was brought in by the rain at 4:30 this morning. I got no sympathy at all. Everyone said, "Well, of course, what do you expect?"

I did some washing and typing in the morning and sat on the boat deck all afternoon. Tony had a pullover, the sleeves of which he wanted taken out. I undid them round the armhole, unraveled the wool, and then picked up the stitches round the armhole and knitted a band of ribbing. I am pleased to say it looks quite nice, but it will be a job to get it finished before we get to Penang.

Tuesday, 9th September 1941

We docked early after breakfast, and Tony and I came on the boat deck to watch. There was a horrible feeling of uncertainty all the morning, for no one knew what was going to happen. I had not packed. I was sure that I would go on down to Singapore. The naval people did not know what was in store for them either, though it seemed pretty certain that they would be put off at Penang. But no one was able to tell them anything. We hung about in this uncertainty, not being allowed to land, until lunch, when it became known that all the naval people would have to leave at 10:00 that evening. In addition, five other passengers were also to be taken on the boat leaving for the same destination. As soon as this was made known, the Captain asked me to join his party that was going in a launch to see this other ship off next morning. Tony and I were very thrilled, and it was nice of the Captain to ask me.

Johnny Turk had invited all the Sub. Lts. to a drink in the smoke room, and I was asked to join them. It was kind of him to include me, for I was feeling so miserable. Goodbyes are such horrible things.

We were just sitting in the smoke room after lunch when a Mr. Gilbert came aboard and broke the astounding news that he had instructions to see me on a ship for Sumatra next day. I had nothing packed, and we had been invited by Mr. Morris to join his party at the Penang Swimming

Club in the afternoon. However, I said I would have my baggage ready by 9:00 the following morning.

Tony and I went ashore to post letters and then went to the office at 4:00 to see about passport, etc. We were shown to Mr. Gilbert's desk, and he took me along to the Dutch Consul. I got my papers in order, and then on to the K.P.M. for a ticket. We had arranged that Tony should come with us in the launch next morning.

As we got back to the ship, we saw all the other Subs. going off. Not wanting to be seen, we slunk in over the side amongst the cargo.

I was rather anxious to get some of my things sorted out. We went up to my cabin, where I managed to lay all my things out on the two bunks. Bunty was ashore, so I wrote her a note, asking if she would mind sleeping in one of the empty cabins just for once as I anticipated being up most of the night packing.

By this time it was getting on for 10 o'clock. I was feeling a bit faint from want of food, so we left everything on the bunks and went in search of eats. We took a rickshaw to the E. & O. Hotel where we had a drink and ordered a mighty dinner of gammon rasher [ham]. As soon as this was ready, we were shown into the Grill Rook where the Skipper's party was nearly finishing. Bunty was there, also, with the 2nd Officer, so I was able to explain the situation to her about the bunks. We had a bottle of wine with our dinner, which we enjoyed very much.

Getting a car to take us in the direction of the swimming club, we made a skillful getaway from the rest of the party. We got out before the club, near some hotel, and walked down to the beach, where we bathed in the moonlight. It was grand. One could not swim because of the rocks, but we sat on the edge and let the waves roll over us.

Returning to the ship, we went below for a cup of coffee. There we met Turk, and all three went to my cabin to pack. They wanted me to rest while they packed, but I thought otherwise! As it is, I have left one or two things behind. The two of them draped themselves round the cabin while I packed my trunk, and by 3:00 a.m. I had most things in. The trunk was ready to be closed down. I arranged the things for my suitcases out on the bunk, and we all went to Turk's cabin for a drink. We left there about 4:00. I was too tired to continue packing, so I crawled onto my bunk and went to sleep. I woke at 6:00 a.m. to find poor Bunty screwed up on half her bunk amongst all my things. Apparently she had found the cabin I thought she could use full as Mrs. Thomas had stayed on board, too, for the night.

Wednesday, 10th September 1941

I got up at 6 o'clock and finished my packing. Tony was up, too, and together we got things in. At 8 o'clock we went down to the saloon for early breakfast with the skipper and party. I found it was too risky to go with the others in the launch, for I had to be there to see to my luggage at 9:00. I had to be at the office by 10:00, so it was not possible. It was a pity, but on the other hand, perhaps it was just as well. I went to the gangway to see them off. At least, I said goodbye and then fled to my cabin. Oh, I did feel miserable. It was a sad ending to a very happy voyage indeed, but then the ending was bound to be sad. In any case, it has been a wonderful voyage.

PART TWO

A Teacher in Sumatra

Wednesday, 10th September 1941

What a horrible day Wednesday was—saying goodbye to everyone, most of all to Tony. It was hard to realize that after 3 months together we might never see each other again. As soon as the others had gone and I had packed, I said my last good-byes, and then set off by myself in the pouring rain for the office. I took a rickshaw and arrived on the dot of 10:00. It was nearly 11:00 by the time my passport came through and all was fixed up.

As soon as the passport arrived, Mr. Gilbert, the agent and I set off for the wharf. A launch was to take me to the ship that would sail across the Straits of Malacca to Medan. There I saw several of the passengers also waiting for launches. Pamela was amongst them with Richard. We exchanged a few words, but by that time my launch had come alongside. Carrying my handbag and my precious typewriter, I went aboard. How small the little cross-channel boat seemed after the *Malda*. I was shown straight to my cabin. It was a three-berth one, but I seemed to be the only one in it; none of the other bunks were made up. I must admit that I still felt rather miserable and could not help reminding myself that this really was the end of the trip. After a good cry and a tidy up, I came on deck and was met by the 1st Officer.

About 12 o'clock the ship was ready to sail. The captain now appeared in uniform and took me to inspect the chart room and bridge. I showed my *vast* knowledge of sight taking and was even shown his mathematical workings, but I got lost in the Dutch nautical tables! The bridge was very spruce and tidy. A couple of basket chairs were placed on the starboard side, and I was invited to sit there with the captain. From time to time he turned to the Malay quartermaster and gave a change of course or issued some direction, but I should think they know the course by heart. This was, however, the first trip this particular Captain had made. It transpired that I was the only European passenger on board, hence the privileges. Also, I was the only woman!

About 1:30, by which time I was "starving with hungry" as my young cousin used to say, an enormous meal was served. The upper deck was divided in half, one side having the tables and chairs, and the other a long dining table. We all sat round in state, the officers now appearing in full mess kit! During lunch I mentioned my liking for curry, and at once the Captain ordered the menu changed so that we could have curry for dinner!

Going down to my cabin, I took a nap until nearly 6 o'clock in the evening, by which time we were tossing about a good deal. I appeared on deck once more and was invited to sit with the Captain on the bridge. I think they were surprised to see me up, for it was very rough indeed, and most of the Malay and Chinese passengers were laid low, as well as some of the crew. A drink was served, which consisted of beaten-up eggs and coffee! An antidote for seasickness. It sounded horrible, but it was surprisingly rather nice. We each had a glass and then continued to sit on the bridge. At eight, another meal was served. By this time we could hardly get to the table, it was so rough; everything slipped from us, and we had to hang onto the plate all the time. I must admit that I was not feeling very like curry, but I had to be polite and make some show of eating a little.

After dinner the 1st Officer took the watch, and I sat on the bridge for a little. But there seemed no point in sitting up when it was so rough. I thought I would go below to my cabin and read, so I said goodnight and retired. I had some difficulty in undressing, for the pitch was so quick that one just hopped from one side of the cabin to the other. However, I did manage in the end and climbed into my bunk. Undoing the porthole was another thing. It was very stiff, and the effort proved too much. No sooner had I got the thing opened than I put my head out and delicately disposed of my curry(!), after which operation I settled down comfortably for the night. Although I did not sleep very much, I felt quite all right. I was very glad of the Dutch Wife that was provided, for the bunks were quite wide, and "she" kept me from rolling onto the floor. [A Dutch wife is a long thin bolster held between the knees allowing the air to circulate.]

Thursday, 11 September 1941

At 6 o'clock the next morning I got up and came on deck. We were still rolling a bit, but not so much as the night before. The Captain and Chief Engineer were on the bridge, and I was asked to join them, where coffee was served. We were within sight of land by now, and the pilot launch came alongside to give instructions. There was still some way to go into the harbor; it was getting on for 7:30 by the time we were in sight of the dock. All the way along we passed fishing traps. We had seem them in Macassar but had not known what they were. In the shallow water bamboo stakes are driven into the sand in the shape of a 'V'. The fish get inside these traps and cannot get out. We passed many of these, and the sea was thick with all sorts of little fishing craft.

As we were nearing the quay, a launch came frantically alongside with a message for the Captain, giving him directions where to dock. Within a few minutes we were alongside, and the emigration officials came on board to deal with my passport! They brought a message that the school secretary was waiting for me at the customs. My friend Rosalind and her husband were waiting in Medan, as they were not allowed in port. I said good-bye to my fellow travelers, took my suitcase and went ashore. The Captain came with me as far as the customs to make certain that there was someone there to see me through.

I was met by Mr. Walker, the school secretary. He was a jolly, fat little Dutch Jew, most kind and obliging. He had charge of all the office work at the school and saw to the staff's salaries, their banking accounts and any other business needs. Well, he said that Rosalind and Bill were waiting at the hotel and that we would go straight there. I had no trouble at all with my baggage. A car took it all except my bicycle, and that could wait in Medan until some conveyance could be found to bring it up to Kaban Djahe.

First, we went to the hotel where Rosalind and Bill were waiting. Rosalind was just the same as when she left England; she looked very happy indeed, and Bill seemed such a nice man. They made a charming couple. She had gained much more confidence and jabbered Malay at a great rate, but apart from that she had changed very little. Goodness, how we talked! The words would not come out fast enough! I was kept some time at the Office; however, after signing yellow, white and blue forms, I was allowed to go.

All this business over, we repaired to the Medan Hotel, where Bill insisted on drinking to my success in champagne! We had a very merry party, and they guaranteed to take me in a sober condition to my new boss, Mr. Cookson! After this, Rosalind and I went off to do some shopping and to get my money changed.

An old member of the staff, a Miss Gillmore, was living in Medan, and she had invited us all to tiffin [Anglo-Indian term for luncheon], so getting into the cars, we went straight to her home. She seemed a very nice person indeed. She invited me to stay with her any time I should be in Medan. Rosalind and Bill had stayed there overnight, and I persuaded Bill to let Rosalind come back to Kaban Djahe for the night. He agreed, and it was decided that she should return on Saturday morning. I was very excited at the thought of her coming up and staying all that time. So we went to pack.

Saying goodbye to Mrs. G. and Bill, Rosalind and I climbed into the back of the car where we could talk more easily, and Mr. Walker sat in front and promptly went to sleep! What a lot I had to tell her of my trip. We had not seen each other since my college days.

The run from Medan to Kaban Djahe seemed quite ordinary; I am afraid I must be getting *blasé* after my world tour! We climbed up and up all the time, and the country seemed much greener than anything we had seen so far, and certainly not nearly so tropical as Honolulu or Fiji. At one bend, the car refused to go, so Rosalind and I got out to lighten the load and walked up the road, waiting for the car to pick us up. In a few minutes it came along, and we got in once more. All the way up I felt the pressure on my ears, so that I could hardly hear, but once at the top I became accustomed to the altitude. We went straight up to Brastagi and then down through the village to Kaban Djahe.

The school is practically in the village, and in no time we were at the gates. We drove straight through and up to the Headmaster's house, which stood at the far end of the grounds, right away from the school part, with only the paddock behind. I felt all eyes upon me as I walked up to the house. Here, at last, I was going to meet my boss. For this I had traveled half way round the world. Would I be accepted? Would I like living and working here? These were my thoughts as Mr. and Mrs. Cookson came out to meet me, and we were invited in to tea.

There were some American visitors there at the time, the parents of one of the children at school; they were going back to America at the end of the week. Everyone was very interested to hear about my voyage, and I had to relate how I had been on a world tour! They were all most anxious for news of home and lapped up all I could tell them. Mr. and Mrs. Cookson were very nice indeed, and they showed every consideration to me. Mrs. Cookson was rather quiet and not at all dogmatic as many Americans are apt to be. I thought she and the old grandmother, who was still, by the way, very active, must have started the school together. Mr. Cookson (he is a Yorkshireman from England) joined later. But both Mrs. Cookson and Mrs. Smith were born in the States and lived most of their lives in Honolulu, so they were very interested to hear that I had been there. Mrs. Cookson was educated in Honolulu before she went to college in the States, and Mrs. Smith had charge of a large school there. She is a most charming person, with white bobbed hair. I don't think she does much teaching, although I think she does a little. Also up at the house was Miss Boey, who came out with Rosalind. She is something of a schoolmarm, but *none* of the staff is "old"; they are young, and I should think at twenty-seven, I am one of the eldest teaching members! One of the past members of the staff was staying with the Cooksons for a holiday; she is married and lives on one of the rubber estates some way from the school. She has stayed on staff ten years!

The grounds are very large. The Cookson's house is right away from the other buildings, which are all grouped together. The dining room is the largest, a flat-roofed building, which contains the kitchens and sculleries. A covered path leads to the playroom, my classroom, and the girls' house. Most of the other classrooms are separate buildings arranged in the garden. Some are just sort of summerhouses made of bamboo and woven palm leaves with a thatched roof of leaves. Others are more solidly built of brick and concrete.

My own room is large and simply furnished. I have a balcony with steps leading down to the garden, so that I am not obliged to go through the house to my room. This may prove useful! Many of the staff furnish their own rooms as furniture is inexpensive and very easily made by the local carpenter, with magazine pictures providing ideas. I saw some that was very nice indeed, but I decided not to get anything new for the time being. I have a very nice, large table-desk, also a dressing table, and three basket chairs, in addition to a wooden cane seated chair at the desk. In the center of the room there is a low, round table, and against the wall a spacious built-in wardrobe. Along the wall under the gable is a row of cupboards, which take all my clothes. Just by the door, I keep my wooden box with my woolly things. The bed is one of the wooden type used out here. At first I found it very hard, but once given another mattress, it was more comfortable. There is also a bedside table and a bookcase, so that I feel very well equipped.

Rosalind and I were invited to supper at the house. It was served at 6 o'clock; after that it was dark. It seemed odd not to have to worry about showing lights because of a blackout. We had a very pleasant meal indeed, and afterwards sat and talked round a log fire. I was feeling very sleepy, so about 8 o'clock we said goodnight and went over to bed. Mrs. Cookson said I was not to get up at 6 o'clock with the others, but she would have breakfast sent up to me.

I woke up at 6 o'clock when the children got up, but turned over and went to sleep until the *baboe* (Malay maid) came in at 7:30 with a tray of breakfast. Fried egg, tea, toast and delicious papaya marmalade. I got up, put on my housecoat, and sat at the table to eat it. Then I got dressed and was just doing my hair when Rosalind appeared.

Together we started to unpack—and talk. I found there was masses of room to put all my things. Clothes are best in cupboards rather than in drawers. Rosalind warned me that everything gets very damp and every week they should be put out to air. The *baboe* does that for you. I will have to be very careful about my fiddle, for I should hate anything to happen to that. I decided to ask one of the staff, who also plays the violin, what he does with his instrument.

From 10:00 to 10:30 the children had a break, and we went over to the dining room, where they were served glasses of fruit juice and either papaya or banana. After this Rosalind and I went down to the village to buy some things for my room.

The village of Kaban Djahe is neither picturesque nor quaint, as its name might imply! Like most native villages, it is dirty and smelly! I am rather surprised at this because the villages under Dutch supervision in Celebes [as Macassar] are so clean and tidy. There are about four or five streets with rows of open shops owned, for the most part, by Malays or Indians. All the remaining ones are Japanese—the photographers and toyshops. It is quite marvelous how much you could get at these shops; they all have the American tinned foods, cereals, and material by the yard (or rather, meter), any amount of tobacco, not to mention quantities of lipsticks, face creams, nail varnishes, etc. and haberdashery, as well. Far and away above anything in our little village shops at home! Alas, my watch gave out on the journey. The sea air must not have agreed with it. I plan to have it mended on my next trip to Medan. I bought a cheaper one here in the village and it keeps good time. Next, I purchased some cubes of camphor, which will guard my possessions against cockroaches. I understand they can eat into all your clothes if proper precautions are not taken. I was also advised to get a tin of Flit and a sprayer; this I did, and then leaving the things to be sent over to the school, we made our way back to continue the unpacking. How nice to have this delivery service.

Tiffin is served at 12 o'clock and on free weekends the staff are allowed to sit at the center table; otherwise, they sit at the head of a table and serve the children. It is very nice that on your free weekend, although you are at school if you so choose, you are not expected to have any duties.

From 1 o'clock till 2 o'clock the whole school sleeps, or at any rate, rests and there is quiet. I think the bigger ones might read all the time, but the little ones have to sleep. There must not be a sound during that time! I went up to my room, lay on my bed, and went fast to sleep. At about 3 o'clock Rosalind came and together we went round the school, she showing me where the different things are kept and introducing me to the office and stor room. All stores and school supplies are kept in a separate building. There is a boy in charge of them. Each teacher has a chit book, and she has to sign for anything she wants for her class.

That is handed into the office, and thus they are able to keep a check on all supplies.

I was able to get some name tapes from the office; they are made on a machine, just the initials. I was ashamed of the amount of washing I had when I arrived, but no one seemed to mind. I was told just to throw it into a corner on the floor and the *baboe* would take it away and do it for me. They have a washhouse on the grounds, and the *baboes* do it all. Anything you want washed is left on the floor of your room in the morning, and she takes it away and usually the next day it comes back. The only clean frock I had was the one I stood up in, and I had already worn it two days in Penang! However, I survived and finally had them all washed and ironed. By the time we had finished, it was time for tea, so once more we went to the dining room. Tea is not a set meal; it is served from 3:30 till about 4:30. The staff sits at the center tables and have tea to drink with brown or white bread, toast, and various assortments of jams, papaya, pineapple, peanut butter, and coconut jam. This latter is delicious. Chopped coconut with molasses poured over it—at least, that is what it looks like, and it is very sticky!

After tea I thought I should make some inquiries about work for the next day, so we wandered across the playing field to the house. Some American visitors were there to tea. We were invited in, and I had to tell them about my voyage. After they had gone, I asked Mr. Cookson about work, and he said I could wait until Monday and have the weekend free. This was very nice of him. Poor Rosalind did not have the same considerations; she and Boey arrived one evening at 9 o'clock and had to work next day at 7:30! What it is to have an uncle in Singapore! We were then invited to stay to supper at the house.

After supper we went down to the village. I wanted to have some films developed, and Rosalind wanted to inquire about her bus back to Sianter, where Bill was sending the car to fetch her back to the plantation on Saturday afternoon. Most of the shops were open, but the photographer, who is also the barber, was closed; however, we were able to arrange about Rosalind's bus. A seat next to the driver is usually reserved for Europeans. It is so much cheaper than renting a car, although it takes a long time. The bus comes to pick you up at your house, which is most convenient. On our way back, we called in at the hotel and had a drink. The hotel is just near the school, and the school staff are allowed to use the tennis courts.

On Saturday we were up at 6:15 for breakfast, and then Rosalind and I went down to the village to see about these photos of mine; I had several rolls and Mummy's photo to have framed. Time was short as we had to be back to see Mary Cookson about books and schoolwork, generally. I was very lucky not having to teach straight away, and I think it helped, too, having Rosalind with me.

The work is not of a very high standard, so there is much to be done. At present, four of the boys in my class are in the sick room, so that leaves me with only eight children. They expect more next term; the numbers in the school are down considerably. A Dutch Froebel teacher took my class while I was on the way, so the children were taught along the right lines. Mary, Mr. Cookson's daughter, has the class above, and although she is very keen and slaves away, she has had no training. Her father hopes to send her to Australia the next term with her brother, who is taking his Cambridge School Certificate at the end of the term. He plans on going on to Australia University, but Mary is very obstinate and does not want to go. How very different from Nancy, her sister, who had been on her own for five years in the States and was educated in Honolulu when war broke out. Father summoned her home, much against her wish! She hangs about the school absolutely at a loose end; she is paid as one of the staff and has mostly garden duty to do. She hardly ever goes up to the house and has her room across the landing from me. She is a most charming girl. Rosalind is very fond of her, and I am sure I should get to know her well.

The other staff appear to be as follows: the English staff consists of Miss Boey, Mary, Nancy, Mrs. Cookson, Mr. Cookson and myself; of the Dutch staff there is one teacher, a very nice girl called Neil Coster, and two matrons, one in the boys' house, and one in the girls' house. Mrs. Verdonck is the kindergarten mistress I spoke of earlier, who was filling up for me; she is very young and is here with her two children. The housekeeper is also Dutch, a Mrs. Radders Ma, a most capable and efficient woman, who has charge of all the catering and makes the Chinese cooks and Batek boys fairly dance round! The food is excellent. The Swiss children are taught by the remaining Swiss master, Mr. Bosch. There was at one time another Swiss master, but he was called home for military service. Mr. Bosch is alone amongst a bunch of females. He is very fed up; he came, so I understand, for three years, but was not allowed to land without signing a contract for five years. The poor fellow was stuck and bound to a contract he did not want to sign.

At 1:30 we all saw Rosalind off in the bus, her suitcase packed on top. Her sundry belongings were piled in beside her, including a wooden box containing a Siamese kitten, which was being taken to someone in Sianta!

Four of us decided to hire a car and go up to Brastagi to shop and stay for the pictures. There is even a cinema here in this village and two at Brastagi, and the film changes every night—nothing very new, but we have all kinds, English, American, French, Chinese and Malay films. That is the main form of entertainment. At the hotel in Brastagi one can dance at the weekend.

Brastagi seems little more than another village like

Kaban Djahe. There are, perhaps, a few more shops and certainly a quantity of shoemakers and souvenir shops, but these contain mostly Chinese and Japanese merchandise. There appear to be very little Batak work. The Bataks are not, as yet, commercially minded, so most of their work can only be bought for ornament. I made a note to try to get some decorative items later on, especially some of these beautiful sarongs and shawls; they would be most useful in the room. Bataks do not use a lot of bright colors, but rather somber browns, oranges and reds, brown being the predominate color. The Batak woman has the most curious headdress. It is a large dark blue shawl, which she folds out somehow and piles on top of her head, making it stick out in two points, and on top of this she is able to balance a great baskets of things. In the rain she will often undo this headdress and wear the shawl round her shoulders. The Bataks appear to be a very primitive race, as compared with the Malays. I hope to see more of them. I understand there is a very interesting *campong* near the school, and Mr. Bosch has promised to take me there. I hope to be able to go out on horseback to see some of these places. It is beautiful horseback riding country all round. Rosalind agreed to send up her riding things. Mr. Cookson has offered to arrange with the riding master at Brastagi where they have horses and a riding school. The children only have the rather tiny ponies indigenous to the country, but at present they had no proper instructors. One of the older girls takes them out to ride. This man at Brastagi used to give lessons at the school, so he ought to be good.

Before going to the cinema, we ordered our supper to have as soon as we came out. The cinema was very good. We saw Anna Neagles in *Irene*, quite an old film, but one I had not seen before. There was also a Ministry of Information film about Dover—caused quite a lump in my throat! After the film, we returned to the restaurant for our supper. The taxi had been waiting all the time for us, and it was at the door at the hotel when we came out, so we all bundled in and came straight back to the school. I was terribly sleepy, and it was not long before I was in bed.

There are several Catholics amongst the children. It being Sunday, I got up early with them and went across to the church. The school rents the convent building during the term time, but at holiday time the nuns from Medan come up, so the staff from Highlands has to move over to the school. Next to the convent, but on the other side of the hotel is a small church. We are lucky at that time in having Mass every Sunday, for one of the priests from Medan is here in Kaben Djahe on sick leave. I understand that come October there will be Mass only once a month.

After Sunday breakfast, I retired to my room. It was still pouring with rain, but in spite of this and in spite of the fact that it was Sunday, two workmen appeared, carrying a small washbasin and several lengths of pipe. I showed them where I would like to have the lavatory, and they proceeded to fix it up. The outer wall was the best place, and so I had it fixed in the corner. Later on I hope to be able to get a little screen to hide it. Alas! I can only get cold water, but it is much better than having to use the basin on the landing, for all the children on the top floor use it in the morning. There is usually a long queue, and we only have a quarter of an hour in which to dress. Just below my balcony there is a round flowerbed, which was at one time a pond because there was a pipe sticking up in the middle. From this the men dug a trench in the pouring rain and connected the water supply to my room. All morning they paddled up and down the steps of my balcony and finally got the basin fixed.

At 12 o'clock the bell rang, and we descended to the dining room for tiffin. The children were very excited because there was *rijsttafel*, not, I was told, the full thing, but about ten different dishes of little bits and bobs, including curry over this mound of rice. I slept heavily afterwards until 3 o'clock.

After tea, Boey asked me if I would like to go for a walk. Since I had been in my room all morning, I readily acquiesced. As we ambled back to the school, we met Mrs. Cookson, who again invited us up to the house for supper. I found a boy from the photographer's had been waiting for me all the time I was out; he had my snapshots and would not go away until he had given them into my hands. I was dying to see them, but I had to wait until after supper before I could look! They were, for the most part, very good indeed. I had Mummy's photo framed and the one of the group that we had taken in Hollywood. They look very nice on my wall.

Monday, 15 September 1941

This was my first day at school! I was dreading it. After three months on the ship, work did not seem right at all, but it does not take long to get into the routine again. I got up at 6 o'clock and came down to the dining room, where I was asked to sit at the elder girls' table. There are about twenty girls whose ages range from 14 to 16; they are a very nice set indeed, some Americans, some English, and the others Dutch and Swiss.

At 7:30 the bell rang for class, and I came down to the kindergarten. Monday morning is always letter writing for the kindergarten class, and Mary had very kindly set the copies for me. All I had to do was to see that the letters were written, then help the children read the letters from home. At 9 o'clock there was a five-minute break; afterwards, they went back into class until 10:00. After that came a long break of half an hour. During this time both children and staff were served glasses of fruit juice and either bananas or pieces of papaya. I went back to my classroom, and then the morning, for me, was finished. My little children went for their baths.

During the morning, I was asked by Mrs. Cookson if I would give a talk to the bigger children about my voyage. I was in a flat spin and spent all the rest of the time preparing notes from my journal. At 2 o'clock I came down in fear and trembling to Mr. Cookson's office where the "lecture" was to be. I got together all the suitable photographs that I had taken on the voyage, and together with my Fiji souvenirs they made quite an interesting collection. I was quite appalled at the number of children there seemed to be, especially the huge boys in the front row! I managed to hold forth for an hour, and it appeared afterwards that they were all interested, so that was a relief!

After supper, I went to the office and collected my huge bunch of mail. Oh, what a joy to have a letter from home. I was just in the middle of reading my letters when there was a knock at my door, and Mr. Bosch appeared to see my fiddle. He is a very keen musician and, I should think, plays a good deal better than I do, but we hope to be able to play together sometimes. There is very little music in the school, and there are no concerts to go to, except occasionally in Medan, and so for those who love music, the only thing to do is to make it for ourselves! We sat and talked for awhile, and I showed him my snaps of the voyage.

16 September 1941

Lessons, as usual, in the morning, but during the 10 o'clock break the shoemaker came to do the children's shoes; he both makes and repairs shoes. He took my measurements, and I got him to make me a pair of white lace-up shoes for garden duty. I also had him copy the pair I got in New York. I need these to wear with cotton frocks. I find that my heavy walking shoes are just the thing here for garden duty in wet weather, and as it is the rainy season, I find them most useful. Also, my winter clothes are not too much for the cold mornings. Usually by 11:00 I am ready to put on a cotton frock, but in the early morning it is quite cold enough for skirts and blouses or short-sleeved jumpers. I am so glad I brought all mine. We do not have to wear stockings, which is a blessing, for they are terribly expensive.

During the week, the shoemaker came again and brought my shoes for a fitting. They are very nice and fit so well; it will be a joy to have shoes that fit round the ankle and are large enough in the toe. I also ordered a pair of bath shoes. Taking a bath is an ordeal, and the first time I nearly died with laughter.

The bathroom is on the ground floor; you open the door and descend six stone steps to a tiled floor. The "baths" are down each side, and in the center is a paved section with gutters on each side. This is, as often as not, under water! The room on either side is divided into sections as for shower baths, each bath divided from the next by a low stone wall, so that standing up one can quite comfortably look over into the next compartment! As for the baths themselves, I have never seen anything like them! The bottom of these compartments are lined with white tiles, built up to the height of one tile. A small sunken area comprises the bath itself, this being one title in depth and roughly two tiles by six in length and breadth! There is just room for me to sit with my knees drawn up. One is provided with a small hand bucket for the purpose of pouring water over the body. Getting the water is not an easy matter. First, you have to drag the long black hose which is connected to a tap high up on the wall; this is usually trailing into one of the other baths and has to be lifted up and twisted round to the bath you have chosen. Next, you turn the tap on and wait for the water to get hot; when this eventually happens, a small washcloth provided for the purpose has to be stuffed into the hole to serve as a plug; slowly the bath fills with water. As soon as you remove this washcloth, all the water spurts over the floor. One can see why it is essential to have bath shoes! These are just leather soles, with straps of leather across the toes, and you slop along, heels flapping! Altogether, taking a bath is quite an undertaking, and there is a great inclination to put off the ordeal as long as possible!

Nancy came and sat in my room one evening, and we did some sewing and knitting together. She is trying her hand at dressmaking but is having great difficulty to getting the colored thread. It is running very short, and even in Medan it is scarcely obtainable. That evening we both went across to the hotel for a drink, she to celebrate the departure of a tiresome boy friend, and I to celebrate the end of duty weekend!

These duty weekends are terrible! The matron is off from tiffin time on Saturday until Monday morning, so I have to be in charge in the girls' house, where I also have my room. Lessons finish for me at 10 o'clock on Saturday. I have been asked to take the seniors for drawing in the morning, so I have them for the first part. Then Mrs. Verdonc has mine for the last part, so I really do very well! From 11:30 till the bell rings for tiffin, I have a garden duty, which means that I have to be in the garden during that time, walking about and generally seeing that the children do not break their necks on the swings and bars. After tiffin they all rest until 3 o'clock. On Saturdays and Sundays, they take off their shoes and dresses and lie down on their beds. It is rather tiring for the person on duty, for she has to be about all the time. I find it very hard on Saturday, but on Sunday afternoon they settle down at once, and most go to sleep. I am able to get a good deal done to my knitting. At 3 o'clock the bell rings, and they all get up. The little ones have to have help with their dressing, and on Sunday they put on their best dresses for church service. We take it in turns to be on garden duty from then until 6 o'clock. This Sunday I had to go to church service, which was held in the play room and conducted by Mr. Cookson.

Straight after supper, the little ones begin to go to bed. It is 8 o'clock before all the lights are out and the house is quiet and settled down for the night. There are two of us on duty after that, and I think we are supposed to sit in the house all the time. At any rate, one of us must be there. Nell and I sit together in my room with the door open. At 11 o'clock each morning, they have baths, and the one on duty has to supervise these, see that the little ones are dry and that they put on their own clothes! Two *baboes* paddle about in the bathroom itself, so we do not have that messy job to do. But duty weekends are quite full. Most people get right away on their free ones! I am planning to go for a long walk next weekend and should probably go to Brastagi in the evening. Nancy and I, unfortunately, do not have the same weekends free, but she is trying to change with Nell for the weekend after, and we were going to Medan together.

Yesterday I went down to the village to buy my sewing materials, and I was most successful in my purchases. It is quite marvelous the things that you can obtain there. My sewing class with the big girls went quite well. They are such a nice set of girls and are so keen on learning. We made mats for the table, with a drawn thread border, and they later designed their own appliqué pattern for the center.

Once again this morning, a man came to readjust my washbasin. When they installed it last Sunday, they fixed the tap so that it stuck right out over the basin, and I could not get my face anywhere near the water! Also, the plug did not fit, and I was obliged to wash under running water, for none of it would stay in the basin! All these things have been attended to, but the tap still drips furiously.

Mr. Bosch came up the other night and fixed two hooks on my wall for the fiddle. He says it is best to keep it hanging on the wall, open to the air as in any case it is liable to get very damp. Strings are very difficult to get, and most people here are obliged to use wire ones. These are not so nice but, on the other hand, stand up to the strain of temperature changes much better. Here it gets quite cold and chilly at night or early in the morning, but by 10 o'clock it is boiling.

Wednesday, 24th September 1941

Just as I was changing, Nancy came up to my room to know if I had got my letters. She said there was a bunch for me; she had seen the postman put them into my box. I rushed down and there, sure enough, were three fat ones: one from Mummy, one from Singapore, and one from Tony. Was I excited! And I had to sit all through tiffin with them unopened by my side!

The moment tiffin was over, I rushed up to my room, and there sat and read my letters. Oh, how lovely it is to get news of home. I read and re-read all the letters; it does help so to lessen the distance from Sumatra to England!

After reading my letters, I came down to earth and prepared my needlework for the afternoon. I found some blue cotton material in the village, and with Clarks' colored cotton embroidery thread, the little ones are going to make bags for the backs of their chairs. Then they can keep all their books together, for they had no desks, only large tables with little colored chairs. Now that I have gotten some of my things up on the walls and some drawings and work of the children, the classroom looks very nice. It is quite large but inclined to be rather dark on dull days.

After tea, Mary came down to the village with me. We paddled round the shops, and I bought a basket such as the Batak women carry on their heads. It is quite a small one and very ordinary, but it makes a nice wastepaper basket, of which I was badly in need. I also got several little tiny dishes, two of which I use on my dressing table for hair pins and bobby pins; the other I use as an ashtray.

I have to learn Malay as hard as I can, for the girls at my table are not allowed to ask the boy waiters for anything. The mistress at the head of the table must give all orders. This is really a good thing, for with the children asking, the boys are inclined to get cheeky. I simply loathed it at first, but since then I have become resigned to the fact that I have to do it. It is very good for me, and like Oliver Twist, I am always asking for more. *Minta lagi* is the phrase which means politely "I ask you to bring." The real Malay or Rajah Malay is quite different, a very eloquent language. I have learned that many of the words used in Sumatra are different from those used in the Straits, but the general foundation is the same. It appears to be merely a matter of stringing words together; there is little or no grammar. Nancy offered to help me, and I am taking advantage of her offer now that I have settled down and sorted myself out.

Nancy came up after supper, and we had a cigarette together. Then I spent the evening sorting my letters and getting the pages sewn together for posting today. The Dutch ai mail rate is very expensive, and I can only send three of these thin sheets—5 grams is the allowance, and that is very little. No doubt later on as news gets less, I shall have less to say!

Another lovely surprise at tiffin time when I got a large letter from Singapore containing the two missing letters from Mummy. Reading them, it was so frustrating to realize she did not know where I have been. I thought the stamps would be a sure guide, but apparently not. By now she will have learnt about my wonderful journey, and I am looking forward to hearing her comments on it.

Thursday, 25th September 1941

My day for garden duty. Yesterday I got all my letters off to post by tea time and then came up to my room to prepare some work for today. I intended to get a lot done, but after supper I went to Mrs. Verdonc's room. We talked over the question of having a concert at the end of the term, and that took until nearly 9 o'clock. This usually takes the place of graduation exercises. I came back to the girls' house and gossiped further with the matron and Nell. Finally, I went up to bed. But before I could get into bed, I was obliged to clear up the mess I had left, painting things all over the bed, etc. I got into bed and lay on my front, reading Mummy's letters again, so it was nearly 11 o'clock by the time I put out my light.

I was certainly not ready to get out of my bed this morning at 6:15! I staggered down to breakfast feeling very sleepy indeed; however, a drink of hot fruit juice revived me. It is rather nice; we have this hot orange or lemon juice every morning. The staff, in addition, have tea, but I rather favor the fruit juice. The morning passed uneventfully. It was very cold and pouring with rain, so that I was glad of my knitted skirt and coat, my mother's handiwork, which has been greatly admired! By tiffin time, the rain had stopped, and the sun appeared.

During rest time I made a superhuman effort and washed my hair. It was no easy matter. First of all, it has to be done in the bathroom, for there is no hot water anywhere else and no receptacle to carry any upstairs. Accordingly, I paddled down to the bathroom and ran the hot water. The hose was trailing in a convenient bath, so, as soon as it was hot, I selected a towel on which to kneel and just got down to the business of washing. This means that you have to kneel on the tiles by the edge of the bath and lean over the gutter into the bath. It is a little difficult, but I shall get used to it in time. And I must say the hose is most useful for rinsing. Having accomplished this feat, I returned to my room. I set my hair and then went out to the balcony for a short time before the bell rang for afternoon school. I still had to descend with a scarf tied round my head.

It was pouring with rain, and all the children were indoors. Some of the girls were playing in a room just outside mine, which is used on wet days as a kind of playroom. They were dancing about to a gramophone. Others below were rushing about in the playroom, where they are allowed to make as much noise as they like. Still others were in my classroom, where the piano was going unceasingly, just strumming. I thought yesterday afternoon I should go mad—it never stopped the whole time!

Rain, rain, and again rain! Goodness how it rains! but it is the rainy season. We had a bright morning, but during the rest time it started and has continued every since without stopping.

Last night I prepared my books for the next day. It was about 8 o'clock then, so I took courage and my violin over to the music room, which is a little summerhouse building in the middle of the grounds. The bigger girls use it as a sitting room on wet days. One side is practically open, and there is a colored blind to let down. This helps, in some measure, to keep the sound in. I stayed there for over an hour and had a very good practice. I was relieved to find that I had not forgotten as much as I anticipated. Nevertheless, I still need a great deal of practice, and now that I have broken the ice, so to speak, I can venture there another evening. Mary has offered to come and play for me, so that will be fun.

A party of about five of us are going down to Medan tomorrow, and we are sharing a car. Otherwise, if you go by bus, you have to stay the night. The bus from Kaban Djahe only gets into Medan at 3 o'clock, and the one returning leaves at 4 o'clock. That does not give one any time for shopping. We are leaving in the morning after school at about 11:30 and shall combine shopping with a cinema and then home the same evening. There is talk of going to

Brastagi swimming pool on Sunday. I am assured that it will be terribly cold, for the water comes straight down from the mountain. However, I have pointed out that I am used to the freezing waters of the English seaside in summer!

A fortnight yesterday since I arrived. It seems more than only two weeks, and I have quite settled down. The children are so nice and really very easy to manage, although those in my class are terribly noisy, as indeed they all are. They just shout at each other, but in time I hope to get them quieter. Some of the older ones are having a party over at the other house. They have decreed to wear fancy dress, so I was asked this afternoon if I could find something for two of them to wear. I have produced my famous housecoat and slacks, together with a blouse and promised to help them dress after supper and fix on mustaches! The gramophone is on just now outside my room, and I can hear them dancing. They are busy preparing some sort of surprise. Every time I walk through, I have to look the other way!

Mr. Cookson met me yesterday and asked if I would like a larger basin in my room as he thought the man had found one. I went to inspect it and decided to accept it, instead of the tiny one I have at present. They altered the tap, but it still sticks out over the basin a good deal. As there was the offer of another one, I did not say no. Mr. Cookson says I am to ask for anything I want! So I asked for a towel rail and a little glass shelf!

What a night we had of it in Medan. We got back this morning at 5:15 AM. I had an hour's sleep and then got up for Mass at 7:00. We had good fun, quite like old times on the *Malda*! In fact, the Grand Hotel at Medan was so like the one at Macassar that I felt there ought to be parties of passengers sitting around. How I wished that had been true and that we were still on the way—a voyage that we never wanted to end!

School for the first part of Saturday morning. I had to take the bigger ones for drawing. It was rather a shock when Mrs. Cookson broke the news of it to me last week, but I was thinking of the standard of art in an English secondary school for girls of that age. Of course, that is a different thing; here they work for the Royal Drawing Society—a much more standardized approach! Lynn Cookson is, however, taking Design for his Senior Cambridge and is in rather a funk about it, so I have offered to help him.

At 10:30 I had to go on garden duty for half an hour, so first having changed, I went out until the car came at 11:15. We arranged to take an extra dress down to change into for the cinema, for you get so hot shopping. We all packed into the car—Mary Cookson, Mrs. Verdonc, Mr. Bosch, and myself. On the long ride down, many people are carsick. The road twists and turns so much, and at the same time the gradient is quite steep. For this reason, Mary dreads the journey and, therefore, seldom goes. However, we arranged to stop the car at intervals and get out for a walk. As it turned out, this was not necessary. She got down without stopping, not feeling sick at all.

The journey down was most interesting for me, and this time, not having Rosalind to chatter to, I took in more of the countryside! First you have to go up the hill to Brastagi, then over the top and down to Medan. The road winds and twists the whole way down, and I learnt that every year they do something to improve it. As we passed, we could see where a corner had been taken off here and a bridge built across a small ravine there. Not so many years ago, I understand, the road was little more than a bullock track, but gradually they have worked on it. Now it is a very good road all the way up.

Coming down to the first plain, the vegetation is not very tropical, although everywhere the hills and mountains are densely wooded. One can see the banana trees, which seem to grow like weeds along the roadside. They have little fruit on them. Unless they are properly cultivated, as they are on the plantations, these wild ones never do very much. We passed several villages on the way down. Those nearer the top are very dirty and untidy. I was told that the Bataks are the most primitive of the Sumatran tribes and quite different from those on the West coast. However, as we got nearer to the plains, I thought the houses of the natives were better made and the villages looked better cared for. But probably there was not much to choose between them! I did, however, notice the way in which the houses were made. The main supports were of bamboo, and the walls were of strips of woven bamboo, like those of the classrooms in Kaban Djahe. In some cases, the strips were woven so as to give a zigzag effect; in others, they looked like parquet flooring. The roof was made of *attak*. I am not sure what this is, but it looks like the leaves of palms tied in bunches and laid on as thatch. Here the houses are built right on the ground and not on piles.

We passed rubber trees and little stretches of teak trees with their white trunks and broad green leaves. We also saw clusters of bamboo trees. Nearer the foot of the hills, we passed rice beds and tea plantations, but I was told that neither of these products can be seen at their best in this part of Sumatra. That is as it may be, but, nevertheless, it was all very interesting to me. They grow three kinds of rice, one of which grows in water, and the other two seem to be just sown on the slopes in little squares divided by poles of bamboo.

Just outside Medan we came past huge barn-like places, very high and thatched with *attak*. I learned that these were drying sheds for the tobacco. We saw some in the process of being constructed, and the inside looked one mass of bamboo scaffolding right up to the roof. Once these scaffoldings are erected, the whole is covered by a roof and the walls of woven bamboo with windows opening from the bottom.

By the time we got into Medan, it was getting on for 1:30, and we were all very hungry indeed. First, we went to a girls' hostel where we took our suitcases and booked a room for changing after shopping. This is a very good idea as one gets so very hot shopping. I think, really, the hotel is for members only, but the subscription is very little and I think it will be well worth joining. Also, members can stay there for as little as one guilder a night. Should we come another time by bus, it will be more convenient to stay the night. Well, having left our things there, we all went across to the restaurant *Te Meulen,* and there we certainly had a good meal. Really, I have never seen anything like the portions that are served for one person; they are literally enough for two people. Bosch and I ordered a Malay dish *nasi gorang.* It consisted of a huge mound of rice, and round the

edge there were bits of cucumber, mangos, ham, fried banana, beans, and on top of all four fried eggs! We were so
hungry that we consumed most of it! The other two had
salad and fish mayonnaise.

During lunch we decided to separate, each doing our
own shoppings, and then meet for tea at the Tip Top Cafe.
As soon as the meal was over, we got into the car, drove to
the shops, and then separated. I stuck to Mary since I
couldn't speak enough Malay. We wandered down the main
street and into some of the Bombay shops. Here, of course,
they all speak English and are most offended if English
people speak Malay to them. There were some lovely materials, mostly from England and America; they say that the
price is going up all the time and soon many of these materials will be unobtainable. In Medan there are several big
European shops, but most of these close on Saturday afternoon, which is a pity, as that is the only day we can get into
town. I found a very palatial looking stationer's and went
in to inquire for carbon papers. There were some beautiful
machines in the window and other office equipment, so it
looked hopeful. Yes, I was lucky and came away with a
vast supply which will last me a lifetime. It is expensive to
buy it in the village, for it is only sold by the sheet.

Our shopping completed, Mary and I repaired to the
Tip Top and there awaited the others. They eventually
turned up, but Mrs. Verdonc had still so much shopping to
do. She would not wait and said she would meet us at the
hostel. We sat so long over tea that most of the shops were
closed by the time we had finished. However, that did not
matter much, and as it was beginning to get dark and we
had arranged to eat at the same place at a quarter to seven,
we thought it best to get back to the hostel to change. We
arranged to pick up Bosch in the car as soon as we were
ready. It started to pour rain before we got back to the hostel. We changed and sent the car out to look for Mrs. V.;

however, we were ready by the time she arrived, a dripping and bedraggled spectacle. She announced that she still had shopping to do and did not want to eat. She would meet us at the restaurant and come with us to the cinema after we had supped.

After a hasty meal, we returned to look for the missing link, but she was still not ready. We took the car to the cinema and then sent it back to wait for her. It was a most depressing film, *Flight from Destiny*, that film we saw in London of the German attack on the lightship. There was, however, a very good Walt Disney to cheer us up, and the suggestion of a beer at the Medan Hotel had even more effect! The rain had stopped by this time, and it was a beautiful evening. We sat out under the stars and drank our beers. The place reminded me so much of the Grand Hotel at Macassar where we also sat out at little basket tables. I felt there ought to have been groups of passengers, but, alas, there were not! The tables were arranged round a stone dance floor, and an orchestra of six was playing gypsy music on a raised covered platform at the back. We sat there for some time, and then there appeared to be signs of dance music. The orchestra put away their fiddles and took up saxophones instead, and an overhead light was switched on. So we decided to just wait until it started!

The place was quite crowded, but still no one got up to dance. At last, Bosch and Mrs. Verdonc broke the ice and had the floor to themselves! Next, Bosch and I took a turn, and afterwards, Mary, the unfortunate young man having three ladies to cope with, an unheard of thing in these parts!

Next, they played a Viennese Waltz, and B. and I once more took the floor. This time two other couples got up to join us. Bosch can only go one way round(!), so we both got very giddy. After the second dance, I could hardly stand; I rolled drunkenly to a chair, caught hold of it, but toppled

over, much to my embarrassment! However, I quickly recovered and walked as soberly as I could to my place!

At this point we ordered another drink and decided to
stay! The Army must have thought I needed escort, for no
sooner had the music started than a Dutch officer came up
and asked me to dance! It turned out that he had lived five
years in England and spoke perfect English. It does make
one ashamed to think that almost every foreigner you meet
can speak English while we make no attempt to learn any
other language than our own and expect everyone to understand us. By this time, the place was quite crowded,
and many more people were on the floor. My next partner
was a Dutchman from Java. He was in Medan for a short
business visit, and as he asked for the following dance, there
was nothing for it but to ask him to join the party! He was
most insistent that we should all go to the Club. But, as it
was getting rather late by that time and Mary was looking
a little tired, we were firm. Anyway, I for one was quite
happy where I was, and so were Bosch and Mary. It was
Mrs. V. who wavered, and this made the young man the
more insistent. This rather upset poor Mary as it was then
3:30 AM and we had a long drive before us. The party broke
up, and we all clambered into the car. It was cold coming
up the hill, and we were all very sleepy; we had coats, however, and another time I shall bring my rug. Really we had
had a very pleasant evening, and it would have just spoiled
it, having gone on to this club. I, for one, was quite ready
for a sleep in the car. Had we been going back to the ship,
instead of up to school, no doubt I should not have thought
twice about staying up all night! Oh, what marvelous times
we had on that voyage. I shall never forget them as long as
I live. If only the voyage could start all over again!

It was 5:15 AM by the time we crawled out of the car at
the side gate of the school. There was already a light in the
kitchen, where the baker was hard at work. We staggered

out and went our respective ways to very welcome beds. Alas, I was only to have an hour in mine, for at 6:30 I had to get up again for Mass. But by this time I have got somewhat accustomed to late nights, and felt none the worse this morning!

The doctor called and invited me to come over to a *rijsttafel* for tiffin; it is most kind of him to include me in the party.

Tuesday, 30 September 1941

The *rijsttafel* was marvelous, but what a quantity of food! One is expected to consume a great plateful of rice and goodness knows how many other dishes of tidbits, all most delicious and, I was assured, full of vitamins! After this enormous meal, we staggered to armchairs, drank coffee and ate ice cream. There were four of us ladies. At about 2:00 that afternoon, we left, intending to get a good sleep in before tea. But on the way back to the hotel for my coat, we met a French family (the mother and father were up to see young Paul) and so Rash introduced me to them. They were very pleased that I spoke to them in French, and we both had to sit down and take a cup of tea with them.

It was the next morning that Mrs. Cookson asked me if I would like to come up to the house for tea. The English teacher from the Brastagi school was coming, and also a family from Singapore, who would probably know my uncle. It was also Boey's birthday, so we were first invited to the dining room to partake of a beautiful birthday cake. Mrs. Verdonc was sitting next to me, and imagine my horror when she told me that "our" boy friend of the night before had called that afternoon. Just at that moment we saw Bosch making for the dining room, accompanying the said gentleman!!!! We both of us were on duty, so there was nothing for it but to give him tea and then tactfully send him away! He quite happily sat down to tea with the rest of the staff, who were much amused. Then we explained that we were both on duty and—well, there it was. He is most anxious to call again in three months when he will be back in Sumatra.

We then went up to the house to eat a further tea, only here it is just a polite one, "afternoon tea," in fact!!

While I was up at the house, the mail came in, and there was a letter from Tony; he has at last reached Bombay and seems to be liking it very much. Letters are only taking a week by air, and that includes getting through the censor, which is not bad.

Tuesday, 30th September 1941

On Monday evening, I was sitting in my room after supper, contemplating an evening's work, when Nancy came in to ask me if I would like to go over to the hotel to have a drink. There were two Americans up from the jungle, old fogies, and she wanted me to help to entertain them. The party assembled in Rash's room. She, these two Americans, a Danish girl, who is at the school studying English, the assistant controlleur, who, by the way, attended Rosalind's wedding, a serious-minded young Dutchman who sat and said nothing the whole evening, Nancy and myself—that completed the party. We sat there for some time, and then they thought they would like to go to the local flicks, that film with Irene Dunn and Charles Boyer, *When Tomorrow Comes*. It was quite amusing to see it again. We were out about 10:00 and went back to the hotel for another drink.

After tea, Nell and I went down to the village and wandered about together. She had various commissions to do, and I enjoyed following her round. There is a very good dressmaker in the village; he is making an evening skirt and blouse for Nell. He has made some very pretty dresses for Rosalind. They have no idea of style on their own but will copy anything, if only you have a picture.

During break, the shoemaker came. He calls every Tuesday, and this time he brought my evening shoes to be fitted.

They will look very nice indeed. Those old brocade ones of mine have tarnished so that they are no longer wearable. I had the pretty little clips taken off and am having them on my new ones. The shoes are silver, with a tiny bit cut out at the toe and the upper stitched in lines radiating from the center of the foot to the outer edge. The effect is quite pleasing and pretty. The heel I am having made not quite so high as the old pair, but in the same style, with the band across the back of the heel. Two other pairs of white shoes that he made for me have been a great success. They fit beautifully. Nearly all the shoes are made to the pattern of American wedge heels, and I am beginning to get rather tired of them; personally, I thought the ordinary heel was so much better. I had, however, one of the white pairs made thus, and the others are just sandals, like the ones I got in New York.

Wednesday, 1st October 1941

It rained most of yesterday and still doesn't look much like clearing up. They say that all this rain is exceptional for October, even for the rainy season! I am assured that the spring is lovely in the island, so I am living in hopes. But this rain is every bit as bad as England. Of course, here it does not rain all the time, and usually there is a fine spell some time during the day when it really gets quite hot again.

Nancy came up to my room after tea for a surreptitious cigarette. I understand that we are not really allowed to smoke in the girls' house; however, we sit on the floor and blow the smoke out the French windows onto my balcony! These doors are not glass but only fine gauze, which is supposed to keep out the midges and mosquitoes, but very often in the evening I have to chase round my room armed with a Flit spray. So far I have not seen many cockroaches, only one or two, which have been promptly squashed under the mat! One finished in this way was discovered the next day to be in the same place, so I took it up and deposited the body in my waste paper basket. By the morning I found the basket swarming with ants, and the body of the cockroach practically disappeared! I hastily put the whole thing out onto the balcony and there let them eat in peace, but in future I shall fling the bodies out into the garden!

Last evening, I was invited up to the house to dinner and so had to make myself respectable. Mr. C. had been in bed for the last two days, crippled with arthritis in the knees. We stayed up at the house until nearly 9:15, toasting our toes in front of a huge log fire. Nancy and I wandered back to the house together, and she came up to my room. We were trying new hair styles in front of the mirror when we were alarmed to hear whistling outside my window! Turning off the light, we peered out but could see nothing. The whistlings appeared to have stopped, and Nancy went off to her room. However, it was not long before she appeared at my door, trembling like a leaf and saying that there was a man outside her room on the balcony! We consulted together what was best to do. We decided to go down to Nell and see if she had heard the whistlings. We all three watched from Nell's room. It was rather alarming because here everything is quite open. After a time, we saw the said man pass the window as if he were going, and we looked out to see. It transpired that he was the assistant controlleur, a past boyfriend of Nancy, with whom she has quarreled!!! However, we were not sure. Having ascertained that he was off the premises, we both went upstairs and decided that Nancy should sleep with me. So we took one of the mattresses off my bed, and fetching her sheets, we made up another bed on the floor beside me.

No further alarms tonight! The young man wrote a note to Nancy today saying that he called, saw her through the window, and was surprised that she did not come out! It appears that he is soon going away and she will not be troubled any more.

My garden duty today, so, of course, it had to rain the whole afternoon. Nancy and I hung about, first of all, in the garden until it started to rain, and then we had to get all the children in, and they roller skated in the playroom. This is, no doubt, great fun for them, but goodness, the noise! Later the rain seemed to stop, so in desperation we got them all out again to have a really good run. However, before 6:00 it started again, and in they all had to come again. We were thankful when at last the bell rang for them to get ready for supper.

After supper, Nancy came up to my room, and suddenly I felt the urge to tidy out my cupboards. They had not really been arranged since I unpacked, and I was afraid of cockroaches, for they eat into such things as net, silk stockings and the like. I got everything out, laid it on my bed, and spent until after 9:00 arranging it all. I also unpacked my wooden box and re-packed it with things I am not likely to need at the moment, thick jumpers and such like. These I liberally sprinkled with camphor.

After these exertions, I thought I would continue the good work by having a bath, so I paddled down to the bathroom and maneuvered the hose with success.

Friday, 3rd October 1941

Oh dear, rain again! Will it never stop? It is 11:30 and class is finished for me until 12 o'clock. It is my duty weekend, and so I must prepare in advance, for there is absolutely no time during the weekend. One is on all the time. Tomorrow I am taking the top class for design and must also prepare the lesson. All the artwork in the school is so formal and seems to lack expression. I long to be able to get hold of large sheets of paper and plenty of paint and thick brushes, for the little ones at any rate. We could do so much. But drawing paper is impossible to get, and the stuff they have at the moment is so poor for painting. The older children never have painting at all. Goodness, when I think of the marvelous art room at Harrogate and the work that the girls there produced!

At break today the shoemaker called, and he has brought my silver shoes. They look marvelous and fit perfectly; I am so pleased with them. He has charged only ten guilders, which is not bad, considering the price of silver leather at the moment. My other shoes were four and six guilders, respectively. I see that he has put another clip on my old shoes, and I had intended throwing them away. However, perhaps they will come in for some occasion, so I will keep them.

I had a letter from Rosalind, and she and Bill have invited me to the St. Andrew's Dinner and Dance, which is being held this year in the Medan Hotel—it will be on 15th November. What fun it will be! I see that it falls on a duty weekend. Perhaps that can be handled, but I don't think they like our changing much. Mrs. Verdonc has asked so much lately that the last time she was refused. However, I shall see what can be done. One of the Dutch matrons announced the other day that she is getting married and will be leaving before the end of the term. She is getting married some time in January, so I do think it is hard on Mr. Cookson. Mrs. V. is also getting married, but that was, of course, known in the first place. Anyway she is only here temporarily. She took over my class until I arrived.

Saturday was a busy day. My design class went quite well for a start. The children appeared to like using paints and produced some surprisingly good results. They finished about 9:30, and at that time they are allowed to wander out into the garden. My duties started with a session in the garden until tiffin. After tiffin, the long rest until 3:00. A short break until 4:30, when I had another session in the garden until 6 o'clock. It poured with rain the whole time, so at 5:00 we had the gramophone and played musical chairs, bumps, etc. in the playroom. Supper at six, and straight afterwards, the little ones started going to bed. They are allowed to get undressed, and then play about till it is time for the lights to be turned off. It would be so much better to let them run about in the playroom, for they make such a noise in the house, get hot, and find it difficult to settle for the night. However, by 7:30 I had all except the bigger ones settled and with their light out. Those upstairs read quietly until 8 o'clock when I turned off their light, too.

Nell had been invited to go up to the dance at the Brastagi Hotel. Having settled the children, I went to help her get ready. She wore the new one she got the other day. Poor soul, she goes out so very little and was so excited last night. Her escort called for her at 9 o'clock and off she went. Nancy, too, had been invited to go to the flicks by the afore-mentioned controlleur but had refused after the other night. I must admit I was glad of someone else's being in the house. Nancy came up to my room, and there we sat on the floor and talked.

There was no Mass this Sunday morning. I had to get up before the children and be downstairs to supervise their dressing and hair-doing. On duty weekends I sit at one of the baby tables and serve out all the food. I quite enjoy it, for I have more courage to speak Malay to the serving boys than when I am with the big girls! I am getting on fairly well and can ask for most things for the table, such as knives, spoons, food and the like. I still find it hard to un-derstand the Malay spoken in the shops; they seem to speak so fast.

After breakfast I went down to the village with five of the older girls; they are such a nice group. We had great fun wandering round the shops. Then we walked round past the golf course and back to the school by a quarter to ten. I was then to be on duty.

Monday, 6th October 1941

Once again it is pouring with rain. It was very cold this morning first thing, and I was glad of my green long sleeved jumper. By 10 o'clock break, however, the sun came out, and it became quite hot. I changed into a blouse but still kept on my skirt. This afternoon I sat in the summerhouse over at the big girls' house, taking a sewing class, and we all got frozen. Well, now it has started to rain again, but it may not last long.

Last Saturday a terrible thing happened. I was sitting in my room typing when I heard a crack, and seeing that it came from my fiddle on the wall, I concluded it must be a broken string. It came again, and again I looked but could see nothing. A third time, and to my horror I saw the fiddle slowly coming to pieces before my eyes! I rushed over to the dressing table and was just in time to catch the pieces! I shall have to send it to Medan to have it re-glued. That will take time. It is annoying, just as I was beginning to get some practice. On Friday night Mary and I did some play-ing together, and it was great fun. Alas, I shall have to wait for some time before I get any more. Bosch has offered to lend me his fiddle; he uses Mr. Cookson's. But I am scared to use anyone else's instrument. They are such precious things.

The children settled quite quickly last night, and I sat for a bit in Mrs. Michaelson's room knitting until I was sure they were all asleep. Then I came up to my room, and after a hot bath, settled down to letter writing. However, Nancy appeared before long, and we sat and talked for a bit, and then she decided to get out her new dress material and pattern. At my suggestion, we pulled the table back and spread the material out on the carpet. We spent a very pleasant evening together. She is a nice girl. I do hope that next term we shall be able to get our free weekends together.

Monday mornings are always boring, for the children have to write letters home. Mary used to set beautiful copies, which they laboriously duplicated. I consider that far too much work for teachers. We have made little books with patterned covers and in there I write the words they want to use. I find they are well able to do this. And I have noticed that, in several of the parents' letters, there have been remarks to the effect that they hope "dear Douglas" will soon be able to write his letter all by himself. So teacher has taken the hint, and it is far less work for her!

After morning class, I went across to Miss Lenie's house, where I could use her sewing machine, and I got my blouse put together before tiffin. I must get the sleeves tacked in and try to machine it tomorrow.

Native campong within walking distance of the school

Nancy on the balcony of the girls' house

My classroom in Sumatra

Kindergarten class at Kaben Djahe

Swimming pool at Brastagi

In the outback at Bencubbin, Australia

THE AUSTRALIAN BROADCASTING COMMISSION

presents

ISADOR GOODMAN

in a

PIANOFORTE
RECITAL

~

ALBERT HALL, BRISBANE

Monday, 19th February, 1945, at 8 p.m.

Recital program, 19 February, 1945

Mr. And Mrs. Jesse McCullough, 1946

Wedding party in front of St. John Berchman's Catholic Church, Shreveport, Louisiana

Wednesday, 7 October, 1941

A wet and depressing afternoon! Such a change from the morning, which was really hot. Getting up as one does at 6:15, it is difficult to know just what to wear. At this time it is usually quite chillsome, and you think to yourself that a jumper and a skirt will be the thing. By 9 o'clock break, it begins to get hot, and a blouse seems more in keeping. Again, by 10 o'clock you are quite certain it is! Usually it is too much bother to change before tiffin, since you know that, as soon as the meal is over, you go up to your room and rest until 2 o'clock. Often it does not start to rain until the middle of the afternoon, and by that time you have already changed into a cotton frock, which means freezing until ten! I am so glad I brought my raincoat with me. It has proved to be one of my most useful garments. I am thinking that I will get a mackintosh cape, as they, too, are very useful. At first I thought "how on earth can people go out in this weather?" but now, along with the rest, I take no notice and just paddle about from place to place with my raincoat over my head. My walking shoes, too, have been most useful; I thought they might be too heavy, but not a bit. They are just the thing for standing about on the wet grass on garden duty.

Yesterday there was a very good film on in the village, *Beethoven*, a French film, and excellent, so we were told. We were most anxious to go. But the trouble was that we all wanted to go, and someone had to stay in the house with the children. Mrs. Michaelson had arranged to go over a week ago, so the duty rested with Nell, Nancy, and myself. These matters are always a little difficult to settle. Nell has already been out several times during the week, so Nancy and I thought she would be the one to stay in. In fact, we did not give it another thought. However, that was not what Nell thought! She wanted to draw lots, but Nancy wouldn't agree to this. They had an argument over it, Nancy saying she would stay at home. All these *contretemps* rather damped my enthusiasm, and so in the end I said I would stay with Nancy. Another night we can go out together. I have plenty of work to do. I can see there will be many of these differences of opinion, but, on the whole, we all agree well together. The Cooksons keep open house for the English staff but leave the Dutch girls to get along by themselves. This seems rather unfair, but, on the other hand, they all have their own friends in the neighborhood.

Today Mr. Cookson came to school for the first time after an absence. He was wheeled down from the house in a kind of bath chair to his office, and there he conducted his lessons. It is a handicap, this arthritis.

Nancy is going out to a farewell dinner given by the hotel manager to speed the departing controlleur! She is planning to get away early so we can both go to the Greta Garbo film that is showing tonight.

Thursday, 8 October, 1941

After supper last night, Mrs. Verdonc asked me if I would like to go to the film with her. At five to eight we set off for the village, and we went straight in. It was an excellent film, *Maria Waivinski*. Charles Boyer is certainly a very finished and clever actor; his study of Napoleon was wonderful. We got back about 10 o'clock and collected Maggie, who had been minding the house for me, as Mrs. Michaelson was out, too. The three of us went to Mrs. V's house for a cup of tea.

I was awakened this morning about 1:30 by a tremendous shouting and laughing. It appeared to be the party coming home from the farewell dinner, so apparently it was a great success! Several of the children appeared on the stairs to greet them. Being alarmed, they had come out to see what was happening! This made a good story the next day, and we hoped it would not reach the ears of the Gods!

This afternoon, just before rest time, I saw Mrs. Cookson going up to the house, so I ran after her to ask if I could change my weekend on 15th November so as to be free that day for this St. Andrews dance in Medan. I had been assured by Mrs. Verdonc that I would not get it, as she had already been refused. However, Mrs. Cookson said that for St. Andrew's and the Dutch Feast they do make exceptions! I came away feeling very pleased. I also asked if I could change permanently as I wanted to be off with Nancy. She is going to try to arrange it for me. Mrs. Cookson then asked me if I would like to come up to the house to tea. A Mr. Greer, a Presbyterian minister, and his wife, together with a Mr. and Mrs. Clarke were coming up, and she would like me to meet them, so I accepted. It was really my garden duty day, but she suggested that I come up for a little.

The guests did not arrive until nearly 4:30, so I was able to get my turn in the garden before I had to go. They are very nice people indeed; it is kind of the Cooksons to ask me up on these occasions. I think they really do like to have the staff up there from time to time. Mrs. Smith, Mrs. Cookson's mother, is a dear. Anne Boey "lives" up at the house, and I was warned that everything goes back to the Cooksons through her. I think most of us feel rather sorry for her as she is a misfit and doesn't seem to have any friends. But really, she is a most trying person!

In the evening I had a little party; we all met in Mrs. Verdonc's room, and I played my Beethoven records. She provided tea, and I got some biscuits, a cake and a few sweets from the village. Nancy and I went down after supper to get them. It made a very pleasant evening, and I think most of us felt we might repeat the performance at least once a fortnight. Mary has some very nice records up at the Cookson's house, so I thought probably we would go up there next time. They have an electric gramophone, which is always best for orchestral records.

Saturday, 9 October, 1941

On Wednesday, I had a letter from Bunty. She said that she had a very rough time crossing the Indian Ocean but had arrived safely to find her mother and father-in-law most charming, and she seemed to be settling down happily. They are people of some note in Ceylon, I understand. So she should have quite a gay time.

After tea yesterday, four of us had a game of tennis, this time on the school courts, which are much better than the ones over at the hotel. At school, they are of sand with a good run back, but over at the hotel, the court is concrete and the ball bounces so high. We played until the bell rang for supper and then had to fly to be in time for the meal. Only the day before, we all had been asked to come in more promptly! I found all my table had gone to a birthday party, so I sat in state in the middle of the room.

I still have not been able to get anything done to my fiddle. Bosch is lending me his until I can get mine attended to. After supper, he came over to fix it up. We discovered that one of the pegs was broken, so only three strings could be put in. However, it should not be a very difficult matter to get another peg made.

Talking of having things made, Nancy came down to the village with me one morning, and we ordered four cushions to be made for my room. She had two large ones that she never used and kindly let me have them. I plan to get some material and cover them myself; with the use of the machine, it will not be a very large job. I will probably find something in Brastagi, where we go up on Sunday.

This morning I had my drawing class, as usual, and we did a snapshot drawing. Next week I shall go back to design and let them have paints. In the evening, a party of Americans was coming up from Medan, and Nancy had asked me to join them, going up to the Brastagi hotel for dancing.

Sunday, 12 October 1941

We had a grand time in Brastagi, getting back next morning at about 3 o'clock, not so late as I had anticipated. The Americans were tired, having got up that morning at 5 o'clock and traveled in from the jungle, where most of the plantations are. Bosch and I had planned to go for a cycle ride if the weather kept fine. After lunch, I went down to the bicycle shed, and the boy got my cycle out. It appeared to be in quite good condition. A bit rusty, but that is hardly to be wondered at, seeing the hours it stood in the pouring rain on that tender before it was finally put in the hold of the *Malda*. The boy had assembled it and is keeping the crate against my departure! The valve rubber on the back tire has perished, but that has proved to be a simple matter, for he keeps a length of valve rubber wound round a pencil in his pocket. We regarded the weather seriously and decided we would wait until 3 o'clock, for by that time it would be likely to have settled one way or the other.

I came back to my room, but, on the way, encountered Nancy wandering in search of the post. It had not come in, so, feeling we should both have a letter, we went off on bicycles to meet the mailman. Sure enough, I had a fat one from Singapore containing the two letters from England by clipper [air], one from Mummy and one from Uncle Jack. I had not heard the news that David, my cousin, was reported missing. How terrible those days must have been for poor Auntie and Uncle before they heard that he was a prisoner of war. Poor David! How he must have loathed being out of it all! Out here in Kaban Djahe, one feels so out of the war. There is no scarcity of food, no blackout, no petrol rationing, and none of the things that bring the war home.

We abandoned the idea of going out on cycles and decided in favor of a short walk. There was a native *campong* just near, and I was anxious to see it. I took my camera along hopefully, expecting to get some photos, but the weather was too cloudy and dull. As it is not very far away, I should be able to go there another day and take some snaps.

These *campongs* are the most filthy places one could imagine! The houses themselves are quite picturesque, and I imagine that, in the out-of-the-way places where the European influence is not so marked, they are even more so. A *campong* appears to be a large group of Batak houses and buildings clustered round a central shelter where the men of the tribe meet to discuss the affairs of the day. Since this one is so near the village, I expect most of them go there for their gossiping. This particular *campong* is set in a clearing just off the road that winds up to the hill. Grass has long since been worn away, and the ground is quite hard from constant tramping of bare feet, but I can imagine in wet weather it is not quite such an easy matter to walk over it. The Batak houses are more like huge barns. If I remember rightly, there is a picture of one in the booklet I got from the K.P.M. in London. At first glance, most of it appears to consist of roof, and this feature certainly gives charm to the buildings. They are set upon piles, thus making a wooden platform before each door. The walls slope outwards for about four to five feet in height. From this rises a huge thatched roof to about four or five times the height of the walls. The material used for this thatch is black and comes from the maize plant. Most of the roofs are gabbled, each gable rising to a point which, in most cases, is capped by a white head with two horns projecting from each side. The meaning of this I have not learned. The ground all around is quite hard, except underneath the piles, where it is just one slushy mass with pigs snuffing about up to their tummies! And the smell! We tried to get the people to let us go inside and have a look, but they all wanted far too much money. We did not continue to bargain to get them below fifty cents. There will be plenty of other opportunities in the *campongs* farther out in the country, and there they will probably be much better.

Most of the old people speak only Batak and do not understand Malay at all. I went up to one old woman who was sitting out on her balcony, weaving a basket. We exchanged greetings, and I stood to watch her for some time. She was most affable and grinned at me, showing a brick red mouth and lips, discolored by this *betel nut* they all chewed and then spit out. It looks perfectly revolting—far worse than lipstick! The betel palm or vine grows throughout Indonesia. The nut, about the size of a hen's egg, is first boiled, cut into slices, dried in the sun and grated. It is sprinkled on vine leaves, smeared with lime juice and rolled into a wad. This is what the natives chew. The juice stains the mouth bright red. All the while, we were followed by the children of the *campong*. One or two could speak Malay; these were anxious to act as guides for as much as they could get. However, we declined their offers and wandered round ourselves, the train following behind. Near the center of the *campong* was a thatched roofed shelter, under which the young women and girls were pounding the maize and grain under the supervision of one of the older women. Even some quite tiny girls were hard at work. We climbed up and watched them; this appeared to please them muchly. They set to work with a will, one young woman, in particular, showing off as hard as she could, grinning the while and revealing a mouthful of gold teeth. Among the Bataks, this is a sign of wealth. They file their teeth off and have them capped with gold. Occasionally one sees a whole row of gold front teeth, and nearly everyone seem to have at least one.

I understand that the grain grown by them all is put into a common pound. By the side of this shelter are great round basket barrels where the grain is stored. Under the shelter, which is also raised upon piles, are two long solid blocks of wood, and bored in each is a row of hollowed out basins into which the grain is poured. Then the girl standing in front of this basin holds a long pole, which she works up and down, pounding the grain into powder. I should think the process is very slow and most trying to the back; however, they did not seem to find it so. The place rings with the rhythmic beating of their poles and the hum of Batak chatter.

There did not seem much else to see, so after wandering round till we came to the exit, we left and followed the road on a little further. In fact, we made a large detour and arrived back at school just in time for supper.

We had plans to dance again that evening at Brastagi. Since the dancing did not start until 10 o'clock, it was arranged that Bill should pick us up at 9:30. While our partners were having a meal, Nancy and I went to change. This proved to be a somewhat lengthy business, especially the painting of our fingers and toe nails! We had great fun. At length, we were ready. By this time, Bill had arrived, and we kept him waiting a further five minutes on the balcony while finishing touches were made. At last, two ravishing beauties emerged and then came the difficulty of climbing over the stile in evening clothes! This way out at the back was much quicker and could not be seen from the house. Not that the Cooksons minded in the least how often we went out, provided the work was done. Nevertheless, most of us used the back way.

First, we went to the place where Bill is staying, and there had a whiskey and Coca-Cola. Soon Miss Rash and the other Bill arrived. We all packed into the car and drove off to Brastagi. Here we were meeting the other two men. When we arrived, the dancing had started, and there appeared to be quite a lot of people there already. Charles Gyon and a Mr. Davies were there in the hall to meet us, and we all proceeded across the dancing floor to a table on the other side. At the moment, I was under inspection— "that new English girl from Highlands." I think everyone knew of my arrival, and I felt most uncomfortable.

The Brastagi Hotel has a wonderful dance floor, some say the best in the Indies. Anyway, it certainly is a beautiful floor. The room is large and paneled in some dark wood. It gives a cozy atmosphere by artificial light but is rather dark by day. Tables and chairs were arranged round the dance floor and at the back; some of them were set for dinner. Dancing did not start until about 10 o'clock. A trio provided the music for dancing. Most of the men of our party were good dancers, so I very much enjoyed the evening. Two of them had been up since 5 o'clock, having come in from the jungle, by which is meant the plantation. Before long they showed signs of wilting. About 2 o'clock, we decided to go back and arranged to come up the following day for the tiffin dance. It is the custom here to finish off the weekend with a tiffin dance, which is rather a nice idea. Probably it is the custom everywhere in the East, but I have not come across it before. We once more packed into the car and arrived back at school about 3:00 AM. There was no church in the morning, so I had a late morning sleep to look forward to.

Nancy and Bill very much wanted to come up for this tiffin dance, but it was Nancy's duty weekend. She was on duty again at 2:00. It was hardly worthwhile going up for so short a time, so I went alone. I decided to wear my flowered linen evening dress and over it, my evening coat. This latter garment is most useful, for it can be quite chilly in the evenings here, especially going up to Brastagi, where it is very much colder than down in Kaban Djahi.

This morning about 11:30, I wandered over to the hotel in Kaban Djahi and found that Charles had already arrived. Together we went up to Brastagi. Most of the same people were there as on the previous night, and again I had some good dances, including a Viennese Waltz with Punt, the tennis instructor here. He was somewhat merry the night before, celebrating his call-up to military service! However, he is a marvelous dancer and has a most charming French wife. She is going over to Singapore while he is away. Later, Davies arrived, and we all stayed until about 3 o'clock. I was starving with hunger and was dying for some mention to be made of *makan* [food]. However, soon after this the dance music stopped, and they played classical music for the diners. We then departed and went to the hotel where Charles was staying. Here we made short work of native food. After this, we consumed *blanc mange* and finished up with coffee and fudge.

This hostel was built for the employees of Messrs. Goodyear and Co., the rubber people, and it was Mr. Marsh, the father of one of the children at school who had invited Charles. But he was taking him back to Medan at 5:30, so I suggested that we should be getting back to Kaban Djahe. With half an hour to spare, we went into the hotel there and had a game of what the Americans call "checkers," or in other words, "draughts," accompanied by a cup of tea. About 5:30, the car arrived, and I was introduced to Mr. and Mrs. Marsh; they seemed such nice people. I arrived back at school just in time for supper, but I was not feeling like eating anything else at the moment and did not go into the dining room. Nancy came up to my room later. We sat and talked for a bit and then decided to have an early night.

How I loathe the sound of the bell on Monday morning! I roll out of bed about twenty-five past six and have to rush in order to be down in time for breakfast. Monday is always a boring morning, for the children have to write their letters. It is a struggle to get them done. We are usually at sixes and sevens all morning. In the afternoon, I have the older ones for sewing, and we have got on well with the book I am reading aloud to them, *Three Men in a Boat*.

All afternoon I played tennis with Bosch and Bridgit, one of the older girls is here studying English. We thought Nell was coming to make a fourth. But she did not turn up, so we played threes. When Bridgit had to go, Bosch and I had practice together. My tennis has sadly fallen off over the last few months.

In the evening, a party of us went to the local flicks. *Boom Town* was on here in Kaban Djahe, and we were anxious to see it, so Nancy, Bill, Mrs. Michaelson, Bill, the other American I mentioned earlier, and I went. I was terribly bored and nearly went to sleep, and should have, had it not been so cold in the cinema.

On Tuesday, as soon as the children were in bed, I took my violin and went over to the teachers' sitting room, where I scraped and scratched for nearly two hours. If felt as if my arm was broken at the end, but it was grand to get such a good practice.

Next week is officially the half term. There is a rumor that we may have a half-holiday on the Friday, but I have heard nothing to confirm this. I doubt if I shall get much written on this tomorrow, as it is my garden duty.

Saturday, 18th October 1941

Officially half term. Since it was very bright and sunny all morning, Bosch and I took about fifteen of the children up to the Brastagi swimming pool. I was practicing last night when Mrs. Cookson came in to tell me that if it was fine, these were her plans for Saturday.

We started off with class as usual until 9:30. I had the big ones for design. Then we all dispersed to collect our bathing kit, finally meeting at the school gates, where the bus was ordered to pick us up. We completely filled one bus, and off we started. The Malay driver drove at breakneck speed until he met an oncoming bus, which signaled to him that the police were round the bend. As these buses have to run to time, we were obliged to stop, and out they got, pretending to fix something on the roof!! They got in again, and we crawled along, the driver consulting his watch every few seconds. At last satisfied that we would not be too early, he sped up, and we drove right up to the hotel. The pool was quite close and was, in fact, part of the hotel property. We all fell out and swarmed up the slope to the entrance. The pool lies in a hollow. Some say it is fed by a mountain stream, but I rather doubt it. Anyway, it is a very nice place, not as large as the one at Penang, but still much bigger than I was led to believe. I didn't find the water very cold. It was certainly colder than at Penang. Personally, I prefer it not to be too warm; it is more refreshing. We were the only ones swimming most of the time. There was a Dutch family, but quite lost among all of us! We had a wonderful swim, then came out and played a hectic game of football-cum-handball on the grass. In for another swim, and then finally home by bus to consume a huge tiffin.

At rest time, the children were very quiet, I must say, and most of the younger ones went to sleep. I had a garden duty in the afternoon. It rained, so we were obliged to be inside. Some of the younger ones played in my classroom, and together we made a "house" in the corner of the room. I was invited to countless meals of counters and erasers, eaten with pencils!

After supper they all have to be put to bed and tucked up. This is a somewhat lengthy business as they are allowed to play first. They nearly always choose to dress up and act plays, which I am invited to watch. However, this night most of them were in bed with the lights turned out by 7:30. The bigger ones upstairs were all quiet after that, and I only had to go up and turn their lights off at 8:00. At the moment, they all have the knitting fever and are busy making sweaters. This keeps them remarkably quiet.

Wednesday, 22nd October 1941

Hari Riah—The Malay New Year. For three days the estates close down, and with the exception of one assistant manager, they all go away, either up to Kaban Djahi or down to Medan for the week, or at least the three days at their disposal. The result is that Brastagi and Kaban Djahe are crowded out, and I should think that any female who can put two feet on a dance floor gets a date!

I was sitting at tea when Cranie Cookson came to tell me that I was wanted on the 'phone. I thought it must be Charles Gion as there was a possibility of his coming up for the holiday. I was, therefore, most surprised to hear Punt's voice at the other end. He wanted me to come up to the Brastagi Hotel for the dance. I made various excuses as I was not very keen to go out with the gentleman—and certainly not alone. In the end I said I would go, provided he could find another partner for Nancy. This he promised to try to do and said he would 'phone me later on in the evening. As the afternoon wore on, Nancy and I grew quite excited at the prospect of an evening's dancing. There would be sure to be quite a heap of folk up at the hotel, and the dance should be quite fun.

After supper we both came up to my room to get ready. We were not sure then if we really should be going, and I refused to go alone! It was not until nearly 8 o'clock that he rang up to say he had found someone, and were we excited! He was an American whom Nancy already knew, so that was nice. We finished our dressing and were just putting on the finishing touches when Punt arrived. We set off for Brastagi, leaving Nancy and Tom to follow. They arrived soon afterwards and joined us for dinner. The place was packed. There was not much room on the floor, but it was good fun, and I got some really good dances. I was wearing my washable evening dress. And, my goodness, how useful my evening coat was! I do not know what I should have done without it. We danced in between each course, and as soon as dinner was over, we repaired to a reserved table on the edge of the dance floor. Nancy and I danced every dance, and it was grand. About 3 o'clock, we went over to join a party of Americans from Wingfoot, people off one of the Goodyear estates, a very jolly crowd. The dance music stopped at 3:30 AM, and soon after that it was suggested that we should all go to the Bungalow and have breakfast! This suggestion was hailed with enthusiasm. Packing into the cars, we set off; it was only a little distance from the hotel. As soon as we arrived, the boy brought logs, and we were soon sitting round a blazing fire. I was about ready to drop with sleep by this time. However, the smell of scrambled eggs, tomato and bacon kept me going until the steaming dish arrived. I became fully conscious and fell to with a will, consuming large quantities of bacon, egg, toast and coffee. It really was delicious at that time in the morning!

With the prospect of teaching in a few hours, for me at any rate, both Nancy and I suggested that we should be getting back. We came out into the cold morning, packed into the cars, and started off down the hill to Kaban Djahe. It was light by this time and a perfectly heavenly morning. Someone thought it would be wonderful to see the sunrise from Piso Piso, one of the mountains in the district. Breakfast at school was at 6:45, which meant that we should be back at 6:30 at the latest; it was then about 5:00, so we decided to risk it. Off we set for my first visit to Lake Toba.

It was a most wonderful drive up, up, up until we came to a little cart track. There was just room enough for the car to pass. We went as far as possible; then, just within sight of the lake, the road stopped. It only enabled cars to turn round and stopped. We got out and just stood and gazed. To the right, the hillside fell away into a deep ravine, and from the opposite side we could see the water just tumbling into it. It was far too steep to see the bottom, but we watched the clouds of spray sent up by the falling water. Straight in front lay the lake, as quiet and calm as a millpond, completely surrounded by mountains. These looked rather dark and green in the morning light and came down to the water's edge in great spurts. Far below us on the water was a speck which we took to be a fishing boat, but it was too far away to really distinguish. From this point, there was a little footpath by which you could descend to the lake itself, but that, I understood, would take about two hours' walking.

Time was getting on, and we were anxious to be back before the rising bell rang. Getting into the car once more, we sped home as quickly as possible. We arrived at the stile about 6:30 AM and wondered how we should get back as the children were already up! However, we crept up to Mrs. Michaelson's room on the ground floor at the back and saw Nell, who came to our rescue. She went up for a couple of dresses while we proceeded to undress in Michey's room!! Leaving our evening dresses there, we flew up to our own rooms just as the bell rang for the children to go down to prayers. Goodness, what a rush! I just had time to comb my hair and stroll in to breakfast as if nothing out of the ordinary had happened!

Class was rather trying next morning. I found it so hard to keep awake, and the thought of going to the pictures again in the evening did not help matters. However, I went in with Nancy to early tiffin. I was on my bed by 12:00 and slept solidly until 2 o'clock when I woke up feeling like death warmed over. I had to go down and take painting! Just as I walked into class, I was called to the 'phone. It was these Americans asking if we could possibly make it the late show, and thinking "Oh well, *Hari Riah* only comes once a year," I said it would be all right. After class I was on garden duty with Nancy. This meant that we hung about the garden until 6 o'clock! When suppertime came, I certainly did not feel much like going out again that evening. However, by the time we had dressed, we felt a little more like it. Foreseeing the prospect of going up to the hotel again, for there was dancing also that night, we put on afternoon dresses. I wore my black dress, which I had cleaned in Medan.

The second show of the cinema did not start until 9:15. Our escort called for us about 8:30, and after a little drink, we went across to the cinema. It was quite a good show, the life of Reuter. Afterwards we went up to the hotel where the dancing was in progress. Not nearly so large a crowd as the night before, and the dancing was much better as a result. I was sleepy in the cinema, but as soon as I heard the music, I woke up and really enjoyed the evening very much. We stayed there until the music stopped at 2 AM. Then, not wanting to have another all-night session, Nancy and I proposed going back. Even so, it was late enough by the time we eventually got to bed. It was arranged that we should come up to the dance on Saturday again.

Nancy and I had a long consultation over what we should wear to the dance this evening. I had already worn my linen frock twice and could not appear in it again. The only alternative was my blue evening dress, which I rather wanted to keep for the dance on St. Andrew's Day in Medan. In the end, I decided to wear my blue frock, and Nancy wore a rather similar one in black. The children were most interested in our "date," especially as two of them were also going, their parents being up for *Hari Riah*. I had a good sleep in the afternoon. In fact, I came straight up after tiffin and did not wake up until 5 o'clock when I went down for a bath. Goodness, what a business it is taking a bath in this place!

After supper, we came up to dress. Our escort was arriving at 8:15, which meant that we had only an hour and a half in which to dress! About 8:00, two of the girls came up to see us off and waved us down Nancy's fire escape! We had dinner at the hotel. Dancing did not start much before 9:30 to 10:00 PM. Really, it was a grand evening, although I must admit I was a bit tired towards the end. My new shoes were most comfortable, and I was very pleased with them. The two girls appeared to be having a grand time, too. Their parents were in the group of Wingfoot people, all connected with the Goodyear Company, and there was a crowd of them there. Later some of them came across and joined us, but that was not until 2:30 AM, when the dancing stopped. It was then proposed that we should repair to the bungalow of someone in the party and there continue the dancing to records. This we did; Nancy and I were not very keen, but since it was *Hari Riah*, we fell in with the majority decision. The bungalow belonged to a young married couple, and they were most anxious to continue the party, so we rolled back the carpet and put on the gramophone. The fire was made up, and we proceeded to herald the dawn.

About 4 o'clock, they began to talk about bacon and eggs, and I was quite ready for something to eat. Before long, a large plate of scrambled eggs and tomatoes arrived. Drawing chairs up to the fire, we did justice to yet another plateful. It was quite light by the time we had finished, and as time was getting on, we made a move to go. It was six o'clock by the time we climbed over the stile. Nancy and I crept up her fire escape, and I had just enough time to change for church! We had a long sermon in Dutch, and it was all I could do not to fall asleep.

Mr. Cookson told me that he would be going down to Medan on Wednesday and that he would take my fiddle to see if it could be repaired. So, during the morning, I packed it up in its case and took it to his office.

I have had several changes in my timetable, and now I do not have much free time in the morning. I have been given Miss Boey's class for handwork and painting, which takes two morning periods and one whole afternoon a week. Lynn Cookson is taking design for his Cambridge in December and knows very little about the subject. I offered to give him what assistance I could, and we have arranged three extra periods a week. This will be only just enough, for there is an awful lot to get through before the exam.

Nancy went out to a picture in the evening, but I did not feel able to cope. Besides, I rather wanted to get in a few moment's practice. Accordingly, after the children were in bed, I took my music and fiddle over to the teachers' sitting room and spent quite a profitable hour and three quarters.

Wednesday, 28th October 1941

This evening the children were allowed to go to the cinema. *A Midsummer Night's Dream* was being shown at one of the cinemas in Brastagi, so two buses were ordered for after supper. Quite a large part of the cinema had been reserved for us, and we all crowded in, causing quite a stir! What a rotten film it was, to be sure! I never got to see it in England when it was on, and I had always wanted to, for there had been so much controversy and talk about it at the time. I thought most of the parts were grossly over-acted, and so much of the script was left out. Puck was quite good until he opened his mouth! Then, goodness, what an accent! No, to my mind, at any rate, it was not Shakespeare.

We were out rather late, about 9 o'clock. Nancy and I had said that we would mind both the boys' house and the girls' house so that the matrons could go to the late show. As soon as we got back, we took a walk round to see that they were all in bed and asleep and then sat in Michey's room, where she had left us coffee and cake. Taking periodical walks round, we stayed there until the others came back at midnight.

Thursday, 30 October 1941

My day again for garden duty. It was fine, and so we were able to be outside. I knitted most of the time and have nearly finished my sock. This is a pair of navy regulation knee length socks I am making for Tony. Later Mary came over to ask me if I would like to come up to the house in the evening to listen to some gramophone records. She gave me a list of the ones she has. Nancy came in, and together we sat on my balcony and had a "wee puff." About 8 o'clock, we walked up to the house. The others had already arrived, so we went straight into the back room where the gramophone was. We made ourselves very comfortable on divans and easy chairs. Unfortunately, the party came to an untimely end when a fuse blew and there was not another one available. However, we had heard some very nice records. Mary fortified us with ice cream before we returned to school.

Nancy and I are invited to a party tomorrow evening at the boys' house. Miss Lenie is leaving to get married, and she is throwing a party—fancy dress and native *makan*. Just the staff from the two houses are invited. Nancy and I have decided to go as the two ugly sisters.

Friday, 31st October 1941

At lunch, Mrs. Cookson asked me if I could come up to the house for tea in the afternoon. All the staff were coming, as they were giving Lenie a farewell tea. At 4:30, we all appeared. Really, the Cooksons are so kind; I must say I have never found them anything else, in spite of the stories that are circulated. We sat round and tucked into sandwiches, cake and ice cream until the bell rang for supper!! With the prospect of another "tuck-in" at 8 o'clock, all I could do was just to sit at the head of my table and not eat anything at all.

After supper, I went up to my room and did some preparation for class on Saturday. I cut out several of the children's drawings and stuck them into two large sheets so that they could be displayed tomorrow in the classroom. By that time Nancy came up, and we began to think about dressing for this party. Both of us wore our housecoats back to front. We made very fine bustles by pinning the belt to a small cushion and tying this round our waists. Then Nancy used a sarong and I took my bed cover, and we draped them round to cover the "bustle." The effect was quite good—and certainly funny! We did our hair up in the Edwardian style and perched little hats on the top. Just as we were making up, all the children burst in with Mrs. Michaelson, who was also in costume; they were much amused and assisted in the preparations. Mrs. Michaelson was in men's clothes, and Nell in a bright red garment with frilly cap and sleeves. Once the children were in bed, we all three went round to Lenie's house. She had locked the door of her room and erected a kind of ladder at the window, which we were expected to climb! With great difficulty, we managed to get into her room through the window and were able to see each other's costumes. Lenie was dressed as a pirate, with black wool stuck on her arms and showing at the neck of her shirt. Maggie had borrowed a suit from one of the Batak boys who wait at table. She looked very sweet with white jacket, trousers, and a colored sarong showing below the jacket. On her head was one of these colored caps they wear, folded out of a head square and perched on the side of her head. The furniture had already gone from the room, as most of it was Lenie's own and had been packed up. She had decorated the walls with drawings of each of us and sundry articles of underwear pinned artistically around! A large sheet of paper was spread down the middle of the room, and on this was arranged the *makan*— a kind of *rijsttafel* you could order from the village. They delivered it in cans which rested one above the other like double saucepans. One of these contained little bits of cooked meats, dried fish, vegetables, curry and goodness knows what else. A large enamel tureen of rice sat in the middle, surrounded by various dishes of dried things, like nuts and Bombay duck. Each person was provided with a sheet of newspaper and one plate. We all sat on the floor cross-legged and fell to with our fingers. It was a little difficult at first, but one soon got used to the way of eating with fingers. The thing to do was to get a good handful and to use the thumb to push it into the mouth! It was a grand meal, and I did enjoy it.

Afterwards, we came back for my gramophone and

Nancy's Hawaiian records, and we sat on the floor and listened to them. It was not a late party. Soon after 10 o'clock, we broke up and went to bed.

Saturday, 1st November 1941

Lenie went off this morning, and I think, in the end, she was rather sorry to be leaving. The new matron is not very interesting—a middle-aged Dutch woman. I should think Mr. Cookson is tired of sweet young things. They all go off and get married. Dutch are easier to replace than English staff!

My drawing class finished at 9:20, and Bosch and I took a party of the children up to Brastagi to swim. Nancy came, too, and she and I took our bicycles on top of the bus. We were free after 11:30 and had decided to do some shopping in Brastagi and have tiffin there. We had a grand swim; these children are such sports. We played catch in the water and had great fun with a large ball. Then we came out and played football on the grass.

Having seen the children off in the bus, we got on our bicycles and went down to the village of Brastagi. We looked in the only possible shop for some material for evening clothes, but they had nothing suitable. At least, the only suitable material they had was slightly damaged, and we could not get them down low enough to make it worth while buying it. I wanted something for an evening skirt, but no luck. We thought perhaps we should do better after tiffin, so we went to the Ritz Hotel, which, by the way, was not as grand as it would sound from the name! There we made short work of a plateful of *naci goreng* and a bottle of beer between us. It is chiefly fried rice, with various odd bits sprinkled over the top and a fried egg, most filling and very nice indeed. We had one portion which was ample for two of us, allowing two helpings each. What one was expected to do with two such platefuls, we could not imagine!

Next, we went across to a shop where I got a beautiful Batak sarong. I planned to use it for covering my four little cushions that I had made out of the 2 large ones Nancy gave me. I also got one of these head squares to use as a tablecloth on the little round table in the middle of my room. It was very dark blue, almost black, with a border of brown and white flowers and a design of conventional Javanese figures in the center with the long arms and the turned up feet.

Having completed our purchasing, we got on our bicycles once more and came home. It was a wonderful spin back down hill, free wheeling most of the way. The sun was quite hot, and I began to feel my back and arms burning from the bathing in the morning. My face, too, was getting steadily redder and redder.

We were home by about 3:00 and able to get a little rest in before tea. Charles Gion rang up to say that he was coming up for the weekend and would I like to go out. I asked him if he could bring a friend up as I wanted Nancy to come, too. However, he didn't know if that could be arranged. I was very pleased when, at 5 o'clock, he sent over a note from the hotel to say that he had arrived with a friend and would I bring a girl over! Nancy and I went over to meet them, and we decided to go up to the hotel in the evening for dinner and dance. The friend was not very exciting, a young accountant from Medan, an Englishman, and goodness! he couldn't dance a step. Not getting much dancing, Nancy and I were rather bored and left before the music stopped. We all came back to the Frisia Hotel and sat talking for a bit, but I was so sleepy that I could hardly keep my eyes open. Was I glad when we made a move for home!

Sunday, 2nd November 1941

I was up surprisingly bright and early this morning. I woke up when the rising bell rang and lay contemplating the ceiling for some time, trying to make up my mind which I wanted most—sleep or food. In the end, I decided breakfast had the greater attraction. I got up, put on my slacks and a shirt, and came down to the dining room. Staff is allowed to dress as they want on an off-duty weekend, which is certainly very nice; most of the staff wear slacks on these occasions.

I took up a cup of tea to Nancy, but she was asleep. I did not wake her. About 11:15, we wandered over to the hotel, but the boys were not up, so we went off to the village. Charles appeared about 12:00 and soon afterwards, the other boy. We went up as we were, in slacks. There were several people attired likewise, but I must say I do not like slacks for dancing. We did not have tiffin until the dance music stopped at 3:00. Some of the party from last night were up, and they joined us. We all sat round a large round table. After tiffin, we did not stay very long. Charles and friend then had to go back to Medan, so we returned to school, both of us very sleepy. It did not take long to get into bed, and still less time to get to sleep.

Monday, 3rd November 1941

Yes, I have had quite enough of going out to last me some time; I shall be contented to sit at home and knit! Anyway, until St. Andrew's on the 15th, and the fortnight after that, Nancy and I are going to Rosalind's. I had a long letter from her the other day, and at long last, she has sent me her riding breeches. Now I shall be able to start my lessons. Helen, one of the older girls here, who takes the children for riding, was going to take me a few times. But I think that during the holidays, I will go up to the riding school at Brastagi and get some proper coaching.

About 8 o'clock, I decided to go over to the teachers' sitting room and have a little violin practice. Mary asked me tonight if she could come and play for me. Mr. Cookson took my fiddle down to Medan Wednesday and learned that they will be able to repair it. It will be ready in about a fortnight, so I can collect it when going down on the 15th. What a joy to have it back again!

Wednesday, 26th November 1941

On Sunday, 23rd, while the children were at church service, Nancy and I went down to the doctor about my throat; he looked at it and pronounced strep throat! That is what Mrs. Michaelson had. I suppose I caught it from her, although that has been a fortnight. I had a slight temperature, so after listening to the B.B.C. news on the doctor's radio, we came back. My throat was very sore, and I did not feel like eating anything. Halfway through supper, however, Mrs. Raderama sent me off to bed, and there I stayed all Monday and Tuesday. As soon as I was in bed and knew that I should not have to get up the next day, I was better and then felt a fraud at being there, letting other people do my work. The doctor came on Monday evening, and although my temperature had gone down, he said I should not mix with the children. That meant another day in bed.

I got up this morning for breakfast and was in class all day. I certainly feel better, but it is surprising how weak one can feel, even after so short a time in bed. Two of the parents are staying at the hotel in Kaban Djahe for a few days, and they asked me to go over for dinner, but I put them off, thinking an early bed was indicated. They are very nice folk indeed, a Mr. and Mrs. Briggs from Johore; they had asked me to come over before, but, of course, it just would be my duty weekend. On those occasions, one does not have much free time. However, I expect I shall have another opportunity, as they quite understood.

Thursday, 27th November 1941

Not such an early bed last night as I had anticipated. In fact, it was quite late by the time I had finished setting work for today. It was a joy to be able to put the lights on last night, for we'd had two days' blackout. I have almost got out of the way of worrying about closed curtains, but I guess I shall be reminded again in Singapore. It was only for two nights here, and so the children had a high tea at 5 o'clock and then went straight to bed. There was no need for them to have any lights at all. In fact, the bulbs in their bedrooms were taken out altogether. Really, this is not being practical, and should the necessity arise, Mr. Cookson will have the place properly blacked out. We were given the option of buying cardboard shades for our lights or sitting in darkness. As I was in bed, I chose the latter course. But the others went over to the hotel, while those on duty ate in one room downstairs. Tonight we have all been invited over to the hotel by the Americans to bid them farewell. Two of them are leaving tomorrow for their jungle stations after a short leave here in Kaban Djahe.

Friday, 28th November 1941

The party last night was fun, but I did not get to bed until 1:30. That was my own fault, for after we got back at 12:30, Nancy and I sat gossiping! There was Nancy, Nell, Rash, myself and three Americans. We all sat round talking and devouring huge plates of turkey sandwiches and pickles. It had stopped raining by the time we started to come back to the school. Nevertheless, it was a wet job maneuvering the stile and paddling through the wet grass to Nancy's fire escape, where we could creep in unseen. Tonight I shall get to bed early and get a good sleep in. Thank goodness, we have a free weekend in front of us!

All the staff are furious because today we had a typed letter circulated amongst us from Cookson. I admit the letter was justified, but we are wild with Mrs. Verdonc. Apparently she makes a habit of being out until the small hours every free weekend, going down to Medan and coming back at 6:00 AM. Well, this is all right once in a while. No one minds. But the silly ass was seen by Mrs. Cookson coming in at 6:15 after the rising bell had rung, and the children were up and about! Of course, it was unfortunate my being in bed just those two days, for normally she has quite an easy time. But on Monday she had to take my class all morning, and it proved too much for her. On Tuesday morning after breakfast, she fainted! Hence the circular, asking all the members of the staff to be in by 10:00 on Sunday evening!!

Saturday, 29th November 1941

Alas, I have a return of my sore throat with the accompanying white spots. Still, I can stay in bed all tomorrow if I feel like it. Oh, no, I can't! I have promised to meet the English teacher from the Brastagi school in the morning. I must needs be up betimes and go up the hill. I am afraid it was foolish to wash my hair on Friday, but I felt I simply had to. Straight after tiffin, I went downstairs and performed the usual operation of bending double over the gutter into the bath and washing my hair; then up to my room and just time to set it before the bell rang for afternoon class. It rained hard all afternoon just after class had started, so my hair did not get a proper chance to dry. Hence my sorry condition today, and do I feel sorry for myself!

I had just got back to my room when Nell knocked at the door to ask me if I would like to come downstairs for a cup of coffee. This sounded very welcome. I came down to Michey's room where I found a whole crowd of the staff; they had been sitting round listening to gramophone records. Before long, I was persuaded to go upstairs for my records and we had quite a recital, for with the fiber needles one can play practically any record without the children's being disturbed. We finally broke up the party at midnight! Gone my intentions of an early night! Michey had some very good stuff with which she painted my throat before I finally went to bed.

Sunday, 30th November 1941

Sunday, 30th November has been such a nice day after all, in spite of my throat, which, by the way, is much better. I got up for Mass, and by the time we returned and had breakfast, it was almost time to get ready to go up to Brastagi. It was beautifully sunny, but I decided to put on my slacks. We were cycling back, and it can be cold on a bicycle coming down the hill. We finally got under way about 9:30, the time I should have been in Brastagi. However, it did not take very long, and we had our bicycles on top of the bus for coming home.

We called at the school for Miss B. [teacher from Brastagi]. We went for a short walk with her, and then came down to the village where we sat and had a beer before coming back. The run back is usually about half an hour on bicycles, down hill all the way; it is really a grand spin. We were talking so hard, however, that it took us an hour. We had to go straight to the doctor's, where we had been invited for *rijsttafel*, without changing. As a matter of fact, one can go to *rijsttafel* in anything one likes, dressed up or not, as one chooses; both are correct, so I have been told. Anyway, my slacks did not seem out of place. It was grand *makan*. I do so love these dishes, and the doctor's *rijsttafels* are always so very good. Afterwards, we sat round drinking coffee and eating ice cream. We all left about 2:00, some with the intention of sleeping. Neither Rash nor I felt like it. She asked me to come round to her house, and we could sit outside and knit and then have tea. First, I went back to school to get something cooler on and to collect my knitting. I also took my photos round to show her, for she had never seen them. We sat there talking and knitting until 7:00, drinking copious cups of tea. By this time the effects of *rijsttafel* had worn off, and we began to feel like supper. We searched around and finally procured some hunks of bread and slices of cheese; these we devoured and then went to make inquiries about when *Un Carnet de Bal* was showing. We had seen it advertised in Brastagi for Sunday night, but then, of course, it was too late to go and also not worth it if it would be coming to Kaban Djahe. It appears that it is to be shown at 8:00 tomorrow evening. The doctor has asked us to join him and then go back to this house for a snack afterwards.

Monday, 1st December 1941

Christmas will be here before we know it, but everyone here at school is scared by the war news. We heard on the B.B.C. that the Air Force had been mobilized and all re-servists called up.

Lynn Cookson started his school certificate exams to-day. He had to go up to Brastagi every day for the papers and did them at the house of a friend, a retired English schoolmaster. His drawing will be the following week, and so I shall have a chance to have him once more before then. I want him to do well.

The time gets nearer and nearer every day. Oh, how I am looking forward to Singapore! But, of course, I know that there is always a chance that we will not be able to go if things get any worse. In fact, I should not be surprised if some of the parents ask for the children to stay here during the holidays, in which case we should offer to take turns in looking after them. After all, it could be looked upon as a small contribution to the war effort.

Another very late night, I am afraid to say. As often happens, there will be two good films on successive nights and then a lull for several weeks! *Pride and Prejudice* is showing at the local cinema, and some of the older girls went to the first house; we, that is, Nancy and I, were going with Karl to the late show but had to wait till the others came back. It was a most glorious night, bright moon, and we sat outside Michey's room smoking our cigarettes.

How nice it is to have the tailor and shoemaker come up to the school for fittings. Time means nothing, and they wait endlessly until you are ready. The tailor came to try on my blouse, but I was a little disappointed with it, for it does not look anything at the moment. Perhaps when he makes the several necessary alterations, it will look better; the skirt is very nice indeed.

Wednesday, 3rd December 1941

I very much enjoyed the film last night. Michey came running back as soon as it was over, and we set off just as the others were coming back. It was quite late when we came out, and we went back to the hotel where Karl had ordered sandwiches for us. We stayed there talking until we discovered it to be in the region of 1:30, so thought it best to be getting back!

We anticipated that Friday we should be getting up at 4 AM and going down in the 'bus to Balawan. Nell and I shall have to behave ourselves as now Pa Cookson is coming with us to Singapore, while Ma goes to Penang. [Alas! this never happened.]

I took some of the children out for a walk in the afternoon. Nature study is such a difficult subject here because I do not know the names of the flowers and trees. Nor does anyone else. Added to this, all the books which might be of some help to me are in Dutch. Also, it is not tropical up in Kaban Djahe, so that books dealing with tropical nature are not much use. I regret so much not having brought more of my own books, but it is too late to worry about that now. I shall see what I can find in Singapore.

An end-of-term concert takes place on Friday, and I have masses to do for that. Verdonc is in sole charge. I don't think she has organized the thing, so I fear the consequences. My own two items are very poor—in fact, I wish the end of term would come!

J

Thursday, 4th December 1941

I am frantically trying to get in all the handwork so that I can press it over the weekend. We are having an exhibition on Monday. Though Mrs. C. rather wanted it to be on Friday, I asked for it to be postponed as it was utterly impossible to prepare for the concert *and* the exhibition at the same time. So Monday it is to be.

Friday, 5th December 1941

Well, the concert is over, and how! It was a terrible show and reminded me of the unrehearsed effort on the *Malda*. Really, I was ashamed—it dragged on and on. Luckily my items were at the beginning, and then I came and sat with Nancy and Begita at the back. To make matters worse, the lights went out in the middle, and they had to ring up for the electrician from the village. At the interval, St. Nicholas arrived with Black Peter. According to the Dutch custom, various children were called out to him, and he read a report from a large book, good or bad, as the case might be. It was frightful, and half the children were in tears! The only person they could get to be St. Nicholas was one of the older girls, and as she was a Dutch child and the performance had to be in English, it was difficult, to say the least of it!! By this time it was 8:30, and still another half of the program to get through!

At long last, the concert came to an end, and the children went to the dining room for hot cocoa and bread and butter. We took Helen Alison home and then went to the hotel. On the way, we met Bosch feeling as fed up and bored as ourselves, and so we invited him to join us. First, we listened to the B.B.C. news, and then I began to feel hungry. My suggestion of sandwiches was hailed with enthusiasm. Before long, a huge plate of sandwiches appeared, and we set to. Someone then suggested that we should play billiards. We ordered another gimlet, from which the winning stroke should take a sip. We had more fun over that glass! About 1:30 Bosch suggested that on the next winning stroke we should pack up. Of course, no one could begin to score, and it was a quarter to two before Nancy made a winning shot! Really, it was a grand finish to a disappointing evening.

Monday, 8th December 1941

Well, that is that, as far as my seeing Singapore goes. The whole school is bursting with the news of Pearl Harbor.

Tuesday, 9th December 1941

What a day yesterday was! While she was getting up, Mrs. Cookson heard the news that war had been declared, so we were told before breakfast. The bigger ones were asked not to let Lynn know, as he was in the middle of his school certificate and was going up to Brastagi for history paper. Nancy had to take him up. She had quite an adventure keeping the news from him, but succeeded marvelously and he did not know a thing until he got back for supper.

Of course, we knew at once that we should not be able to get away for the holidays. Today, sailings have been officially canceled, and only the Sumatra children will be going. The rest will stay here, and we shall take it in turns to look after them. Ships may carry passengers later. It is terribly disappointing, but then we are all in the same boat. I am being terribly busy here, being looked upon as chief air raid warden at school. I am most anxious to hear from Singapore, for the news of the bombing is most worrying.

Friday, 12th December 1941

Alas! It was this morning at 4:00 AM that we should have set out for Belawan for a week's holiday. What a disappointment. The children have been marvelous! Most of the parents have cabled to Cookson to keep them at school, so it was only the Sumatra children who were going in the morning. Mr. Cookson went round to each class earlier in the week to explain to them all. The very little ones could not fully realize just what it meant. At the moment, they all seem quite excited at the novelty of remaining at school during the holidays, and the bigger ones started to make plans of what they particularly wanted to do. I saw Mrs. Cookson's class out yesterday morning, marking out a deck tennis court. Some of them are to be allowed to keep pets. They are to have a Christmas tree and some sort of party, no doubt, so I hope that we can keep them happy.

It poured with rain solidly for the whole of Monday and Tuesday. We put off having the exhibition of handwork, as it would have meant carrying all the things in the rain to Anne's classroom. I was quite glad of the extra time to get last minute things done. So, on Wednesday morning during my class time with the older children, we started to get the classroom ready, putting the desks together and covering them with sheets. Mary brought her exhibits along, and during rest time, we got them set out. When all was finished, the room looked quite gay, and the work spread out over the tables made a good display. All available wall space was covered with the children's art, and when all was ready, it was quite a fair exhibition, all things considered. One has been hampered with lack of materials, more so since the war. With the top class I took potato cuts, and they printed large sheets suitable for Christmas wrapping paper. These helped to fill up a good deal of space, besides lending contrast to the other drawings. Both Mr. and Mrs. Cookson were very pleased when they saw it.

My class spent Wednesday morning writing invitations to all the staff, and after break, we borrowed the post box and went round delivering the letters! In the afternoon, they each had someone to take round the exhibition, and they certainly saw to it that they came!

School finished officially on Thursday afternoon. It was quite impossible to get any of the children to concentrate on lessons this week, and with the first wet days, it was terrible—the days just dragged. However, since we had some sunny weather the last part, they were able to go outside.

On Tuesday afternoon, they assembled in the playroom to sing carols and to watch a little nativity play done by Miss Mary's class. We intended to have it at night, all sitting round a Christmas tree, but with blackout regulations in force, this was impossible.

In the evening, I went over to Anne's room. We made out lists of the children for A.R.P (air raid practice) and planned some organization in the event of a raid. Next morning, we collected them all in the playroom, giving them places, each group with a staff member. They were given a practice during the course of the morning. Mr. Cookson is having trenches dug out at the back. I hope we never have to go to them, though it is always best to be prepared.

We have had a staff meeting and have come to an amicable agreement as to who shall be off and when. To help matters, we have been given an extra week, thus making six weeks in all, each group getting three. Nancy and I are off together, which is very nice indeed. We shall organize hobbies, walks, picnics, and the like, so it should be quite fun and will help to pass these anxious times.

Tonight we are going to see *Komrade X*. It should be very good, for even the Cooksons are going. Now there are two shows, one at 4:30 and the other at 7:15, this on account of the blackout.

Saturday, 13th December 1941

I was awakened very early this morning by the Sumatra children who were going home and had many last minute things to pack. We were all down by 7:00 to see the first 'bus off. The little ones were very brave, and no one cried, although some were very near tears, I think! After the second 'bus had gone, we all went in to breakfast. I was not down for any duty this morning, although we are not off really until midday. However, after 9 o'clock, Nancy and I went up to Rash's to listen to the news.

By 6:30, we were both so hungry, having missed supper, that Nancy went up to the house to see what she could find in the icebox. She came back with the message that we were both to come up and see what we could find. There was a large jar of strawberries and plenty of cream. We also opened a tin of sardines and had a wonderful meal by torchlight!

Monday, 15th December 1941

What a morning! I had two hours garden duty by myself from 8 to 10. I was about ready to pass out when the bell rang for fruit juice! It was very hot by this time. I went up to change into something cooler, then went with Mrs. Black to the village, where we looked round the shops, chiefly for blackout paper and drawing pins. I have got some dark blue material and have run up curtains on the machine, but I fear that they are not altogether successful. Mine is quite an easy room to black out, but so far one cannot get the right material. What a job it's going to be fixing up the whole school!

Tuesday, 16th December 1941

We decided to wait until Wednesday morning before going to Prapat. There seems so much against our going. In fact, we dropped in for the news after supper, and while listening, both came to the conclusion that we could put off the holiday. Everyone seemed to be working, and it seemed selfish to take a holiday and spend money. We now have quite definitely decided to stay and volunteer for some sort of war work, either hospital or canteen.

We came back to school rather subdued and depressed! Mrs. Cookson was sleeping down at the school, so we went in to see her. She was already in bed, but we sat on the floor, telling her our plans. About 9 o'clock, we phoned Mr. Alison up on his estate—Prapat—to tell him that the bungalow was off. He quite understood, for, in the first place, we had booked it on the understanding that it might have to be canceled at the last minute. Well, having done that, we both felt better and determined to see the person in charge of the canteen organization in the morning. She is the controller's wife, and it is rumored that she won't have any young people helping, but only staid married women, so I guess there is no hope for us! Still, it can never be said that we did not offer to help.

Rosalind rang Mrs. Cookson this evening. She was on her way up to Brastagi for a few days when war was declared, and she went back to the estate. In fact, I don't think she even got as far as the 'bus! She has offered to come up here if the Cooksons need any more help, and she has offered to have Nancy and me for our free week if we have nowhere else to go, which is very sweet of her.

Wednesday, 17th December 1941

We moved into our new quarters this morning, and very cozy we are. There are two rooms. We have had two beds put into the end room, and have blacked out the middle room as a sitting room. We have only brought over just what we need. It is not worthwhile bringing over everything for the rest of the week, for we are on duty again on Tuesday.

Thursday, 18th December 1941

Well, after breakfast, attired in slacks, we went over to the hospital and found quite a number of ladies working at rolling bandages and the like. Mrs. Van Ray was not there, but the sister-in-charge said, "Oh, yes, you can help!" and straightway handed us a triangular bandage to hem! We were a little taken aback but sat down at once and got on with the job. There is no mention of canteen, so we think it best to prove to the old dears that we can work and are really willing to do so before we ask to be transferred! We sat there all morning working as hard as we could, rolling bandages, cutting butter muslin for swabs, etc. In fact, we went over again after rest time and stayed there until 5 o'clock, promising to come over tomorrow.

We felt very dirty indeed after our work at the hospital, and so after tea, we were able to get into a hot bath and change. Then at 9:00 we called for Mrs. Black and went over to the hotel to listen to the news.

We were over at the hospital again this morning and spent most of the time rolling bandages. We had a good deal of help from the soldiers who were all waiting there! It was really quite amusing! About 11:30, we came away. Nell, too, is with us, but she is doing Red Cross nursing. She returned with us to our suite, and we all three sat on the balcony and had a beer.

Nancy has a rotten sore throat and so did not go over again this afternoon. We were sitting here just before high tea when Mrs. Cookson came to join us. Mrs. Cookson told us we should have to clear out of the girls' house and move over to our new quarters permanently; they are trying to consolidate space and keep everyone nearer together. We spent the morning sorting out all our junk and packing it up in cases to move over. I am very pleased, for it is so nice being over here with Nancy; we have two rooms, and now with suitable furniture, it is very nice indeed. We sleep in the end room and use the middle one for a sitting room. Straight after breakfast, I went over to the hospital to say that we could not work but that we would try to come in the afternoon. It took us all morning to move—goodness, the rubbish! When all our things had been moved, both rooms seemed as full as they could be. We felt that we just did not know where to begin to tidy. However, gradually we got things straight and by 2:30 I had had enough. I thought I would go over to the hospital, but Nancy preferred to stay and get all her things in order. So I left her in a perfect sea of clothes and went to roll bandages instead!

I had a letter from Tony today, the first for some time. He is in Calcutta and has been chartered to a ship with Arthur. I am so glad they are together. I expect it will be a long time before I shall hear from him again.

Sunday, 21st December 1941

There was no church, so we again had a long lie in bed, then went up to the house for breakfast. Being Sunday, there was no hospital either. After breakfast Nancy and I went round the village on bicycles. I have been making vain efforts to get those socks posted to Tony, but they do not seem to know anything there about the postal regulations regarding packets sent overseas. I shall have to take them to Medan with me on Monday. We decided that a day in Medan would be a nice change and would enable us to get some Christmas shopping done. I had offered to make some dolls' clothes for those children who did not get parcels from home, so we went along to the children's room, took two dolls and proceeded to cut out dresses. These we carried over to the hotel to sew while we were waiting for the news. It now appears that they may not have the 10:30 news any more; the hotel is full and certain important guests require quiet at 10!! This is a blow, for we cannot get over for the B.B.C. news at 7:30, and we have not been able to hire a radio ourselves. Maybe later on this will be possible, but at the moment we are absolutely dependent on second-hand news, which is never a good source of information.

Tuesday, 23rd December 1941

The last two days have been very hectic, to say the least. We decided to go to Medan and so, on Monday morning, got up for breakfast at the right time, or only a little late anyway! Nancy ordered the 'bus for 8:40. Mrs. Black said she would come as far as Brastagi with us. We set off with lengthy lists of shoppings to do for the Cookson family, mostly Christmas shopping for the children. Several parcels have already arrived for the children, but some will not get anything, so the Cooksons are buying little presents for them. At Brastagi, Mrs. Black left us, and we went all round the market in the 'bus that was picking up people and packages. If you are in a hurry, as we were, it is the most irritating thing, this going backwards and forwards, canvassing passengers. We had already been round Kaban Djahe market, but as it was market day, most of the Bataks were staying and did not want to go down to Medan. One boy sat at the back of the 'bus and shouted continually, "Medan! Medan!" at the top of his voice, while the driver twisted and turned through the market, up and down the road. At long last, we seemed to have collected enough to set off on the two hour drive down the hill to Medan. This was my first experience of such a long drive by Batak 'bus, and I must say I was very agreeably surprised. One certainly gets a little cramped and the seats are rather hard, but it is much more airy and I don't think one feels the twisting so much as at the back of a car. It takes very much longer, of course, for there were so many stops *en route*, people getting out with all their *barang*. At one stop, the wheels had to be cooled and the radiator filled up with water. However, when you think that it costs only 60 cents (or ?1.20) return, as against seven or eight guilders, one willingly puts up with the spitting and native tobacco!

It was about 11:00 by the time we arrived, for there had been several stops on the way. The shops close in Medan on a weekday from 12:00 to 1:30, so we did not have time to do much shopping before everything closed. However, we managed to do a little and were walking down the main street when whom should we meet but Karl King, the American who has been staying at the hotel. He had come in to collect all his *barang* from the office, for he was being evacuated. He asked us both to tiffin at *Ter Moulin's* Cafe, so as soon as the shops closed, we made our way to the restaurant. We sat for ages while the steaks were ordered, but at last they came and they did look good! We had just taken the first mouthful when the sirens sounded! We dashed to the shelter, but before long the "all clear" sounded. It was a false alarm—the plane proved to be Dutch, so once more we sat down and were able to finish our tiffin in peace.

By this time, it was nearly 2 o'clock. We had to fairly scurry around to get all our shoppings done before 3:30 as we did not want to attempt that 'bus ride in the blackout. Nancy and I had thought of the possibility of staying the night at the de Boer hotel; still, we did not want to do this unless it was absolutely necessary. However, it soon became evident that we should not get all our commissions done before dark. We took time off for a much needed cup of tea and then went to the hotel to book a room. Goodness, it is hot work shopping in the heat. Up in the hills, one does not know what heat means, but as soon as you come to Medan, why, you simply melt. We had been shopping round all afternoon on our own flat feet, so by 4:30 we were about done in. Of course, we had nothing to change into, nor had we anything in the way of washing equipment! I have never felt so dirty in my life! We did manage to buy a cake of soap, and a splash in the hand basin certainly made us feel much better.

We went round to the desk to put a call through to Kaban Djahe and say that we would be up in the morning. That call took an hour to get through. All the time we sat outside at tables which were arranged round what used to be the dance floor, I suppose. It was a heavenly night and beautifully cool after the hot day. Karl joined us, and later we all had dinner together. Again, we returned to the open and were joined by another American, a Mr. Dale. We sat there together until the party was broken up once more by the air raid siren. We adjourned to the hotel shelter and sat there listening to the radio. We were about an hour without anything happening and were joined by yet another two Americans. As soon as the "all clear" sounded, we came back to our original table and had a nightcap before retiring. We were rather tired after that long 'bus ride in the morning.

Up early on this morning and down to a delicious breakfast of scrambled egg and bacon and hot coffee. (The Dutch breakfast of cheese and cold meat does not really appeal to me. I stick to the conservative eggs and bacon, or at any rate, eggs.) We went round to telephone for the 'bus, but at the same moment, the siren sounded again, and we had to wait till the "all clear." Even then, the 'bus arrived half an hour late, at 9:30 instead of 9:00, and of course, there was the inevitable trailing round the market, so it was 10:00 before we were under way. We were so mad, because at this rate we would not be home till 12:00, and the others were wanting to go off duty. However, nothing could be done about it, and we just had to sit there and hope that we would get moving soon. Round and round we went, picking up people here and there, piling huge bundles of vegetables and all sorts of things on the roof of the 'bus. At long last, we left the market and went round to pick up a Malayan family with thousands of children, who all proceeded to pack into the back of the 'bus. Later, they were sick! This time we really did get away but had to stop at the first village for petrol. There were several other stops on the way up, but eventually we did get home and arrived only just after tiffin had started. I am glad to say that the others had not waited for us, so all was well.

There was, however, another surprise in store for us—for me at any rate. We evacuated the girls' house, in which Michey had installed all the girls—no, I mean the boys' house, where the girls were then living. Poor Michey had just got all their clothes put in the new house, and now they have all to be moved. We have to go to a house a little farther up the road. It is quite a nice house with a good-sized garden, already fitted with swings and see-saw. The school beds have been taken over, and the children will just sleep over there and come back in the morning for breakfast and all other meals.

After tiffin, then, I collected the girls together, and we set out in a little crocodile, each child carrying a raincoat and an armful of dolls! Although it is not very far away, it was quite a business getting them all over, complete with belongings. They were all thrilled to bits at the novelty of it all. I eventually got them all settled on their various beds, and some even went to sleep! At 2 o'clock, Bosch brought the boys along, and they all played in the garden until it was time to come back for supper. I left at 2:00, however, and came over for a much-needed bath! Nancy and I sat and wallowed in boiling hot water, and, as a result, felt very much better.

At 5 o'clock, they all had supper, and then over once more to the house with further junk. They were all settled by 7:00, and Mrs. Black and I sat in Anne's room where we made coffee.

Wednesday, 24 December 1941

Christmas Eve. Nancy and I spent the morning together in our sitting room, sewing as hard as we could. In Medan yesterday, we found a McCall's pattern for stuffed animal toys. She is busy making a handsome giraffe.

After supper, the children sat round the Christmas tree which Lynn had fixed up in the dining room, and they sang carols before going to bed. There was great excitement over the hanging up of socks. I went round to all my little girls, pinned a sock at the end of each bed, and placed one in the shoe, "in case Father Christmas wants two!" They were all asleep quite early, and Anne went round to fill the socks. As soon as they were in bed, I came back to the Cooksons' house. They were all busy up there doing up parcels, and the room was a perfect sea of colored paper and presents. We sat round the table and joined in. Soon everything was wrapped up, and it was seen that each child had at least one present to be handed from the Christmas tree in the morning.

It was nearly 11 o'clock by the time all was ready, and Mrs. Cookson and Nancy insisted on seeing me home; it was pouring with rain, but we put on mackintoshes and paddled in the dark up the road to my new quarters.

25 December 1941

Christmas Day. I was awakened in the small hours, long before it was light, by one of the tiny girls, who had discovered her stocking. It must have been only just after midnight. Hard heartedly I made her put the sock back, and go to sleep again! They all woke up very early. We all came down to school by 7:00, and they put their presents for the others round the tree. Mass was at 7:30. We started the handing of presents as soon as they were all assembled, for we had to be over at the church by 7:25 at the latest.

After Mass we came back and had our breakfast. Tiffin was not until 1 o'clock. My goodness, what a spread it proved to be! Three huge turkeys and I don't know how many plum puddings. The children stuffed and stuffed and really enjoyed their Christmas dinner. The bigger girls had made the table so nice, too, with little cards in each place, homemade crackers, and paper hats—it was really a very good effort indeed. It was quite late by the time all the eating was over, and we had had several pauses while photographs were taken. But when everyone was ready, we went out into the garden and had one more photo taken. Then over to rest, a much-needed rest, I might add. None of them wanted much supper, and an early bed seemed indicated.

Monday, 29th December 1941

I have been terribly busy. Thank goodness, another free week begins tomorrow, and both Nancy and I shall not be sorry, for this week has been rather hectic. Now that we have got things organized and in swing, so to speak, it should be better. There is always the possibility that we shall have everything changed and upset, but at any rate, for the time being, we are all set. One simply cannot plan for more than a day ahead.

Mummy must be terribly worried today, hearing over the BBC that there has been a raid on Medan. Nancy was on her way down to take a child to the airport, but luckily she was stopped on the road and given the information and so was able to turn back. The news came through this morning on the radio from London. We are a good way from Medan, and I do not suppose that they will bomb us up here. Anyway, all precautions have been taken at school, and Mr. C. is in constant touch with the Consul. There seems no need to evacuate. [Alas! it did happen.]

The Epilogue

Although 29 December 1941 was the last entry in my diary, that was not the end of my adventures. How I traveled across Australia, married an American sailor and came to live in Louisiana will have to be told from memory. Although memory can sometimes be evasive, I have dated pictures and souvenirs to help me keep on track.

It was the next day that Mr. Cookson came to tell me that he had arranged for me and his daughter Nancy to evacuate. In fact, he told us that a car would be leaving in two hours' time and that we should pack a suitcase weighing not more than 14 pounds. How do you pack all your possessions into a small suitcase? Of course, you can't, but the selection of what to take and what to leave is an even harder choice. The things you grab up first and then realize that, of course, you would have no need of them—then common sense takes over. I left my beautiful violin hanging on the wall, took up my camera and then decided it might be confiscated, so left it, too. I packed my photo album, a few clothes, and that was it.

We left on time, also taking two children with us whose parents were in Singapore. We took the now familiar road to Medan. I had traveled this road many times and once even by native bus. But this time the journey was made more hazardous by having to observe the blackout, for we could not use headlights and the jungle looked forbidding!

The airport was also in subdued darkness. I remember being ushered onto a plane already nearly filled to capacity. Not only was every seat taken, but the aisle down the center was packed with squatting humanity. This was my first experience of flying, and I had serious doubts that the plane would be able to take off. But it did!

We landed in Java, and I am afraid that I do not remember the name of the hospitable family that took us in. It was on a tea plantation, probably run by a parent who had children at Kaban Djahi. I don't know how long we stayed there. Probably only a few days before we were on the run again, driving across the island by winding jungle roads, still in the blackout, to the southern port of Tjilatjap in Java.

This little port was a seething mass of people, everyone trying to get off the island and onto a ship. Camp cots had been set up in every available building, and somehow through the courtesy of the kind authorities, we were able to sleep and be fed a meal till we embarked the next day.

The men folk had come in from the jungle to put their wives and children on the ship, hoping they would be out of danger and reach safety. What heart-rending goodbyes there were, and some of those couples never met again. Cabins and some sleeping arrangements were to be had for the women and children, particularly those with small babies. The rest of the able bodied had to fend for themselves. The soldiers, of which there were many, had to form lines on the deck and simply sit cross-legged for the entire voyage. I was advised that the famous war correspondent Knickerbocher was on board, but I did not get to meet him. It was a bright moonlit night when we pulled out of the Tjilatjap harbor, and I offered a silent prayer that this trip would be without adventure.

Of the trip itself I remember very little. It was not very long. The first port of call was Freemantle, Australia, and here we were put off the ship unceremoniously, perhaps even "dumped" would be more descriptive, for the Dutch were not in sympathy with the fleeing English. I think this was partly due to the fact that Englishmen who came to work in the Indies stayed their time and then returned to England, their home, whereas the Dutch settlers did just that: they settled, married native women and considered this their home. They stayed, even in the face of invasion, and were resentful of our leaving.

We landed. Nancy and I and the two children stood on the dockside with our little possessions, wondering what to do. By a miracle, the parents of the two children were there to claim them; one mother so delighted to see her child that she demanded to know what he had done with his coat! The Refugee Committee was fabulous; those ladies met every ship that came from Singapore and the Indies and arranged overnight housing for the refugees. We were assigned to a dubious hotel across the tracks, but we left our things there and decided to take a walk and survey our surroundings. We were on our way back to the hotel when I saw someone on the sidewalk waving and jumping up and down. My cousin Barbara! She had come down from Singapore three weeks earlier and had been on the lookout for my name to be posted. She was staying at the home of some family friends that I had never met, a Mr. and Mrs. Brisbane, friends of my aunt and uncle in Singapore. She took us to meet them, and they immediately opened their home to us. Nancy wanted to be independent, so she did not stay; but I stayed many months with this kind family.

My first concern was to get a job. I was lucky enough to be employed by a mapping company engaged in making an ordnance survey map of Western Australia. We worked on a very small section, how small I did not realize until we saw the finished map. It certainly was a tiny reward for all our hard work, but we were also proud to be on the map at all. We worked from strips of aerial photographs, sliding them carefully through a device (I don't remember the name of it) that brought the landscape into three dimensions. On this we marked possible streams and rivers and circled clumps of trees that might give protected cover. It was fun and interesting work, but, of course, with the finished map the work came to an end.

Next, I returned to my original occupation of teaching young children and somehow managed to be accepted in the small Church of England school for girls, known as St. Hilda's. This was significant since I was probably the ONLY Roman Catholic ever to be employed at that school! I spent several very happy years there. My class was a varied group of children. Two I remember being very, very shy; they would not mix with the other children. They had been in virtual seclusion on a remote sheep station and until then, they had had no contact with other children. Eventually they became part of the group.

On about 21 June 1942, since Singapore seemed likely to fall and the threat of a Japanese invasion was very imminent, it was decided to take the whole school, at least those children who had come from Sumatra and Singapore, into the outback for protection. Accordingly, we packed up everything and went by train 200 miles up the tract to a remote place called Bencubbin. It really was in the middle of nowhere. I don't think the Japanese would ever have found us, even if they had landed in Australia!

Bencubbin consisted of a main street, rather like the movie pictures of the Wild West (minus the shoot-ups). There was a hotel, in fact, two, I think, a row of shops, a church with a hall back of it, a post office and a railroad station. That was Bencubbin! But what fun and excitement we had in that place. We took over the shops and converted them into sleeping quarters for the children. Barbara, who joined our staff, commandeered the kitchen in back of the church. There she cooked on a wood-burning stove, having to chop and cut the wood herself. I took over a small building and converted it into a one-room school.

Barbara and I became very friendly with the Episcopal priest. We all spent much time together, and he became familiarly known as Peter.

For a short time in early spring, Western Australia is a riot of color; the wild flowers are unbelievable, and the wattle trees make a sea of yellow . . . but the flies!!! A short walk in the evening, or any time for that matter, and your back is black with flies; nothing seems to faze them. And with no protection at the windows to keep them out, one has to wave a napkin constantly while serving meals. These are the blowflies that do so much damage to the sheep and livestock.

I was introduced to the chip heater. This is a device over the bathtub. You collect twigs or small chips of wood, place them in the heater, together with some newspaper, light them, and in time, the water running through the coils comes out hot. But you had better be quick with your washing, for the water will not stay hot very long. One gets used to anything, and there is a never-ending supply of chips to be had for the picking up.

Saturday nights we were off duty; at least, we took it in turns. We had become very friendly with all the young farmers and their families who came into town every Saturday to get supplies. Sometimes a group of us would get together, climb into the back of someone's truck, evening dress and all, and drive 40 or 50 miles to some town that had a dance. Upon arrival, all the men would gather round the trucks, where the beer was, no doubt. The women, all dressed up, would sit on benches round the walls. When the music started, the boys would come through the door, check out the possibilities, single out a partner and make a beeline for that person! We did all the old time dances—Pride of Erin, Paul Jones, etc. It was so much fun. After the dance, we would pile up in the truck again and head for home, snatching a few winks before getting the children up for Peter's church service.

The children and I had fun, too. We were studying the Norman period in history, and one afternoon while on a nature walk, we came upon a deposit of clay. So we brought some back to school, made little bricks, which we dried in the sun and fashioned into a Norman castle.

I don't remember how long we stayed in Bencubbin, but it was a wonderful experience. We visited some of the farms. My, how the Australian women worked, taught school via radio, helped run the farm, grew their own vegetables and cooked the most delectable meals! One family we stayed with overnight would make bread dough, and when the family got ready for bed, would set the pan of dough in the ashes to rise, and we had fresh baked bread for breakfast. Barbara and I also witnessed the necessary slaughtering of a sheep. It is rather grisly, but it is true that the sheep makes no sound; its jugular vein is severed and the carcass hung up to drain. Then we took part in skinning the carcass. This is their only source of meat, and Australians eat a lot of mutton and lamb.

Before we left Bencubbin Barbara joined the Army and was subsequently sent to New Guinea. Upon returning to Perth, I, too, felt that I would like a chance to see some more of Australia before the war ended. I did not want to go to sea again, so I decided to request a release from my reserved occupation and see what was available on the other side of the continent. Of course, I had to have a job to go to first, or I would never get a permit.

I applied to Loreto Convent, Brisbane. The Mother Superior of this convent had known me at the convent back in St. Albans, England, where I had gone to school, so she was influential in getting me the job and also in securing living accommodations for me with a family in the town of

Cottesloe, a suburb of Brisbane. It took a little while, but I did get permission to move to Brisbane.

Meanwhile, I really enjoyed my stay in Perth. It is a beautiful city with many large and stately buildings, and it has a spectacular harbor noted for the black swans that swim around the bay. I went sailing several times with some of the Navy boys. Perth was overflowing with the American Navy, and the housewives were competing to entertain them. Consequently, single girls were in great demand! Tennis parties almost every weekend, and sometimes we would have crayfish picnics on the beach after dark, for that is the best time to catch them. Crayfish are larger than the Louisiana crawdads I have come to know. A kerosene can of salt water would be put to boil on a fire made from driftwood at the edge of the water. Then we would wade into the water with nets to catch the crayfish, drop them into the boiling water and wait for our meal. Fresh from the ocean indeed!

Two of the other teachers at St. Hilda's and a fourth girl rented a house near the school. The houses in Australia all have verandahs round at least three sides of the house, and the bedrooms open out onto these verandas, which are used for sleeping on hot nights. They are appropriately called "sleep-outs."

Probably around February of 1943, I made a train trip across Australia to Brisbane, passing through Melbourne and Sydney. It took at least five days to cross the continent. Each time the train came to a state line, we had to pile out and change trains, even if it was in the middle of the night, because the rail gauge was different in each state. I understand that now all rails are of uniform gauge.

The first part of the journey crosses the Nullarbor Plane, and never let an Australian hear you call it a desert! But that is really what it looks like, because for as far as the eye can see on either side of the train, it is low scrub and saltbush. And the heat! We had no air conditioning on the train, and that was the first time I had ever seen butter melting in a dish on the table. (I came to Louisiana later!) A troop train passed us on the double track. It was nothing but a cattle truck with the sides removed and a wooden bench placed down the middle. On this were seated soldiers returning to Perth. How they made the trip, I shall never know; we heard that the temperature reached 120 degrees.

We eventually got to Sydney, and the first thing I did was to find a public bathhouse. It was heaven, believe me! I was met by a friend from England who took me to her apartment. Sydney is so like San Francisco, built on hills with steep roads that fall down to the harbor. My friend had her little girl with her, whom I had not seen since she was a baby. We went to the zoo, and they showed me koalas sitting up in a tree eating eucalyptus leaves, which are its only food. We had a really nice visit. Then on to Brisbane.

Mother Superior had arranged for me to take a room in the house of an elderly lady from the parish. We became very friendly during the time I lived there with her. The houses in this part of Brisbane were built up on stilts, which gave space underneath for lawn mowers, bicycles, etc. But there was not indoor plumbing! However, "When in Rome", one can adjust to anything, and everyone was so very friendly.

While in Brisbane, I spent a wonderful week at a summer vacation camp somewhere in the beautiful Green Mountains north of Brisbane. The group of guests met and traveled together by bus as far as the road would let us. We then got out and piled our gear under a tree to await the pack mules that would carry it the rest of the way. The camp was virtually isolated. We made the rest of the journey on foot. This camp was run by an Irish family who made the week so much fun for the guests.

Campers slept in individual cabins, but we ate in a group in the dining room. At night we would gather round a huge open fireplace for conversation, reading, word games and ghost stories. On the stove in the kitchen sat an enormous blue enamel teapot which never emptied! You could drink the strong black tea at all hours of the day or night.

We went in groups on daylong hikes, carrying a picnic lunch provided by the camp. Sometimes it meant following a rocky riverbed up to a lookout point where the view was stupendous, or climbing down the rocks to the valley. Looking out over the valley, it almost seemed that the mountains appeared to have giant hands whose fingers were reaching down for the water below. One night we had a special surprise; our hosts led us down a dark path by lantern light to the bottom of the hill where there was a cave. We were allowed to enter the cave two at a time. The surprise was fantastic, for the inside of the cave appeared bright as day, lit by thousands of fire flies clinging to the walls. It was a sight I shall never forget. Yes, this was truly a memorable vacation.

It was June 19, 1945 when I decided to go to a Chopin recital at the Albert Hall in Brisbane. It was a well-known local pianist, and I was interested, but I did not have a ticket. However, the girl at the box office suggested that I come early and then perhaps get a seat unclaimed. This I did, bringing a book and some knitting, in case I had a long wait. It grew late, and still no one had come to claim my seat. Just then an American sailor came to my row and murmured, "Pardon me," as he stepped across me and sat in the next seat to mine. This is the sailor I followed to Louisiana! We talked after the recital and went to get some refreshments; we exchanged programs, and he asked me for a date. I accepted and then got cold feet when I got home. I thought about it . . . what would my mother have said!

We dated several weeks, and then Jesse was shipped up to the Philippines, but the night before he left, he called me on the phone five thousand miles away and he proposed. I said "yes" and named the little kitten on my lap at the time Louise after Louisiana. But she turned out to be a he, so I called him Louis.

On the 6th December 1945, the nuns presented me with a beautifully inscribed Book of Prayer, the Loreto Manual, which I greatly treasure.

We were, of course, uncertain about the future, so wedding plans could not be made in stone. We decided that if Jesse were sent home via Australia, we would be married in Brisbane. But it was not to be. Soon after the war was over, he was sent directly to the States. It was left to me to get gone as soon as possible, by ship either to England or the States, whichever opportunity came first.

It so happened that a passage to England came first, and once in England, I was united with my mother and family. It had been almost five years since our fairwell at Greeenoch. Straight away, plans were made for a wedding in Shreveport. My mother could not come, but two years later, she visited us and doted on her first grandson.

I secured a passage on a cargo ship, one of Lykes Brothers boats, the *Charles H. Herty*. There were only eight passengers on board. We carried a cargo of lamp black and Scotch whiskey. The crew, I understand, got into the whiskey one night, and we had a stowaway on board. We landed June 30, 1946, and I thought New Orleans must be the hottest place on earth. I was scared that I would not recognize Jesse out of uniform—it had been so long!

On July 6, 1946, Jesse and I were married at St. John Berchman's church in Shreveport, LA, a fitting conclusion to an exciting wartime journey. It was the beginning of another adventure that lasted almost 46 years and produced three wonderful children, J.G., Michael and Justin, whom I refer to, as in the old TV show, as "**MY THREE SONS**". J.G. still signs his cards, "From your No. 1 son."

Yes, I have been greatly blessed and have much to be thankful for.

Appendix

Name of Ship   "MALDA"   Date of Departure JUNE, 1941

Steamship Line   B.I.S.N.CO.   Where Bound   SINGAPORE

NAMES AND DESCRIPTIONS OF BRITISH PASSENGERS AT THE PORT OF Greenock

Port at which Passengers have contracted to land	NAMES OF PASSENGERS	Last Address In Kingdom	Profession, Occupation or Calling
Singapore	ANGUS, W.	Government	Government
Colombo	ATKINS, W.L.	•	•
Colombo	ALLEN, Mrs.W.T	•	•
	ALLEN,Miss	•	•
	BRAKES,SubLt J.	•	•
	BENTLEY,SubLt A.R.	•	•
Singapore	BANKS,Mrs.	•	•
	Master	•	•
	Miss	•	•
Colombo	BONES, J.	•	•
	BUFTON, W.V.	•	•
	BLAIR,R.Y.	•	•
Singapore	BURST, A.V.	•	•
	BELL, W.W.	•	•
	BARKER, J.	•	•
	CHISHOM, F.S.B.	Crown Agents	Crown Agents
	CLARK, T.	Government	Government
	CASS, R.	•	•
	CARTER, L.	•	•
	COTTRELL,F.H.	•	•
Colombo	CRABB, W.L.	•	•
Singapore	COLERIDGE,A.F.	•	•
	CHASE,A.B.	•	•
Colombo	CROSLAND, G.	•	•
	DUNCAN, J.C.	•	•
	DICKINGS, J.W.	•	•
	PRITCHARD-DAVIES, Sub.Lt. A.R.S.	•	•
	DAVIES,SubLt S.	•	•
	DAVIS,Paymaster Lt. C.E.	•	•

Port at which Passengers have contracted to land	NAMES OF PASSENGERS	Last Address in Kingdom	Profession, Occupation or Calling
Singapore	DUCKWORTH, Mrs. F.V.	Crown Agents	Crown Agents
	EBDEN,W.S.	•	•
	EYRES, G.	Government	Government
Colombo	EARLEY, W.A.	•	•
Singapore	EASTON, H.	•	•
Colombo	ELPHICK,SubLt S.F	•	•
Singapore	FLEMING,E.D.	Crown Agents	Crown Agents
Colombo	FLOCKTON,H.	Government	Government
Singapore	GROVES,Mrs.J.M	•	•
	GARDINER,E.A.	Crown Agents	Crown Agents
Colombo	GARDINER,J.L.	Government	Government
	HORSLEY,Lt.A.C	•	•
Singapore	HALL, L.	•	•
Colombo	HUGHES,F.P.	•	•
	HEAP,SubLt R.	•	•
Singapore	ISSAACS, J.	•	•
	JAMES, F.G.	•	•
Colombo	JONES, C. Mrs.	•	•
	JOHNSON,SubLt P.F.	•	•
Singapore	KITSON,Mrs.G.VL ANE, R.W.	•	•
	LOVE, P.G.A.	•	•
	MATHIAS,Mrs EG	Crown Agents	Crown Agents
	MORRISS,L.A.G.	•	•
	MUMMERY,C.F.	•	•
Colombo	MORGAN,G.W Mrs.	Government	Government
	Child	•	•
	MITTEL, R.W.	•	•
	Mrs.	•	•
Singapore	MANN, T.	•	•
	MILNER, A.	•	•
	MARSHALL,J.W.	•	•
	MARCHANT,H.R	•	•

Port at which Passengers have contracted to land	NAMES OF PASSENGERS	Last Address in Kingdom	Profession, Occupation or Calling
Colombo	MARKHAM,G.R	Government	Government
Singapore	NEWBOULT,A.T	Crown Agents	Crown Agents
	O'MALLEY,T.K.	Government	Government
	ORGAN,A.W.J.	•	•
	PETRA,TANGKU	Crown Agents	Crown Agents
Colombo	PATEL,I.L.	Government	Government
	PARKER,Sub.Lt N.W.	•	•
	PERCIVAL,SubLt H.G.R.	•	•
	PIKE,Sub.Lt.T.S.	•	•
	PONTET,Sub.Lt. J.E.	•	•
Singapore	RILEY, Miss E.	Crown Agents	Crown Agents
	RYDER, J.L.	Government	Government
	REDSHAW,W.L.	•	•
	RACKHAM,F.W.	•	•
Colombo	RILEY, G.W.	•	•
	RUSSELL,SubLt. A.H.	•	•
Singapore	SHEPPARD,MCF	Crown Agents	Crown Agents
	SPRAGG, L.W.	•	•
	SHEARS, A.G.	•	•
	STOCKDALE, D.	Government	Government
Colombo	SOUTHERN,TAR	•	•
	STORER,Sub.Lt. H.M.	•	•
Singapore	TURRAL,Mrs.GR Master	•	•
Colombo	TAYLOR, J.	•	•
	TICE, Mrs.M.A.M	•	•
Singapore	VOLLER, T.	•	•
	WILSON, Miss M.A	Crown Agents	Crown Agents
	WROATH, W.	Government	Government
Colombo	WINDUST,H.A.	•	•
	WESTCOTT,Sub-Lt. D.	•	•
Singapore	YARDLEY,F.R.	Crown Agents	Crown Agents
Colombo	YEADON, K.R.	Government	Government

Port at which Passengers have contracted to land	NAMES OF PASSENGERS	Last Address in Kingdom	Profession, Occupation or Calling
Colombo	ALSTON,Mary Joy	Bowden,Cheshire	Nil
	BRIGGS, John	Highgate West Hill, N.6	Ambulance Driver
	BETTERTON, Stanley	•	Ambulance Driver
	BLAND, Cyril	Harrow	Buyer
Singapore	BUCKELL, Margaret	St. Albans	Teacher
	COLQUHOUN, Andrew	Glasgow	Accountant
Colombo	CHARLESON, William	Trowbridge, Wilts.	Tea Planter
	CLARK, John	Edinburgh	Tea Planter
	DAVIES, Martin	Highgate West Hill	Ambulance Driver
	DEWEY, Edward	Grantham	Tea Planter
Singapore	DOIG, Phyllis Ursula	Dorking	Nil
		•	•
	FOGG, Roger	Isle of Man	Engineer
	GRIFFITHS, Evelina	Southsea, Hants.	Ambulance Driver
	HARRIS, Michael	Highgate West Hill	Ambulance Driver
	HARBOROW, Sarah	Blackpool	Registered Nurse
	HOLMS,Gertrudur	Hampstead	Nil
Penang	LIM, Kgan Chye	Cambridge	Student
Colombo	MACDONALD, Donald	Eastbourne	Tea Planter
	MACKINTOSH, Stanley	Highgate West Hill	Ambulance Driver
	MCAINSH, John	Nr. Walsall	Bank Official
	MCDONALD, Richard	Portsmouth	Tea Planter
	MCINTYRE, Thomas	Bishop Auckland	Ind. State Rlys.
	PATON, Thomas	Abdereenshire	Banking